SPACES OF PEACE, SECURITY AND DEVELOPMENT

Series Editors: **John Heathershaw**, University of Exeter, UK, **Shahar Hameiri**, University of Queensland, Australia, **Jana Hönke**, University of Bayreuth, Germany, and **Sara Koopman**, Kent State University, USA

Volumes in this cutting-edge series move away from purely abstract debates about concepts and focus instead on fieldwork-based studies of specific places and peoples to demonstrate how particular spatial histories and geographic configurations can foster or hinder peace, security and development.

Available now

Post-Liberal Statebuilding in Central Asia
Imaginaries, Discourses and Practices of Social Ordering
By **Philipp Lottholz**

Doing Fieldwork in Areas of International Intervention
A Guide to Research in Violent and Closed Contexts
Edited by **Berit Bliesemann de Guevara** and **Morten Bøås**

Surviving Everyday Life
The Securityscapes of Threatened People in Kyrgyzstan
Edited by **Marc von Boemcken**, **Nina Bagdasarova**, **Aksana Ismailbekova** and **Conrad Schetter**

Forthcoming

Navigating the Local
Politics of Peacebuilding in Lebanese Municipalities
By **Hanna Leonardsson**

Unarmed Civilian Protection
A New Paradigm for Protection and Human Security
Edited by **Ellen Furnari**, **Randy Janzen** and **Rosemary Kabaki**

Shaping Peacebuilding in Colombia
International Frames and Local Contestations
By **Catalina Montoya Londoño**

For more information about the series and to
find out how to submit a proposal visit
**bristoluniversitypress.co.uk/
spaces-of-peace-security-and-development**

SPACES OF PEACE, SECURITY AND DEVELOPMENT

Forthcoming

Memory Politics after Mass Violence
Attributing Roles in the Memoryscape
By **Timothy Williams**

Development as Entanglement
An Ethnographic History of Ethiopia's Agrarian Paradox
By **Teferi Abate Adem**

International Advisory Board

Rita Abrahamsen, University of Ottawa, Canada
John Agnew, University of California, Los Angeles, US
Alima Bissenova, Nazarbayev University, Kazakhstan
Annika Björkdahl, Lund University, Sweden
Berit Bliesemann de Guevara, Aberystwyth University, UK
Susanne Buckley-Zistel, Philipps University Marburg, Germany
Toby Carroll, City University of Hong Kong
Mick Dumper, University of Exeter, UK
Azra Hromadžić, Syracuse University, US
Lee Jones, Queen Mary University of London, UK
Louisa Lombard, Yale University, US
Virginie Mamadouh, University of Amsterdam, Netherlands
Nick Megoran, Newcastle University, UK
Markus-Michael Müller, Free University of Berlin, Germany
Daniel Neep, Georgetown University, US
Diana Ojeda, Xavierian University, Colombia
Jenny Peterson, The University of British Columbia, Canada
Madeleine Reeves, The University of Manchester, UK
Conrad Schetter, Bonn International Center for Conflict Studies, Germany
Ricardo Soares de Olivera, University of Oxford, UK
Diana Suhardiman, International Water Management Institute, Laos
Arlene Tickner, Del Rosario University, Colombia
Jacqui True, Monash University, Australia
Sofía Zaragocín, Universidad San Francisco de Quito, Ecuador

For more information about the series and to find out how to submit a proposal visit
**bristoluniversitypress.co.uk/
spaces-of-peace-security-and-development**

PRECARIOUS URBANISM

Displacement, Belonging and the
Reconstruction of Somali Cities

Jutta Bakonyi and Peter Chonka

First published in Great Britain in 2024 by

Bristol University Press
University of Bristol
1-9 Old Park Hill
Bristol
BS2 8BB
UK
t: +44 (0)117 374 6645
e: bup-info@bristol.ac.uk

Details of international sales and distribution partners are available at bristoluniversitypress.co.uk

© Bristol University Press 2024

British Library Cataloguing in Publication Data
A catalogue record for this book is available from the British Library

ISBN 978-1-5292-1522-9 hardcover
ISBN 978-1-5292-1523-6 paperback
ISBN 978-1-5292-1524-3 ePub
ISBN 978-1-5292-1525-0 ePdf

The right of Jutta Bakonyi and Peter Chonka to be identified as authors of this work has been asserted by them in accordance with the Copyright, Designs and Patents Act 1988.

All rights reserved: no part of this publication may be reproduced, stored in a retrieval system, or transmitted in any form or by any means, electronic, mechanical, photocopying, recording, or otherwise without the prior permission of Bristol University Press.

Every reasonable effort has been made to obtain permission to reproduce copyrighted material. If, however, anyone knows of an oversight, please contact the publisher.

The statements and opinions contained within this publication are solely those of the authors and not of the University of Bristol or Bristol University Press. The University of Bristol and Bristol University Press disclaim responsibility for any injury to persons or property resulting from any material published in this publication.

Bristol University Press works to counter discrimination on grounds of gender, race, disability, age and sexuality.

Cover design: blu inc, Bristol

Front cover image: Construction of makeshift shelter in a resettlement area in the outskirts of Bosaso. Photo taken by Nuurow, a resident of the area and a research participant, July 2018.

Contents

List of Figures and Table		vi
About the Authors		viii
Acknowledgements		ix
1	Introduction: Researching Precarious Urbanism and the Displacement–Urbanization Nexus	1
2	Histories of Conflict and Mobility: The View from the City	26
3	Camp Urbanization and Humanitarian Entrepreneurship	52
4	Improvising Infrastructure: The Micropolitics of Camp Life	78
5	Techno Relief? Connectivity, Inequality and Mobile Urban Livelihoods	107
6	Liminal Durability: Belonging in the City and Enduring Solutions	138
7	Conclusion: Living at the Precarious Edges of Planetary Urbanization	173
Appendix		187
Notes		189
References		192
Index		220

List of Figures and Table

Unless otherwise stated, all photographs featured in the book were taken in July 2018.

Figures

1.1	Photograph of a camp at the edge of Baidoa	5
1.2	Photograph of view from within Statehouse in Hargeisa, Somaliland	6
2.1	Map of the Somali Horn of Africa	28
2.2	Photograph of the 'Ex-Health Ministry Camp' in downtown Mogadishu	36
2.3	Photograph of the Statehouse neighbourhood in Hargeisa	47
3.1	Satellite images of the north-western outskirts of Mogadishu in 2012 and 2017	56
3.2	Photograph of camp urbanization in north-west Mogadishu	57
3.3	Photograph of a newly built house in the vicinity of a camp in Mogadishu	64
3.4	Satellite images of Statehouse in Hargeisa (2002 and 2017)	69
4.1	Photograph of toilets established before the growth of an outskirts camp in Baidoa	83
4.2	Photograph of toilet in a camp at Mogadishu's outskirts	85
4.3	Photograph of dilapidated toilets in resettlement neighbourhood on the edge of Bosaso	87
4.4	Photograph of a water point at the outskirts of Bosaso	91
4.5	Photograph of girl/young woman fetching water in a Mogadishu camp	93
4.6	Photograph of a maternal and child health centre (MCH) in Bosaso	97
4.7	Photograph of a Quranic school (*dugsi*) in Mogadishu	102
5.1	Photograph of a woman doing laundry in a camp in Mogadishu	108
5.2	Photograph of manual workers waiting for jobs in Bosaso	113
5.3	Photographs of cow and milk container, Baidoa	114

5.4	Photograph of laundry in Mogadishu	116
5.5	Photograph of woman making gravel in a Baidoa camp	117
5.6	Photograph of women and children searching a rubbish dump on the edge of Bosaso	118
5.7	Photograph of shoeshine boys, Bosaso	120
5.8	Photograph of children in a resettlement area in Bosaso playing with worthless paper currency	123
5.9	Photograph of camp sign at the outskirts of Mogadishu	126
5.10	Photograph of woman holding baby and mobile phone in a Mogadishu camp	131
6.1	Photograph of a woman from southern Somalia in a (re)settlement area in the northern city of Bosaso	139
6.2	Photograph of the resettlement area at Bosaso's outskirts	148
6.3	Photograph of camels in Mogadishu	159
6.4	Photograph of painting in a community centre of a Mogadishu camp	163

Table

A.1	Subclan self-identifications by interviewees (where given) in first round of narrative interviews	187

About the Authors

Jutta Bakonyi is Professor in Development and Conflict in the School of Government and International Affairs at Durham University. Peter Chonka is Lecturer in Global Digital Cultures in the Department of Digital Humanities, King's College, London.

Acknowledgements

A large team of collaborators was involved in the research project that this book is an outcome of. Along with the authors, Kirsti Stuvøy and Abdirahman Edle Ali were part of the core research team, and this book would not have been possible without their contributions. We are also grateful to the researchers who conducted interviews in the four cities: Mohamed Abdiqadir Botan, Ahmed Abdulahi Dualeh, Ismail Abdullahi Moalim, Mohamed Ahmed Takow Hassan, and Mahad Wasuge. Sincere thanks are also owed to Omar Dirie, Mohamed Yusuf Salah, and another person (who wished to be anonymous) who assisted us in the photovoice components of the research.

The exhibitions were an outcome of the photovoice methodology. They were held in the cities where the research was conducted and were organized in partnership with UN Habitat. We are grateful to Sagal Ali, Teresa del-Ministro, Amun M. Osman and Ishaku Maitumbi for their collaboration and assistance in facilitating these. We would also like to thank the government officials, representatives of international and national organizations, and other experts who participated as panellists at these exhibitions in the Somali cities, as well as in Kenya, Ethiopia, the UK and Norway. We are grateful for their reflections on the research findings and their engagement with the people who produced the photographs and testimonies featured in the exhibitions. Among others, these included Abdirahman Omar Osman 'Yarisow' (AUN), Abdisalaan Bashir Abdisalaan, Mohamed Cilmi Aden, Mohamoud Yusuf Aden, Asha Mohamed Ahmed, Mohamoud Yusuf Muuse, Ali Wardheere Abdirahman, Abdullaahi Ali Watiin, Maryam Abdi, Fathi Egal, Omar Degan, Pauline Skaper, Hannah Stogdon, Muna Ismail, Nick Bass, Rubbina Karruna, Safia Y. Abdi Haase, Stein Erik Horjen, Martin Suvatne, and Abdirashid Ali Warsame. We thank the organizations and institutions that hosted different versions of the exhibition, including the Rift Valley Institute, King's College London's African Leadership Centre/War Studies Africa Research Group, and KCL Somali Society. We would like to also express our thanks to the anonymous reviewers for their detailed, thoughtful and critical engagement with our manuscript. We are also grateful to the team at Bristol University

Press for their efficient, flexible and supportive collaboration throughout the publication process.

Thanks are also owed to the UK's Economic and Social Research Council (ESRC) and the Department for International Development (DFID) which provided the funding for the research (ES/R002355/1). An additional generous Leverhulme Fellowship (RF-2018-642) provided Jutta Bakonyi with the time necessary to write this book. Jutta is grateful that they did not impinge on her academic freedom to deviate from the topic of the original proposal.

On a personal level, Peter would like to thank Isabelle Sykes for the love and support that allows us to juggle our respective obligations to (often distant) colleagues, alongside care for our wonderful boys. He is also grateful for the support from Clifford and Elizabeth Chonka, and John and Marigold Sykes. Jutta would like to thank George Karanja, Ali Mihava and Mohammed Kariuki for providing numerous distractions and occasionally forcing her to move away from her desk.

Finally, we both wish to thank the many people living in marginalized urban settlements whose interview and photographic testimonies underpin our understanding of precarious urbanism in Somali cities. This book is dedicated to these people's strength and innovation in conditions of acute poverty.

1

Introduction: Researching Precarious Urbanism and the Displacement–Urbanization Nexus

Over the last two decades, the 'internally displaced person' (IDP) has become an increasingly central figure in policy, humanitarian and media reporting on violent conflicts and wars. The United Nations Guiding Principles on Internal Displacement, defines IDPs as:

> persons or groups of persons who have been forced or obliged to flee or to leave their homes or places of habitual residence, in particular as a result of or in order to avoid the effects of armed conflict, situations of generalized violence, violations of human rights or natural or human-made disasters, and who have not crossed an internationally recognized State border. (UNOCHA, 2001, 1)

Based on estimates that globally '80 percent of all IDPs are living in urban areas' (Muggah and Abdenur, 2018, 1), internal displacement is increasingly discussed in the context of urban studies and the intersection of violence, mobility and urbanization (Beall et al, 2011; Bartlett et al, 2012; Potvin, 2013; Sanyal, 2016; Darling, 2017; Büscher, 2018; Büscher et al, 2018; Pech et al, 2018; Muggah and Abdenur, 2018; Şimşek-Çağlar and Glick Schiller, 2018; Bakonyi et al, 2021). We aim to contribute to this literature with an empirical focus on the Somali Horn of Africa, a region characterized by its relatively low levels of urbanization (in global comparison) but very high rates of urban growth (Massy-Beresford, 2015), which UN Habitat has recently estimated at approximately 4.23 per cent (UN Habitat, 2020).

Somali cities constitute near exemplary cases for studying the nexus of displacement and urbanization. Over 30 years have passed since the collapse of the central government in Somalia, and these three decades have been characterized by recurrent armed conflicts and waves of mass displacement, involving different actors and levels of violence. The four cities focused on in this book – Baidoa, Bosaso and Mogadishu in Somalia, and Hargeisa[1] in the de facto independent Republic of Somaliland – have, over the years, been characterized by both phases of mass in- and out-migration. At the time of our research (2017–19), large numbers of displaced people were living within and at the outskirts of these four cities.

Neither displacement nor urbanization are abstract or universalizable phenomena. We aim to present and analyse perspectives from the urban margins, foregrounding the views of people who escaped violence and environmental shocks and sought refuge in cities where they now live in conditions of acute precarity. Displacement, although a dreadful experience, does not automatically lead to abject poverty. *Burburkii*, 'the destruction' of the Somali state in the early 1990s, and the decades of political instability that have followed were accompanied by multiple waves of displacement, several of which were experienced by the people we engaged with in the research for this book. Nonetheless, many examples demonstrate that people uprooted by violence can manage to rebuild prosperous lives elsewhere, whether in Somalia or across international borders. Eastleigh, a neighbourhood in Kenya's capital Nairobi where a large number of Somali refugees settled in the early 1990s, is often framed in terms of its transnational economic dynamism (Carrier, 2016). Within Somalia, there are many people – usually those who already had access to various forms of social and economic capital – who have been forced to move to new areas because of conflict and have been able to establish themselves and prosper. Although internally displaced – as, at one time or another, a significant proportion of the Somali population has been since the late 1980s – such people are not usually associated with the figure of the IDP and are thus not captured in the policy and humanitarian discourse that aims to deal with displacement and 'displacement affected populations'.[2] The IDP label is synonymous with poverty, vulnerability and marginalization. A large part of this book shows how this figure is (co)produced by a wide range of actors operating at different scales, and how the displacement label intersects with other vectors of social differentiation around ethnicity, race, gender, caste, class and place.

There are multiple stories to tell about the relationship between displacement and urbanization in the wider Horn of Africa, where many cities are experiencing rapid transformations and rapid growth. Carrier and Scharrer's recent volume (2019), for example, highlights the multifaceted impacts of Somali international migration on urban landscapes in countries such as Kenya, and how these cities can shape further patterns of mobility (see also Bakewell and Jónsson, 2011). We explore the transformations entailed in such 'mobile urbanity' from the perspectives of the urban margins of cities within Somalia and Somaliland. In doing so, we tell a story about the emergence of a particular form of precarious urbanism and the relations of power in which the precarious urban lives we describe and analyse are embedded. The book therefore also contributes to a continuously growing body of research that engages with the 'everyday' and 'ordinary' experiences of urbanization and urban life at the margins (Simone, 2001; Mbembe and Nuttall, 2004; Simone, 2004; Robinson, 2006; Wacquant, 2008; Hahn, 2010; Myers, 2011; Roy, 2011; van Noorloos and Kloosterboer, 2018; Aceska et al, 2019).

These everyday experiences are neither exceptional nor peripheral. Many, if not most, of the 2.9 million displaced people that UN agencies currently estimate for Somalia (including Somaliland) live in dilapidated settlements where they struggle to make ends meet (Hujale, 2021). We have used narrative interviews and photovoice to capture how these city newcomers have inhabited, appropriated, built and experienced the city. The focus of the book is on the multiple ways people attempt to rebuild their lives and in doing so (re)construct, often quite literally, the same cities that offer them a very limited range of opportunities and resources. Forced displacement can be both disruptive and generative. It induces hardship and disorientation and is associated with multiple losses. At the same time, displacements produce new social relations and orders, transforming how, for example, things, bodies, spaces, resources or money are assembled (Hammar 2014, 4). The generative effects are especially visible in the political economy of displacement (Hammar, 2014; Bakonyi, 2021). In Somali cities this involves small-scale humanitarian entrepreneurship (camp gatekeeping); the establishment of infrastructure; the commodification of land and the emergence of new urban land and labour markets; as well as the use and commercialization of technologies that connect marginalized populations into multiscalar networks and circuits.

Our methodology emphasizes a locational perspective and has attempted to work 'from the ground up' (Ettlinger and Bose, 2020, 517), albeit with important limitations that we reflect upon later in this introduction. From the start of our research, initial observations and conversations with people living in or familiar with marginalized settlements in the cities pointed to the geographically and politically stretched-out spatial and social relations that characterize the places and lifeworlds of urban in-migrants. Signs of international engagement – both literal and figurative, such as humanitarian NGO branding, newly built mosques, discussions of remittances from relatives in the diaspora, the ubiquity of mobile phones and mobile money – all immediately draw attention to the entanglements of specific (urban) places in 'more general social processes' (Massey, 1996, 102). Even if these places are marginalized, they remain embedded in and linked to the world (Massey, 1991; see also Mbembe, 2000; Robinson, 2016). The 'politics of location' (Roy, 2016, 201) is central in this book, and we aim to develop an analytic approach that makes visible the many multiscalar connectivities that are unevenly developed across and within marginalized settlements in the four cities. Prominent among these are international humanitarian and state-building interventions; investments in land and housing often through ventures from the global Somali diaspora or financial institutions; or continuously expanding information and telecommunication industries that enable mobile phone and internet access, as well as mobile money. These connectivities epitomize what Tsing (2005, 2) describes as capitalism's messy, uneven and 'makeshift links across distance and difference', and they intersect with gender, race, ethnicity and clan as they reconfigure social relations and shape urban experiences. These links are also part of the developments that have encouraged a more celebratory positioning (or 'hashtagging') of Somali cities in a broader 'Africa Rising' narrative (Hammond, 2013; Momodu, 2016; Chonka, 2019a). Such framings risk eliding the violent logics and differentiated experiences that accompany urban reconstruction and economic growth. Throughout this book we explore the specific processes and politics of urban renewal and reflect on tensions that manifest in how Somali cities are represented in various accounts (including our own).

First and foremost, though, our focus is on what people who have been displaced actually do when they arrive in the city. Here we are studying practices of moving to and being in the city that are immersive, non-systematic (what cannot be known in advance) and performative (where the rules are only given in action) (Cadman, 2009, 457). In this respect, de Certeau's (1984, 29ff.) 'art of doing' and 'making use' of the city have been helpful concepts. De Certeau described tactical movements and forms of 'making do' with conditions and places that are imposed upon people, but which nonetheless provide possibilities (within constraints) and enable, to some extent, changes to be made to what is found. This understanding of the everyday has contributed to our grounded and comparative perspective on quotidian experiences and struggles at the urban margins and our emphasis on how disenfranchised city dwellers are actively involved in the making of the four rapidly growing Somali cities. Literature on city-making and urban marginalization has developed various terms – such as makeshift arrangements (Vasudevan, 2014; Thieme et al, 2017), assemblages (McFarlane, 2011) or ensemble work (Simone, 2018) – to capture the struggles, experimentations and daily improvisations, but also the social and material contributions that are made by people at the urban margins (Simone, 2004; McFarlane, 2018). We selectively use these concepts in examining the social and material features of urban settlements established by people who arrived in the city and had few other options but to squat in vacant city spaces, conflict-damaged ruins or otherwise abandoned buildings, thus forming inner-city settlements. With most of these city-spaces being reclaimed, people started to erect makeshift huts at the edges of cities. These characteristically emerge

Figure 1.1: Photograph of a camp at the edge of Baidoa

Note: The city's outskirts are visible in the distance.
Source: Photograph taken by Mumino, a resident of this camp and participant in the research.

in the transitory structure of camps, which cumulatively house thousands of people in outskirts areas surrounding many Somali cities. Because these (re)settlement dynamics have played out in different ways across the four cities, the book discusses urban marginality for both geographically peripheral and more central urban locations. Although we emphasize the importance of location throughout, being at the urban margins is not foremost related to the location of a settlement but rather the socio-economic precarity that its residents live in and the social differentiation of these populations through labels such as IDP.

Camp settlements such as the one shown in Figure 1.1 are contributing to both urban densification and urban sprawl. Shaping space in and around the city, this constitutes what we conceptualize as distinctive forms of 'camp urbanization'. This concept has been developed elsewhere (Agier, 2002a, 2002b; Abourahme, 2015; Martin, 2015; Jansen, 2018), along with the related notion of 'humanitarian urbanism' (Büscher and Vlassenroot, 2010; Potvin, 2013; Büscher et al, 2018). However, the city examples we examine display important differences, both in comparison to other global contexts, and between the four Somali cities themselves. The form of camp urbanization analysed in this book does not so much involve the accidental emergence of 'camp cities' (Agier, 2002a, 2002b; Jansen, 2018),[3] nor the (literal) concretization over time of refugee camps as spatially distinct neighbourhoods within wider urban formations (Abourahme, 2015; Martin, 2015). Instead, our examples point to how mobile, constantly shifting patterns of arrival, settlement, transformation, eviction and resettlement are manifest in the

Figure 1.2: Photograph of view from within Statehouse in Hargeisa, Somaliland

Note: This settlement, formed on public land by displaced people and refugee returnees, is now surrounded by the wider city.

Source: Photograph taken by Sucad, a resident of this camp.

morphologies of the city and shape trajectories of urban development and ways of living. We describe the latter as precarious urbanism.

Patterns, materializations and temporalities of camp urbanization vary across the four cities. The settlements and neighbourhoods we examine are associated in humanitarian, policy and popular discourse with the in-migration of displaced populations, even if they persist over decades and transform into 'ordinary' urban slums or informal settlements (Figure 1.2). As we show with the examples from Hargeisa (Somaliland), long-term city residents have increasingly moved into such areas to find affordable shelter. The political categorization of migrants and urban poor is spatialized when informal settlements are defined as 'residential areas or housing units where occupants dwell without any legal claim to land', while camps are differentiated as 'temporary shelters for holding refugees, the internally displaced, and asylum seekers' (Huq and Miraftab, 2020, 351). Nonetheless, the 'IDP camp' remains a locally dominant idiom, and the concept of informality is problematic in contexts where little formal planning or state-driven governance of urbanization has taken place over more than three decades.

Another urban formation that has started to take shape more recently is the resettlement area. Often developing the character of spatially distinct neighbourhoods, these areas have been established through collaborations of international organizations and city governments to find 'durable solutions' for displacement affected populations. We investigate in the following chapters the making of all three of these types of settlements – informal settlements in the city, camps at the outskirts, and resettlement areas – living conditions within them, and their role in the wider processes of camp urbanization of Somali cities.

Although we often differentiate inner-city (squatter) settlements, camps and resettlement areas, distinctions between the three types of settlement are not clear cut, as we demonstrate throughout. Urban places are notorious for their refusal 'to be contained withing pregiven frameworks' (Massey, 2005, 161). Instead, the settlements tend to show how space is not foremost constituted by boundaries and enclosures but emerges through movement and circulation (Thrift, 2006, 141). This is evident in the continuously changing materialities and morphologies of the locations under focus. Although we specifically discuss connections between mobility, materiality and city-making, practices of governing these cities in Somalia or Somaliland (or anywhere else) invariably involve attempts to make places appear static and to define boundaries that delimit distinctions between in- and outsiders: those who belong, and those who don't; and those who don't but are tolerated for now. Discourses of belonging and citizenship are part of an ongoing politics of classification and (spatial) sorting that build on and simultaneously reconfigure relations of clan, ethnicity, race, gender and class. At the same time, they are reconstructing cities in ways that generate and embed marginality and precarious forms of urbanism. While we build at times on conventional differentiations between camp and city, rural and urban, displaced and host, newcomer and local, our exploration of urbanization processes emphasizes the multiple material and social assemblages that transcend binary classifications and illuminate practices of othering implicit in these codifications (see Pratt, 2019). In this way, we attempt to re-engage with the 'worlding' of cites from a non-essentializing perspective (see Simone, 2001, 2004; Ong, 2011; McCann et al, 2013). Worlding emphasizes performativity while taking account of the multiscalar activities, engagements and encounters of institutions and actors. Not all of these institutions and actors are necessarily located in the city and many of them are drawn together only temporarily to fix certain problems that they or others have previously identified (Ong, 2011, 3, 11).

Our comparative socio-spatial analysis of marginalized settlements in the four cities shows, for example, how the categorization of people as IDPs tends to flatten the diversity of experience and identities of in-migrant populations while (re-)producing distinctions between urban insiders and outsiders, the 'locals' and the 'displaced'. Analysing the multiple layers of distinctions that intersect with the figure of the IDP reveals how citizenship is understood, practised, and contested. However, it also shows that the 'art of being global' (Ong, 2011) is not restricted to a jet-setting elite, but is also a characteristic of precarious lives. Simone (2004) and Bayat (2000, 2010) have already shown how marginalized urban residents develop parochial, but nonetheless complex tactics and often mobilize connections across the globe to manage their survival. This literature contributes to the theorization of 'subaltern urbanism' – a body of knowledge that aims at disrupting grand narratives derived from reductionist readings of European and North American experiences. Such narratives often ignored the violence involved in the making of Northern cities and how colonialism and imperialism not only affected urbanity/ism in the global South, but inevitably shaped cities and urbanism at the core of empires (Rabinow, 1995; Jacobs, 1996). The mobilization of transnational links by marginalized populations is also a feature of work on refugee experiences (Horst, 2007), and we observe similar dynamics across the four cities. We attempt to present these cities in a way that 'cares about, and pays attention to, the inter-locking of multiple social-political sites and locations' (Gupta and Fergusson, 1997, 37) which are evident when comparing and contrasting emergent lifeworlds at the margins of the four urban centres. This 'comparative gesture' (Robinson, 2011) acknowledges 'local uniqueness' (Massey, 1983) of places, people and experiences, but also allows for careful generalizations beyond the cities and region under focus. In this way, we hope to contribute to theorizations of urbanization focusing on the way global urban dynamics unfold at the precarious 'edge of the world' (Mbembe, 2000).

A common theme within this adopted perspective is precarity. Although existing in multiple and complex forms, precarity can initially be understood as existential and sustained insecurity and uncertainty (Ettlinger, 2007; Butler, 2009). Such deep-rooted insecurity dominates the narratives and photographic accounts of research participants, as they reveal socio-spatial and relational formations of security (Dillon, 2004) as well as the fragmentation and segregation through which urbanization unfolds (McFarlane, 2018; Stuvøy et al, 2021). Interviewees and photovoice participants have provided testimonies that reveal intimate details and at times also degrading experiences of enforced mobility and poverty. For example, people described how they had been repeatedly exposed to physical violence, exploitation, extortion, hunger, and sickness, and many presented their lives as ongoing stories of material and social deprivation and distress. We specify and discuss these experiences, but also detail the strategies people develop for surviving extreme precarity, including building-up and mobilizing reciprocal relationships and networks and developing practices of mutual care and support.

None of these relations and practices are devoid of power. We explore how inequalities, struggles, and conflicts are shaping how people settle, make use of land and housing, use information and communication technologies, provide labour, and establish infrastructures while compensating for gaps and malfunctions, and co-produce social distinctions and discriminations to position themselves vis-à-vis powerful actors who may provide support. This all points to the often highly localized and unintentional interweaving of activities, ideas and aspirations that simultaneously activate and remould relations of power, from quite different social positions and scales of reach. Throughout the book, however, we emphasize that displacement is neither peripheral nor temporary but a central part of the rapid urbanization that is underway in the Horn of Africa. Mobile populations and those living at the urban margins are active agents in the making of cities (Şimşek-Çağlar and Glick Schiller, 2018) as they forge social connections, contribute to urban reconstruction, and negotiate their 'right to the city' (Lefebvre, 1996; Samara et al, 2013). The extent to which marginal urban practices can be understood as resistance against relations of exploitation and domination or even have the potential to alter relations of power (Beveridge and Koch, 2018) remains contested. However, our examples point to the reproduction of power relations even while subaltern populations are 'quietly impinging on the propertied and powerful, and on society at large' (Bayat, 2010, 15).

Methodological considerations: displacement narratives

This book presents, analyses and compares snapshots of people's experiences of displacement and (re)settlement across the cities of Baidoa, Bosaso, Hargeisa and Mogadishu. These accounts are presented in the form of interview excerpts and photographs. As with many methodological approaches in conflict-affected environments, ours was not only based on intellectual considerations but was also shaped by the necessities of a research field dominated by security issues and limitations of access (Bliesemann de Guevara and Bøås, 2020; MacGinty et al, 2020). Our research process was heavily influenced by relationships between the securitized environment in which it took place and the technologies it used. Immersive ethnographic fieldwork would have been desirable but remains unfeasible in most of the cities, not only for foreign but also for Somali researchers. Except for Hargeisa in Somaliland, each of the cities presents significant security risks for research. The Islamist militant group Al Shabaab maintains a clandestine presence in Mogadishu, Baidoa and Bosaso, while the risk of kidnapping or targeted violence remains for both international and Somali researchers. These threats can also affect people who reside in ostensibly secure and segregated compounds managed by international organizations (ICRC, 2018; Bakonyi, 2022a) as well as people working for international or Somali NGOs (HRW, 2020). Ethnographic research on displaced populations in East Africa has, therefore, focused on refugee camps in Kenya where a degree of long-term immersive engagement has been possible (Horst, 2007; Jaji,

2012; Jansen, 2018; Ikanda, 2019; Brankamp, 2020). Relatively little research has been undertaken in marginalized settlements of conflict-affected cities within Somalia and Somaliland. Because ethnographic fieldwork in these urban settlements was unfeasible, we considered alternative approaches that could help us to gain some understanding of lived experiences at the urban margins. We chose narrative interviews and photovoice, and reflect here on these choices and how the methods were undertaken.

The oral and visual material that this book is based on was generated between 2017 and 2019 in a UK ESRC/DFID-funded research project entitled 'Security on the Move' (securityonthemove.co.uk). The core research team consisted of Jutta Bakonyi (Durham University), Kirsti Stuvøy (Noragric and the Norwegian University of Life Sciences), Abdirahman Edle (South West Livestock Professional Association, and now a University of Nairobi/Copenhagen doctoral candidate) and Peter Chonka (Durham University, now King's College London). We cooperated with eight researchers based in the cities, including Mohamed Abdiqadir Botan, Ahmed Abdulahi Dualeh, Ismail Abdullahi Moalim, Mohamed Ahmed Takow Hassan, Omar Dirie, Mohamed Yusuf Salah and Mahad Wasuge[4] – who contributed for shorter periods to different stages of the research. Narrative interviews were conducted with 177 people in Baidoa, Bosaso, Hargeisa and Mogadishu, the majority living in either outskirts camps, inner-city (squatter) settlements or resettlement areas as differentiated previously. Forty people, most of whom had participated in the earlier interviews, took part in the photovoice exercise that formed a second step in the research process. We use a selection of these photographs throughout the book.

Most of the narrative interviews were conducted by the Somalia/Somaliland-based researchers. The interviews followed a research guide that the research team had jointly developed during a fieldwork preparation workshop in Nairobi. The city-based researchers, however, were requested not to follow the guide too closely, but rather encourage respondents to talk about their migration biographies and settlement experiences at their own pace and rhythm. Most interviews were conducted with people living in urban settlements associated with displacement, including 68 with men and 93 with women. The ages of interviewees ranged from 17 to 98. Efforts were made to speak with people from the widest possible range of clan groups. Given that settlement practices are often clan-based, a wide coverage of settlements in each city was sampled to account for clan diversity (see Appendix). People were interviewed in fourteen settlements in Baidoa; six in Bosaso, six in Hargeisa and ten in Mogadishu.

Beyond security, the research team had to overcome further barriers, including the negotiation of access with gatekeepers. These are the people who set up and manage new settlements and link incoming migrants, landowners and aid organizations. We were obliged to work with these gatekeepers, and they preselected interviewees following criteria we set out. Depending on individual negotiations, gatekeepers received between $50 and $100 for their service. This provides yet another example of the political economy that underpins camp urbanization in Somali cities (Chapter 3). It also demonstrates how research becomes part of this economy. Gatekeeping, as Spencer et al (2021) discuss, is not merely about getting access to places and people but also shows how power is diffused throughout the research process. Field research and interviews[5] are embedded in multiple forms of negotiations and interactions between researchers, gatekeepers, interviewers and other actors who may try to influence research findings (see Bakonyi, 2018) and become part of the process of (academic) knowledge-generation.

The preselection of interviewees by gatekeepers may have introduced a bias in the sampling. However, to the best of our knowledge, gatekeepers did not try to influence the answers of the interviewees and seemed to have selected people more with respect to their own convenience than the expected answers of the interviewees – many of whom shed light on and critically discussed practices of gatekeeping. We use Chapter 3 to explore the complex role of gatekeeping in more detail and from the perspective of both the new urban residents and these camp leaders.

Interviews were held in Somali and lasted between 45 and 90 minutes. They attempted to elicit people's migration experiences, the reasons why they fled, the routes taken, the selection of destination cities, and experiences on arrival and while living in urban areas. To get a sense of the wider environment of the cities, interviews were also conducted with people involved in different ways with the settlements, including elders who lived in their vicinity; people who played roles in their management but did not themselves reside there; representatives of municipal, federal or central governments; and staff of national and international organizations involved in urban planning or humanitarian support. Interviews were recorded and translated into English. The recordings/translations were reviewed by the Somali-speaking members of the core research team, including Peter Chonka. The interview excerpts we use to evidence and substantiate our arguments have been copy-edited to enable extensive direct quotation (sometimes removing interviewer questions) and to account for nuances in translation. To protect respondents, we use aliases and have removed identity markers and the exact dates and locations of interviews.

The interviews were analysed by the core research team. Immersing ourselves in hundreds of pages of transcripts, we first developed codes individually, but then compared notes, discussed and further fine-tuned these together. These codes were applied across all interviews. For this book, the two authors have developed additional codes and applied these to the original research material. This process enabled us to bring emergent topics of individual accounts into conversation with each other, moving from engagement with personal stories and perspectives to a broader and comparative view of patterns of experiences of displacement and urbanization across the four cities. Before detailing how we facilitated photovoice, the second pillar in the methodological approach, a reflection on the categorizations that we used or avoided is necessary.

The power to categorize and classify

Empirical research always risks developing overly stringent categories, and risks using a political and potentially conflictive language that imposes neat labels onto messy social realities. Discussions at our initial research workshop revealed early on the arbitrariness of commonly used categories of displacement. Differentiations between internally displaced people, refugees, returnees, economic or political migrants, and voluntary or forcefully displaced migrants do not correspond neatly with the lived experiences of mobile populations in Somalia (or elsewhere), or the complex interplay of compulsions and choices that underpin the different forms and scales of movement that is here captured as displacement. These categories imply distinctions in regard to identities, practices and problems of diverse populations (Zetter, 1991; Bakewell, 2008a; Crawley and Skleparis, 2018; Sturridge et al, 2018) that are often grounded in 'methodologically nationalist' views that take the existence of a state for granted and reify this as the quasi-natural political organization (Wimmer and Schiller, 2002). After more than 30 years of state collapse and the emergence of a highly fragmented and contested landscape of political authorities, methodological nationalism jars with experiences of government and associated practices of belonging and citizenship in Somalia and Somaliland. Attempts to quantify and categorize human movement into headline numbers that differentiate 'international', 'internal' and 'return' mobility,[6] are empirically questionable and politically contentious. The Republic of Somaliland provides an obvious example here. Somaliland declared its independence from Somalia in 1991 and operates as an autonomous and independent political entity, albeit one that is not internationally recognized. Because it lacks international recognition, regardless of whether people have been displaced to its cities from within its territory or from Somalia, they are understood by the Federal Government of Somalia (FGS) and its international backers as internally displaced. In contrast, the Government of Somaliland considers in-migrants from Somalia as refugees, at least if they do not belong to one of the major clans that populate its territory. With such a link, they would be considered returnees.

There are many more examples of how political contestation and reconfigurations of government impact on and provide further classifications of the people and places discussed in this book. Governmental actors are currently rebuilding the state of Somalia through a federal model, which

Somaliland rejects joining. Many of the political fault-lines between the internationally recognized FGS based in Mogadishu and its constituent federal member states (FMS) have been shaped by the militarization of clan-based divisions during the civil war and violent conflicts that followed the state collapse in 1991 (Bakonyi, 2009; Kapteijns, 2012). At the time of writing, the FGS struggles to exercise empirical sovereignty beyond Mogadishu and relies on support from the African Union Mission in Somalia (AMISOM, which became the African Union Transitional Mission in Somalia in 2022). The FGS operates in practice through a 'series of city states [...] where aid and the displaced are now concentrated' (Jaspars et al, 2019, IV). The form of the state remains contested and governmental authorities at FGS and FMS levels compete with each other, for instance in relation to processes for transitions of political authority or relations with foreign patrons (Hagmann, 2016). The FGS and FMS also compete with Harakat al-Shabaab al-Mujahideen (Al Shabaab) for control of cities, regions and the wider country. In this context, notions of belonging, the definition of in- and outsiders, internal or internationally displaced, refugees and returnees are an important part of ongoing contestation around government and citizenship.

Foregrounding the views of people who sought refuge in cities, we avoid looking at displacement through the eyes of the state or its humanitarian partners with whom it shares a 'secret solidarity' in the government of unwanted mobility (Agamben, 1998, 133). We decided early on to abandon such categorizations and instead use the concept of displacement widely and without further classification. This also implies that we do not differentiate economic from political or conflict-related displacement, the former often thought of as voluntary, the latter as forced. But how voluntary is displacement caused by the loss of livelihoods due to climate change-linked drought, the loss of employment opportunities, rising food prices or predation by armed groups? Many, but not all interviewees fled in response to violence, others to escape droughts, and most because of a combination of both. The connection between wars and droughts, and the ways violence interrupts coping mechanisms and accelerates the transition from drought to famine are already well documented (de Waal, 1997). Very few interviewees moved to a city only because they expected better economic prospects without first having experienced the (violent) loss of their livelihoods. Some interviewees in Bosaso were strongly driven by the desire to make an onwards journey across the Gulf of Aden to the Arabian Peninsula and possibly to Europe. However, even they were usually first confronted with violence or the loss of livelihoods before they decided to embark on the international, undocumented and dangerous migration path, known in the context as *tahriib* (Ali, 2016). Many interviewees had fled more than once, some had crossed borders in the process, while others immediately settled in a city where they often experienced evictions and, thus, continued displacement.

In sum, reasons for and patterns of mobility in the wider Horn of Africa are complex and comprise multiple intertwined factors, many of which can be linked to violence and ecological insecurity. Directions of migration are seldom linear, and the maps and graphic visualizations produced by international organizations to quantify and present mobilities significantly flatten out experiences and dynamics of displacement.

As mentioned earlier, we have avoided categorizing mobilities and displacement according to a state-centred and administrative logic. However, taking a broader view of displacement risks homogenizing people's experiences of (forced) mobilities, thus generating a reductive view of the multiple axes of individuals' identities. We explore throughout this book the flattening effect of the IDP label (*barakacayaasha* – 'the displaced') which many actors use to identify and talk about in-migrants. They thereby also contribute to the delineation and exclusion of people as urban outsiders, often implying (but avoiding) specific clan, ethnic/racialized, caste or class descriptors. This, we argue, is part of the emergent social stratification of cities in Somalia and Somaliland.

In this respect, Bjarnesen and Turner's (2020) edited volume on African displacements foregrounds the interplay between visibilization and invisibilization of migrant populations as both a form of structural marginalization produced by institutions engaged in administering and managing migration, but also as strategies used by migrants themselves to cope with ascribed labels and roles. Our analysis of camp urbanization in Somalia/Somaliland contributes further to this discussion. For example, it shows how practices of labelling displacement render people and places (in-)visible in multiple ways. The categorization of people as internally displaced, is materialized in camps, the makeshift settlements that are presented as the places where IDPs live. Such camps make some forms of displacement visible while hiding others, for example people who move in with relatives outside of camps. Categorizations are also made visible through a politics of problematization (Foucault, 1998) and the depiction of displacement, urban in-migration and camps as humanitarian and urban-planning problems, while suggesting solutions and designing interventions to address them. The materialization and problematization of displacement contribute to identity formations as they differentiate experiences of displacement, which are often made (in)visible in ways that serve the interests of dominant groups in the cities.

Although we emphasize that using the homogenizing label of 'displaced people' is inherently problematic, we have not been able to develop an alternative lexicon that systematically disaggregates the complexity of human experience with (enforced) mobilities and precarious forms of urban settlement. Depending on the location, topic and analytical focus of the chapters, we therefore use terms such as camp dwellers, inhabitants of the urban margins, refugee returnees, minoritized groups and new settlers (referring to resettlement areas) to emphasize specific contexts, dynamics and relations of power that structure the experiences of migration, settlement and urbanization.

Pictures, visibility and power

The research step that followed narrative interviews involved participatory photography and discussion of these images - a process that made certain aspects of displacement explicitly visible (Bjarnesen and Turner, 2020). The use of photovoice approach was intended to generate knowledge on lived experiences of displacement and settlements at the urban margins, providing photographers with the option to self-visualize their circumstances and perspectives. Displacement and mobility across the Horn of Africa are usually made visible to the world through images taken by photojournalists or international organizations. These photos appear in newspaper articles, blogs, reports, policy briefs and fundraising material. Most commonly, experiences of internal displacement are illustrated by photographs that position people among dilapidated shelters and inhospitable surroundings. Often focusing on women and children (at times also the elderly of both sexes) and portraying people in misery and seemingly without agency, such crisis photography is part of a 'politics of pity' that aims at mobilizing emotions from a distance, often to justify and gather resources for interventions (Boltansky, 1999; Nikielska-Sekula, 2021, 8).

Such imagery is shot through (as it were) with unequal relations of power. Images themselves exert power as they generate and distribute emotions and information while contributing to the production of knowledge. Humanitarian photography often tries to provide a crisis with an identifiable face and thus focuses on individual bodies (Slovic et al, 2017). Photographed people are often neither given the choice of having their picture taken, nor can they decide where and how their image is used. Questions are increasingly raised about the possibility of subjects of humanitarian photography – particularly the children whose faces tug at the heart strings of distant donors (Manzo, 2008) – to give meaningful and informed consent about the use of their images for fundraising. Similarly, commentators in the region have argued that such photography may reinforce tropes of endemic violence and suffering at the expense of more nuanced analysis of economic, political or cultural developments (Kahiye, 2015). Images play an important role in mobilizing aid, but the way human suffering is portrayed often reinforces (gendered) cliches and obscures both the immediate politics of crises as well as the social structures and (international) power dynamics that underlie and shape violent conflicts (Müller, 2013). Many of these photos also invoke fantasies of (white) 'saviour humanitarians' (Smith and Yanacopulos,

2004; Scott, 2014; Ademolu and Warrington, 2019) counterposed with the generic figure of the displaced as powerless, voiceless, miserable and in need of saving.

To some extent, the advent of social media has brought new possibilities for popular critique (Schwarz and Richey, 2019; Chonka 2019b) and has influenced shifts in (post)humanitarian communication strategies (Chouliaraki, 2010) away from the use of reductive visualizations. Nonetheless, the politics of media and photographic framing of crisis and emergency remains a contentious topic. A variety of factors feed into this sensitivity in the Horn of Africa: the recurrent necessity for emergency fundraising for humanitarian campaigns; extensive international engagement; high profile and easily sensationalized spectres of terrorism and piracy; an increasingly active social media commentariat within Somalia and throughout the global diaspora; and contested local narratives about political and economic reconstruction across the fragmented territory (Chonka, 2019c).

We stumbled into the use of photovoice with some naivety, and we reflect on this critically below. Nonetheless, we were attracted to the promise of the method to potentially alter researcher-informant power imbalances, transforming informants into research participants and co-producers of knowledge. Drawing from Wang and Burris's (1997, 370) foundational articulation of the photovoice method, we aimed to support individuals to visualize their experiences; to facilitate dialogue through group discussions of visual material; and to influence policymakers through the dissemination of pictures and their accompanying testimonies. In this sense, we also intended to play on the affective and emotive features of photos, using them as a tool to attract attention of urban planners and policymakers, and to facilitate dialogue between them and people living in dire precarity. At the same time, these methods were also chosen to respond to constraints on ethnographic access to the research sites outlined previously. Participant-generated images made these sites not only visible to exhibition audiences, but also to the core research team who could not spend extended time in many of the settlements where research participants lived.

Photovoice is often used by researchers working with social groups understood as being culturally, politically or economically marginalized (Wang and Burris, 1997; Green and Kloos, 2009; Denov et al, 2012; Sutton-Brown, 2014; Butz and Cook, 2017). The combination of visual and oral testimonies also aimed at overcoming the limits of the written and spoken word and to move beyond constricting categorizations developed in academia and policy. Literacy levels in Somalia are low, partly due to the collapse of schooling in the 1990s (Abdi, 1998; Cassanelli and Abdikadir, 2008). However, the Somali Horn is renowned for a rich oral culture and poetic canon, and research has emphasized photovoice's value in cultural contexts emphasizing non-written communications (Castleden and Garvin,

2008; Maclean and Woodward, 2013). To our knowledge, photovoice has not been used as an academic research method within the Somali-speaking Horn of Africa.

Given that we use photographs and aligned testimonies throughout the book, it is worth detailing the process, the issues that emerged, and how the photos were discussed, interpreted, analysed and eventually selected to be made public. The initial narrative interviews were used by the core research team to identify possible participants and invite ten interviewees from each city to participate in the subsequent photovoice process. The remote supervision of the selection process became a challenge: in Bosaso and Hargeisa the majority of photovoice participants had been involved in the previous interviews. In Baidoa and Mogadishu the need to involve camp leaders/gatekeepers led to the recruitment of participants who had not been part of the initial interview sample. However, as with the narrative interviews, participants were selected to maximize the number of settlements involved, ensure an equal number of men and women, and diverse representation of clan, age and lengths of settlement in the city. In Mogadishu, again, the sample was somewhat less broad, as four of the participants came from the neighbourhood of an influential camp leader (which we came to realize through the photos they presented).

In mid 2018, the authors and the other two members of the core team began the photovoice with workshops for the photographers in each city. Participants were invited to photographically document aspects of their daily lives that they wanted to share with the researchers and wider audiences, including policymakers. They were given a digital camera (Hargeisa) or smartphone (cities in Somalia), received guidance on its use, basic photographic techniques, and ethical and security considerations (to which we return later). After a period of between five and ten days, the photographers were invited back in smaller gender-split groups to discuss their photos. Although participants were asked to present only some of their pictures that they considered meaningful or wanted to share, many decided to hand over everything they had taken, ranging from 20 to 30 photos to hundreds of images. During the workshop, we invited photographers to present and talk about their pictures: what they showed, why they had taken those images, and what they meant to them. Other participants contributed to the discussion while we asked questions either to clarify or to elicit further dialogue. In this way, themes or stories that emerged from the selection and details within the photographs – people, expressions, styles of dress, actions, objects, the built environment – became prompts for group discussions, sometimes eliciting jokes and laughter, and sometimes being received in (rather sad) moments of quiet. These discussions were audio-recorded, transcribed and analysed together with the photos, thus complementing the narrative interviews.

The visual prompts made features of everyday urban life visible that would likely not have been identified in interviews. For example, a photo from Bosaso showed children playing with household waste, including Somali shilling banknotes (Figure 5.8). This initiated a group discussion about the problem of counterfeit currency and policies that rendered much cash in circulation to be worthless. This led to a further discussion on mobile money systems (see Chonka and Bakonyi, 2021).

Some participants apparently photographed everything they came upon, while others appeared to be more strategic in their choice of pictures and presentation. One photographer from Mogadishu focused his pictures on individuals with severe health problems, disabilities or conflict-related injuries and presented these images in a way that showed his expectations for direct support. This revealed broader sociomaterial realities in which research methods (here, narrative interviews and photovoice) are entangled and how these lead to particular emphases of speakers and photographers. Photographs reflect many of the 'discursive and aesthetic assumptions of the camera holder' (Hutcheon, 1993, 248) and have, or are expected to have, affective qualities that influence the (potential) audience in particular ways (Rose 2016, 9ff.). In the same way that we as authors subsequently selected photographs with the aim of sensitizing audiences and allowing viewers to gain some understanding of experiences at the urban margins, some photographers aimed at drawing the attention of the researchers to their most pressing problems. However, in contrast to the journalistic or humanitarian gaze, many photographers also showed photos of happy occasions. In Mogadishu, for example, we were shown photos of women gathering in festive clothes and preparing food to celebrate the birth of a child, as well as pictures of men sitting together in tea shops and discussing daily political issues in the settlements and beyond. Many people took photographs of their children that highlighted them as a source of pride and love that they wanted to speak about. Unfortunately, we felt that generally we could not publicly display such photos due to concerns about anonymization.

The photos, their presentation and the discussions around them spoke evocatively to topics of marginalization, unequal relations of power, fundamental uncertainty, insecurity and fear. However, they also pointed to an art of doing or an art of assembling – cobbling together and making do with whatever one was able to gather, whether materials, bodies or tools. We hope that the way we present the photos and testimonies in this book provides the reader with glimpses into the precarious, hopeful and, at times, miserable, humorous, mundane and dramatic lives lived at the margins of Somali cities.

Corresponding with what was initially the central theme of the research, a particular concern in undertaking photovoice was security. For example, our choice of giving research participants in Somalia smartphones was related to safety considerations. Given the ubiquity of mobile telephony across the cities, the use of a mobile phone to take photos was considered less risky than the use of a camera. However, we also discussed with the participants that the 'blending in' should not be misunderstood as encouragement for them to covertly take pictures, either without gaining consent or putting themselves in danger. Potential risks and the priority of safety were discussed in-depth in the photovoice training workshops. In Mogadishu and Baidoa most photographers therefore only took pictures in their own neighbourhoods or from their workplaces, as they considered it unsafe to take pictures in the wider city.

For security reasons, we decided to use only the first names of photographers who wanted to be identified, and pseudonyms for those who didn't. Although we do not wish to present a faceless world in these images, we have tended to avoid using photos where individuals are clearly identifiable, even if they gave their consent to be photographed. Preserving the anonymity of photographers and subjects alongside the method's aim for (self)representational agency constitutes a challenging balancing act (see Johnsen et al, 2008; Harley, 2012; Evans-Agnew and Rosemberg, 2016; Chonka et al, 2022). We take a cautious approach here, particularly considering security contexts across the cities.

The photographers kept the cameras or phones after the project was completed, a practice that seems uncommon in photovoice studies. This resembled an exchange of sorts: research participation and production of information (pictures and testimonies) for a useful and valuable device. Interviewees (from the narrative interviews) and photographers were also monetarily compensated for their time.[7] All interviewees were living in conditions of acute poverty and relied primarily on irregular manual day labour. Therefore, we felt that we needed to relieve them – for at least the day of the interview or workshop – from the stress of searching for another day job and allow them to focus on participation.

Visualizing security, exhibiting power

The photovoice material became the basis for exhibitions that the core research team co-organized with UN Habitat in all four cities. Academic research in conflict environments often becomes entangled with the aid industry (Stepputat, 2012; Mateja and Strazzari, 2017; Dodsworth and Cheeseman, 2018). However, we did not partner with UN Habitat primarily for security reasons, as we have both conducted prior research in Somalia without such support. Instead, we wished to build on and contribute to this organization's knowledge and experiences of cities and urban planning in the context, and to engage with policy and aid practitioners at the exhibition and dissemination stages of the project. Nonetheless, security considerations did contribute to the remote coordination of significant parts of the research project, particularly at the narrative interview stage. In Somalia/Somaliland,[8] the external research team operated in an environment characterized by what Duffield describes as extreme bunkering and relative detachment from the populations that aid workers are ostensibly there to assist (Duffield, 2018; Bakonyi, 2022a), or researchers to understand. These entanglements, along with remote coordination, undoubtedly contribute to North–South power dynamics in scholarship and enduring colonially inherited patterns of production of knowledge on the global South (Spivak, 1994; Aidid, 2015; Berns-McGown, 2016; Cronin-Furman and Lake, 2018; Eriksson Baaz and Verweijen, 2018).

Duffield (2013, 15) argues that information and communication technologies allow for the increased distancing of humanitarian work in fortified aid compounds as a reaction to emerging security threats. This, in turn, can reinforce the techno-discursive distance between donors and receivers of aid, and related historical power imbalances. Our research engaged with both donors and recipients; urban planners and people affected by such planning. At the same time, our use of networked digital technologies to generate information was probably more reminiscent of the remote-controlled cyber-humanitarianism that Duffield (2018) critiques. Visual representations in the form of participant photos and satellite images provide a remote researcher with a selective but seemingly direct view of research sites. Each provides a way of visualizing and a way of seeing with its own ethical and epistemological problematics (Gregory, 2011; Rothe, 2017), and we discuss this in more detail elsewhere (Chonka et al, 2022). These tensions intersect with contemporary discussions around the decolonization of scholarship and knowledge (Kessi et al, 2020), which, as Mignolo and Walsh (2018) state, remains necessarily incomplete and cannot be achieved through academic practices that take place in institutions which are deeply imbricated in 'the colonial matrix of power'. Our experiences certainly confirm this. The development of ethical partnerships between Northern and Southern researchers and institutions remains challenging (Coetzee, 2019) and given difficulties of access, security, and reliance on international and national interlocutors, Somalia presents a particularly complicated environment for attempts to destabilize the power imbalances that characterize research on the continent. At the same time, the need for this here is particularly acute, considering ongoing international military engagement and the high stakes of knowledge production (Al-Bulushi, 2014; Besteman, 2017).

Among the aims of the photovoice method was to use exhibitions as a distinctive setting to facilitate dialogue between people living at the urban margins and relevant policymakers, and potentially generate longer-term connections. Dilemmas around representation, participation and risk played a prominent role in the selection of images and testimonies for public display. Ultimately, we did manage to engage a wider public, including urban authorities such as city mayors, government ministers and staff from international and national organizations. Attendees had the opportunity to view the exhibition alongside the photographers, some of whom guided them through the displays, sharing their views and experiences.

We came to approach the exhibition process as another research site. Just as the interviewees' and photographers' engagement with the research is indicative of lived experiences and the socio-economic and political relations in which these experiences are embedded, the interactions we observed while organizing and participating in the exhibitions further pointed to power and security dynamics, and made visible the contested nature of displacement and belonging. For example, the curation of the exhibition in Hargeisa (Somaliland) generated tension between the research team and university that hosted the event because the exhibition included pictures from cities in Somalia. Government representatives and staff of the university objected to comparisons between Hargeisa, capital of the de facto independent Republic of Somaliland, and the other cities located in Somalia, in their view a separate state. We had anticipated such concerns, and exhibition materials were carefully selected to highlight Somaliland's separate political identity and distinctive displacement dynamics. Nonetheless, and as we discuss in the following chapter, Hargeisa's experiences of urban destruction, displacement, (re)settlement, reconstruction and growth are connected to Somalia's wider post-independence history of state formation, collapse and the violent conflicts that led to the separation of Somaliland. Both distinctive and shared features of the displacement urbanization nexus in Hargeisa (Somaliland) can be understood through comparisons with Baidoa, Bosaso and Mogadishu (Somalia).

The exhibitions showed marked differences in terms of the public participation and discussion of research participants. In Bosaso and Hargeisa some photographers took the opportunity to raise their voices and even criticized attending officials for their lack of action or unmet promises. In Baidoa and Mogadishu research participants were less outspoken, likely because of their more recent in-migration and overall greater security risks in these cities. One research participant in Baidoa was openly dismissed as a 'fake IDP' by a high-ranking member of the city government when he tried to raise a criticism. In Baidoa fear of Al Shabaab was another reason for people's reluctance to engage in public discussions. After all, Al Shabaab remains active in Baidoa's rural hinterland, and some participants occasionally return to their farms or homesteads in areas under the control of the group. The reluctance to speak openly in Mogadishu was also related to the political and socio-economic marginalization of in-migrants and related discourses of discrimination. The threat that Al Shabaab continues to pose in the capital was felt a few months after the exhibition when Mogadishu's mayor, Eng. Abdirahman Omar Osman 'Yarisow' (who had participated in our event) succumbed to injuries he sustained in an Al Shabaab suicide bombing at his office in the city. While this targeted attack had nothing to do with the mayor's engagement with the research exhibition, it underscored the fact that Mogadishu lacks a secure space for direct citizen–state engagement (see also Chonka, 2018). Overall, in presenting a selection of visual representations from people who live in precarity, the exhibitions and this book have aimed at disrupting traditional discursive framings in photojournalistic and humanitarian photography. Our adoption of the photovoice method was influenced both by security-related constraints of access as well as epistemological and ethical concerns around the external production of knowledge. While we are sceptical that these methods resolved the multilayered power imbalances between and among the researchers and research participants, we attempted to widen the methodological approaches and opportunities for participants to meaningfully participate in the research process. Readers will judge for themselves whether our research approach constituted 'doing things differently' (Marchais, 2020) and the value that our framing of this material will ultimately have for the book's contribution to understandings of displacement, urbanization and marginality. The extent to which this may be beneficial for marginalized populations in the types of settlements we researched also relates to a wider dissemination process that is ongoing and within which this book plays a role.[9]

The structure of the book

The chapters that follow examine the multifaceted relationship between conflict-linked displacement and city-making. They are structured thematically around different experiences of precarious urbanism, and ways in which city-making is being undertaken from and within settlements associated with displacement. Every chapter explores these themes comparatively in relation to each of the cities, albeit in some cases with a more pronounced focus on one location that exemplifies the wider dynamics described and analysed. Part of the distinctiveness of our contribution is grounded in this comparative approach, highlighting both similarities and differences in the way displacement and settlement at the cities' margins are experienced.

Chapter 2 provides a historical background to patterns of displacement and urban destruction during different phases of conflict in Somalia/Somaliland since the late 1980s. It compares the unfolding of violence in the four cities, before focusing on in-migration and ongoing efforts towards political and physical (urban) reconstruction. This chapter shows how patterns of conflict-related migration link each of the cities over the different phases of the wider conflict that both led to and resulted from the collapse of central government. It presents the cities' respective profiles and compares the experiences and motivations of people who have been displaced to (and between) these urban centres over the last three decades. In this way, the chapter begins to account for the emergence and particular morphologies of settlements that in-migrants establish.

Chapter 3 examines the political economy that has developed through encounters of urban in-migration with the destruction and reconstruction of cities. It foregrounds the actors involved in the establishment and maintenance of the different types of settlement and analyses their relationships with each other, focusing particularly on camp leaders, camp dwellers and landowners. These interactions are based on access to and (re)distribution of aid but are also shaped by affective ties of care and ambiguous emotions characteristic of patron–client relations. These relationships are less clear-cut and more complex than wider humanitarian discourses of aid diversion would suggest. Nonetheless, the political economy that accompanies urban displacement reproduces marginality and precarity, and often initiates evictions that lead to further displacements. These cycles of resettlement and (violent) evictions represent a nascent form of gentrification. Such dynamics are most visible and acute in Mogadishu, but comparisons are drawn with the other three cities to explain the socio-spatial dynamics that camp urbanization unleashes and the precarious forms of urbanism it generates.

Chapter 4 zooms further into the settlements and lived experiences of the urban margins, focusing on the micropolitics and improvisations that characterize development of infrastructures and service provision. Sanitation, water and health are assembled for and by people who rely on left-over materials and their own bodies and labour power to compensate for malfunctions and bridge infrastructural gaps. The chapter emphasizes making do and continuous improvisation. It conceptualizes infrastructures at the intersection of material and embodied practices that foster male and female subjectivities and exacerbate urban inequalities. In this way, infrastructures become tools and expressions of social differentiation. They are used to construct and rationalize distinctions between, for instance, those considered locals and displaced newcomers, irrespective of how long the latter had already been living in the cities.

A different kind of infrastructure is examined in Chapter 5. Mobile communicative networks connect residents in marginalized urban settlements with the wider city and the world at large. Mobile phones shape (gendered) labour relations through, for example, the relationship between precarious day labour and the affordances of mobile money systems for workers and employers. This chapter emphasizes how in-migrant populations contribute their labour power to the physical reconstruction and economic growth of the four cities, and details the role information and communication technologies (ICTs) play. Connectivities are ambiguous. They ease many of the time-consuming and potentially stressful requirements of face-to-face interaction as they connect people with job opportunities, enable worker payments, and allow microtransfers within families who have no access to savings. Such technologies sustain precarious livelihoods and can also reinforce divides between digitally differentiated labour pools. This chapter adds to critical engagements with 'ICT for development' (ICT4D) discourses among humanitarian and other policy actors, and problematizes narratives of empowerment centred on the harnessing of the entrepreneurial capacity of displaced populations through digital connectivity. Here we argue that a focus on displaced people's work potential – implicit within many accounts that adopt a tech-solutionist approach to poverty – can render invisible the city-making labour that is already being undertaken by marginalized and mobile people. It may also obscure questions of labour rights and their intersections with inequalities in digital literacy.

Chapter 6 explores the broader politics of belonging and citizenship in the four cities. It focuses on internationally supported urban planning initiatives that are resettling people from camps and inner-city settlements in Bosaso and Hargeisa. Again emphasizing ambiguity and ambivalence, the chapter discusses how resettlement schemes can improve tenure security and thus mitigate risks of evictions. However, these settlements tend to be located at the far periphery of cities, contributing to their distinctly detached and liminal character straddling urban and rural lifeworlds. Distance between city centres and resettlement areas can enable the territorialization of stigma associated with displacement. We show how resettlement schemes can align with locally prevalent stereotypes and distinctions made between people considered to belong to the city and those considered as outsiders. Markers of distinction are used and imposed on people living in settlements associated with displacement, an imposition that is even more powerful if the settlement is spatially segregated from the city 'proper'. Although we try to avoid using state-centred categorizations and reductive labels, as researchers we nonetheless recognize our own role in their co-production. Finding settlements and identifying interviewees, for example, involved a reliance on already existing distinctions and may subsequently contribute to their reinforcement. Therefore, Chapter 6 is also an explicit attempt to unpick some of these labels as it points to the various ways displacement, mobility or poverty can be categorized, contribute to othering, and reproduce or even strengthen existing forms of domination and discrimination.

The conclusion brings together the themes of each of the previous chapters, emphasizing that in-migrant populations are active – albeit marginalized – agents of city-making, as opposed to merely representing a humanitarian or development 'problem', or imposition on these cities that needs to be 'solved'. We reiterate here how Somali cities are sites of camp urbanization and humanitarian urbanism that take distinctive forms in comparison to other global contexts where many of the concepts we use have been developed. We also discuss how the book's experiential gaze at the nexus of displacement and urbanization brings into focus dilemmas and tensions in the representation of urban spaces characterized by economic and population growth, dynamic forms of reconstruction, bunkered international intervention, along with continued urban violence and marginalization.

2

Histories of Conflict and Mobility: The View from the City

'We came [from Baidoa] to a place called Hanti-Wadaag[1] in Qoryoley [around 1991]. We were there for such a long time and the drought had started. People were without food and starving. People were weak and dying, and that is how I lost my parents […] in Qoryoley. I was then living with my aunt for some time. She was poor too, and I decided to leave Qoryoley before I died of starvation. I left and went to Merca […] My siblings had died too. I am the only one left of a family of twelve persons. Merca was under the militant group – the USC [United Somali Congress] guerrillas. They were shocked at how I looked – long and shaggy hair, torn clothes. I was dirty and they gave me a small amount of money and a blanket. I was homeless and sleeping outside. I was there for about two months and decided to leave for Mogadishu where my uncle was. He was 83 years old at that time. The life in Mogadishu was very challenging too. I could not find my uncle and the security was even worse. I joined the street boys, started using drugs and was a shoeshiner. There I met Idris, we were from same neighbourhood [in Baidoa]. I don`t know whether he is alive or dead. He was working in a restaurant, he asked about our family and I told him that they had all died. He was so nice and was giving me the leftovers from the restaurant. I was sleeping in the streets where gangs hurt me many times. I asked Idris to help me find a room to rent to live in while I was working as a shoeshiner. The life was hectic and the sound of gunfire was normal. You would hear "so and so" had died, or was robbed, or was raped.' (Hanad, Bosaso, December 2017)

Hanad is a house painter in his 30s who lives in the port city of Bosaso, in the Puntland State of Somalia. His experiences since childhood of violence, poverty, hunger and continued forced migration – parts of which he recounts – directly connect three of the four cities that this book focuses on. Born in the southern inland city of Baidoa, Hanad was around ten years old when the mass violence and resulting famine that accompanied the collapse of the Somali state in 1991 forced him and his parents to flee to Qoryoley in the Lower Shabelle region. After the death of his parents, Hanad moved northwards along the coast to the capital, Mogadishu, to seek out some form of safety and sustenance with other family connections from Baidoa. As a young man in Mogadishu he met a girl from his home town, and because of continued violence and instability in the capital they left for Bosaso on Somalia's northern coast, around the year 2000. Bosaso offered the possibility of stability, employment and potential onward migration, which he ultimately did not embark upon, across the Gulf of Aden to the Arabian peninsula.

This book presents, contextualizes and analyses testimonies and photographs produced by people living in camps and settlements associated with 'the displaced' in four different Somali cities – individuals like Hanad. This material relates to people's lived experiences of precarity and their roles in processes of urbanization and (post)conflict reconstruction across cities that are linked through multiple mobilities. Some of these migration patterns have been shaped by histories of violent conflict that led to and followed the collapse of Somalia's central government in 1991. In this chapter we examine the concept of displacement through a historical overview of the relationship between forced mobility and different phases of violent conflict in Somalia. The chapter builds on personal experiences shared by research participants, and their memories of the unfolding political fragmentation of Somalia. As in Hanad's account, these memories detail multiple reasons for flight and show how people were moving to – or back to, or between – the cities of Baidoa, Bosaso, Hargeisa and Mogadishu through various periods of instability over the last three decades. The testimonies describe experiences of forced mobility, the ways in which people found and negotiated places to settle in cities on arrival, and how they attempted to rebuild their lives in the urban environment.

As we emphasize throughout the book, experiences of displacement and dynamics of urbanization across the four different cities are diverse. Nonetheless, each city has been shaped by often interrelated legacies of conflict and displacement. In the context of the prolonged political fragmentation of the former Somali Republic, the four cities are located within different political administrations whose orientation towards the ongoing federal reconfiguration of Somalia varies significantly (Figure 2.1).

After a brief overview of political dynamics that have underpinned the construction and break-up of the Somali state, the chapter focuses on each of the four cities. Research participants' narratives of displacement illustrate how different phases of the wider Somali conflict have affected each city,

Figure 2.1: Map of the Somali Horn of Africa

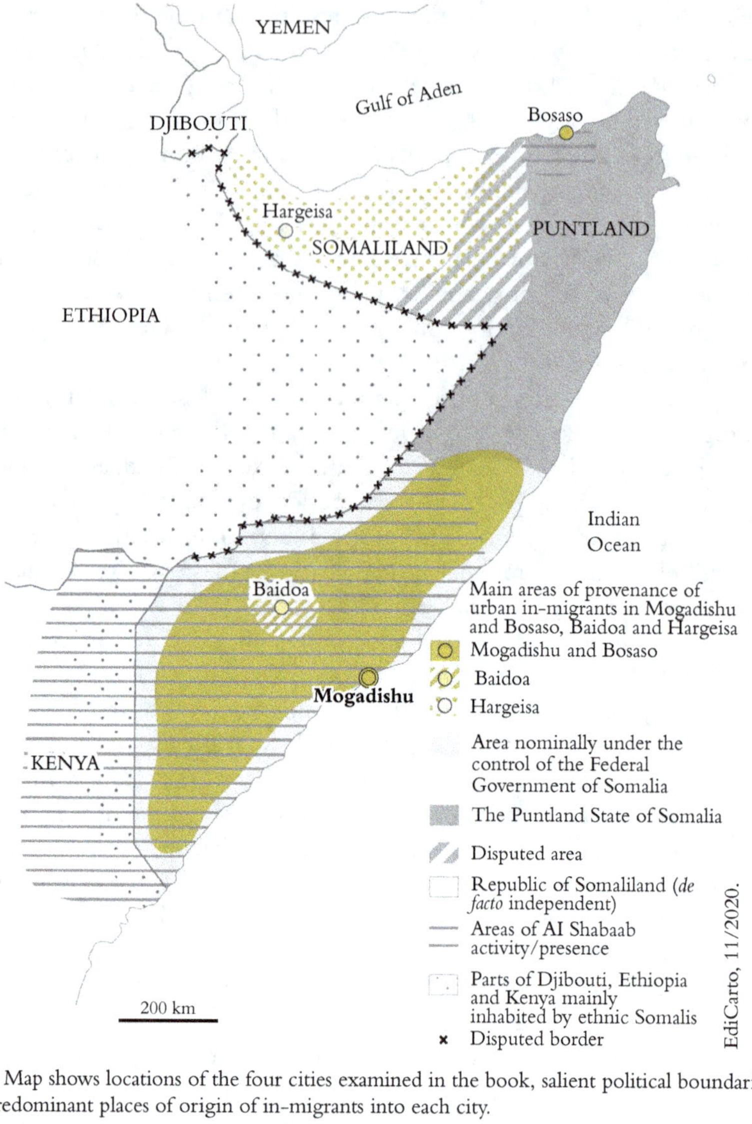

Note: Map shows locations of the four cities examined in the book, salient political boundaries and predominant places of origin of in-migrants into each city.

Source: An earlier version of this map was produced by *Afrique Contemporaine*, for an article written by the authors (Bakonyi and Chonka, 2019). An edited version is reproduced here with the kind permission of the journal publishers.

especially in terms of in-migration and the development of camp-like settlements in urban and peri-urban space.

Contemporary political divisions and continued political instability in Somalia are the product of over three decades of armed conflict. This historical trajectory is underpinned by changes in the political salience of clan relations, the experiences of the post-independence Somali state-builders, and foreign interventions. We begin here by contextualizing the former, clan affiliations and politics, and explain how the collapse of the Somali state in 1991 came to be conventionally (if controversially) understood as occurring along clan lines (Besteman, 1996, 1998; Lewis, 1998). Extensive work in Somali studies has problematized an essentialist view of clan as the primary cause and driver of violent conflict and has demonstrated how the meaning and political salience of clan affiliation has changed in the context of colonial domination, post-independence democratic experimentations, military rule and political contestation following state collapse (Samatar, 1989; Ahmed, 1995; Bakonyi 2009; Kapteijns, 2012). Nonetheless, clan dynamics have long been important for understanding population movements across the Somali populated territories of the Horn of Africa. This came across quite clearly in the ways in which many interviewees articulated their status, sense of belonging (or difference), and citizenship, often in contrast to their understanding of the clan-based character of the cities' make up. Clan affiliations are deeply intertwined in the broader political economy of violent conflicts, including the militancy of Al Shabaab, but also shape practices of reconciliation, peace- and state-building, and have therefore strongly influenced patterns of displacement, settlement and urbanization. One of the central arguments of this book is that interlinked and internationalized histories of conflict, political engagement and humanitarian action have produced a powerful discourse around displacement that marks out certain population groups as insiders or outsiders of cities and political territories that have been carved out since the 1990s. Clan-based discourses and practices inscribe themselves in spaces as they materialize in urban morphologies and shape urban developments through scales and forms of humanitarian urbanism. These factors have significant implications for understandings of citizenship across the fragmented political territories that today constitute Somalia and Somaliland. The categorization of people as displaced not only tends to collapse differences between people who have been forced to flee but also marks out distinctions between 'locals' and 'outsiders'. In Somalia, these distinctions and related practices of in- and exclusion are closely tied to clan affiliations that feed into claims of autochthony: kinship-based claims that are translated into territorial claims to a city. By problematizing in-migration in humanitarian or urban planning frames, the displacement discourse tends to elide political questions of belonging and citizenship. Such omissions and depoliticizations are usually beneficial to people from dominant clan and class groups, and often reinforce the precarity of migrant populations from marginalized clans.

The vast majority of people across Somalia and Somaliland identify as Somalis, and as Sunni Muslims. Somali lifestyles and cultures across the wider Horn of Africa have historically been shaped by nomadic pastoralism (goat, sheep, camel and cattle rearing for subsistence, trade and export) or, in southern parts of the country and pockets across the north, agro-pastoralism (a combination of livestock rearing and farming). Lineage structures of clan were a key mode of social organization within this context. Currently, four main clan families are differentiated, the Daarood, Digil and Mirifle, Dir, and Hawiye.[2] These are further subdivided into clans and subclans based on male descent. Clanship and territoriality have a complex and fluid relationship (Cassanelli, 2015). Some clan groups are closely associated with particular places, while others are spread more widely across the Somali Horn (Barnes, 2006). In general, socio-cultural differences between the major clan families are not highly pronounced. However, the Digil and Mirifle groups that dominate the inter-riverine areas of Bay and Bakool (but also reside in significant numbers in the Shabelles, Jubbas and Gedo regions in the south) have a greater reliance on agro-pastoralism and many speak Af Maay, a dialect or language distinct from the Af Maxaa Tiri that was established as standard Somali in the post-independence era (Helander, 1997; Lehman and Eno, 2003).

Clan labels belie a wealth of internal diversity – not all Digil and Mirifle are agro-pastoralist Af Maay speakers, for instance. The major clan family distinctions also do not cover the many other groups who fall outside this wider Somali lineage structure and are heavily discriminated against. These include the 'Somali Bantu Jareer' (Eno and Kusow, 2014), which encompasses people who inhabited southern riverine regions before nomadic pastoralists spread across the Horn, as well as the descendants of 19th-century south-east African slaves (Declich, 1995; Eno et al, 2010; Menkhaus, 2010; Kusow and Eno, 2015). Also politically and socially marginalized are caste-like minority groups, referred to as Gabooye or Madhibaan. These groups constitute the perpetual Other in relation to Somali origin myths (Mire, 2017, 5), as they are associated with ritual impurity and disdained professions (Luling, 1984; Hill, 2010; Eno and Kusow, 2014). Numbers of minorities and majorities are unverified and contested, and names of minority groups are problematic and often pejorative. Nonetheless, the salience of clan affiliation has translated into a political reality with the so-called 4.5 system of governmental and parliamentary appointments that has been used since the first (post state collapse) formation of a central parliament and government for Somalia in 2004. It has since shaped the allocation of seats in consecutive federal governments and parliaments, allocating equal shares of positions to those who hail from the four major clan families and a half share to so-called minorities.

Clanship has traditionally provided mechanisms of mobilization for both conflict and reconciliation (Lewis, 1994). These processes are based on the discussions and mediations of clan elders and collective responsibilities of compensation payments (*mag/diya*) that have interacted with the changing modes of governance in the region. As in other colonial contexts, European colonizers altered clan relations; for example, in the political empowerment of certain clan groups and elders who worked as intermediaries between the colonizer and colonized, and increased their power significantly in the process (Samatar, 1989). Unsurprisingly, the post-independence era of parliamentary democracy became rooted in clan-based clientelist networks, setting the scene for the military dictatorship (1969–1991) of General Mohamed Siad Barre, who effectively navigated Cold War rivalries while espousing a modernizing agenda pronouncing anti-clanism and 'scientific socialism'. Ultimately, however, Barre's rule remained rooted in a configuration of three Daarood clans. Organized resistance that started to develop after the failed war Somalia launched against Ethiopia over the Ogaden region in 1977, also relied largely on clan-organized networks (Compagnon, 1998; Bakonyi, 2011; Hoehne, 2016), notably the Daarood/Majeerteen-dominated Somali Salvation Democratic Front (SSDF) in the north-east, the Isaaq-dominated Somali National Movement (SNM) in the north-west, and the predominantly Hawiye militias of the United Somali Congress (USC) in the central regions. The state responded by militarizing 'loyal' clan groups to counter opposition and collectively punished clan constituencies that were believed to support the guerrilla organizations (Bradbury, 2008; Kapteijns, 2012).

The geographical reach of Barre's power shrunk considerably over the years. His military government was eventually toppled in 1991 when USC forces carried the fight to Mogadishu. In the immediate post Barre period, many non-Hawiye clans were forced out of the Somali capital, and groups, particularly from the Daarood, who were associated with Barre's regime were killed in large numbers, although many had also contributed to the resistance against the regime (Bakonyi 2009; Kapteijns, 2012). The continuation of clan-based violence and intra-USC conflicts in Mogadishu prevented the re-establishment of a functioning government. Consequently, the state apparatus collapsed as clan militias and gangs marauded through southern and central regions, targeting one another and people from unarmed clan groups, expropriating their land and looting their possessions, including food reserves and international humanitarian supplies. People displaced by ongoing violence and the loss of livelihoods started to seek sanctuary in areas where their clan predominated, a process which has had a lasting impact on settlement patterns across the Somali territories (Hoehne, 2016).

Coinciding with a drought, this violence and looting initiated a massive humanitarian crisis. and set into motion the first ever humanitarian intervention of the United Nations. Military forces were initially led by the United States (1992–93) and later by the UN (1993–95). While these forces de-escalated the violence, they neither managed to bring about peace nor rebuild the state. However, the withdrawal of UN forces by 1995 was followed by the emergence of radically localized forms of governance. Although these led to the political fragmentation of the former state territory, they nonetheless enabled a return to a form of normalcy best classified as the 'no peace, no war' situation that Richards (2005) describes as a common social reality in many contexts.

When this state fragmentation was reinterpreted as global security threat post-9/11 (Bakonyi, 2019) the international gaze turned back to the Horn of Africa. Particular international attention was given to the rise of the Islamic Courts Union in south-central Somalia (Barnes and Hassan, 2007; Skjelderup et al, 2020). A US-backed Ethiopian invasion routed this embryonic and (in Somalia) quite popular movement and supported the establishment of a Transitional Federal Government (TFG) in Mogadishu. This intervention set the stage for Al Shabaab's Islamist insurgency against the TFG and their foreign supporters that continues to this day (Hansen, 2013). An internationally recognized Federal Government of Somalia (FGS) – militarily propped up by a 20,000 strong African Union force (AMISOM) – was established in Mogadishu in 2012, and tangible steps have been taken towards the federal reconfiguration of the Somali state. Nonetheless, Al Shabaab maintains a shadow government, significant territorial presence, and the capacity to engage violently in direct confrontations against foreign and Somali security forces, and in attacks against civilian targets. The frequency of US drone strikes against Al Shabaab increased significantly after 2012, and the United Nations is heavily involved in the diplomatic, humanitarian and security-focused stabilization and state-building process that engages different power holders across a still highly divided Somalia. The following sections introduce the four cities that are the focus of the book while attending to experiences of war, displacement and resettlement from the perspectives of interviewees and photovoice participants.

Mogadishu

The cities examined in this book have all been profoundly affected – albeit in different ways – by the protracted conflict in Somalia, which has evolved and periodically escalated into moments of mass violence since the 1980s. Violence in southern Somalia has partly been driven by conflict over agricultural land (Besteman and Cassanelli, 1996), while property disputes have also often underpinned conflict in the capital city, Mogadishu (RVI/HIPS, 2017). Following its capture of Mogadishu in 1991, the USC immediately split in two. Hawiye/Abgaal factions took control of the northern part of the city, while the southern part was taken over by Hawiye/Habar Gidir militias. Both groups were aligned with other Hawiye and non-Hawiye clan groups, and Mogadishu evolved into a microcosm of the political division that divided the rest of south-central Somalia into a patchwork of competing subclan militias and their leaders (warlords). The period of the warlords (1995–2005) saw the reduction of violence, partly because of the fragmentation of clan militias and the loss of violent manpower, and partly because of the activities of a rising business class.[3] Some business people developed an active interest in the development of the city, and in protecting their land and other properties they had acquired during the war (Bakonyi, 2011, chapter 6.1). Access to land and property in Mogadishu in this period was mainly structured by clan affiliation and available connections to warlords or other armed groups. In this time, much of the public, state-owned land was taken over by armed groups, along with properties of people who had been displaced or fled from Mogadishu in the early years of the civil war. By 2005, the warlords had been eclipsed by the Islamic Courts Union, a movement of local sharia adjudicators who were also backed by those businesspeople with an interest in maintaining trade and protecting property rights (Mwangi, 2010; Ahmad, 2015). The 2006 invasion of Ethiopia, the subsequent insurgency of al-Shabaab, and the war between al-Shabaab and the TFG/AMISOM alliance wrought significant damage to Mogadishu and initiated several waves of displacement that further complicated questions of land ownership and settlement rights.

The intensity of violence changed in Mogadishu again in 2011 when Al Shabaab was forced to withdraw. This roughly coincided with a drought that led to a famine and caused, once more, mass migration of people from the south-central rural regions into the capital city. The TFG and AMISOM forces who nominally controlled Mogadishu, promised access to protection and aid. After 2012, following the installation of the internationally recognized Federal Government of Somalia under President Hassan Sheikh Mohamud and an increase in security in the capital, attempts towards reconstruction initiated a building boom in Mogadishu. This has been driven in part by diaspora real estate investors, the transnational Somali remittance and mobile communication sector, as well as infrastructural developments of international actors.

Overall, Mogadishu has been affected by higher frequencies and intensities of inwards *and* outwards migration compared to the other cities examined in this book. Recurrent phases of urban violence, and the broad spectrum of armed actors in Mogadishu – among them clan militias, state security forces, criminal gangs, international intervention forces, and Islamist insurgents – have regularly caused large scale displacements out of the city to the surrounding hinterlands, where people often wait for a deintensification of violence to return (RVI/HIPS, 2017; Bakonyi, 2022b). At the same time, however, violent conflict and environmental shocks also set in motion centripetal dynamics as people flee from rural areas into the capital city where they hope to find aid and protection. Somalia's vulnerability to the impacts of climate change is further aggravating displacement dynamics. The frequency of droughts and floods appears to be increasing (Ogallo et al, 2018). Severe droughts with acute humanitarian consequences are ongoing at the time of writing, and continue to negatively impact agricultural production (Warsame et al, 2021), especially in the context of shifts from drought resilient sorghum to cash crops for export, such as sesame (Jaspers et al, 2019). Multiple factors, among them climate change, political instability, land-grabbing by powerful politico-commercial actors, and high taxation by Al Shabaab, contribute to a trend where small-scale farmers are displaced from their land and forced to seek aid and new livelihood options in cities such as Mogadishu.

A large proportion of the people in Mogadishu whose testimonies and photographs are presented in this book had come from Bay, Bakool and Lower Shabelle regions. This is representative of wider trends of displacement and settlement at the cities' margins. Durations of residence of interviewees in Mogadishu ranged between one month and seven years prior to the interview. Two of the interviewees had been previously displaced from the city and had subsequently returned. Several had moved between different camps within Mogadishu, often because of evictions. Of the 26 people initially interviewed in Mogadishu camps, a majority (15) belonged to Digil and Mirifle clans.[4] Other interviewees self-identified with various Somali Bantu Jareer, Dir and Hawiye subclans. None of those (sub)clans would be considered to be locally powerful, and none is associated with historical claims to the city. Groups such as the Reer Shabelle are understood to be part of the Bantu Jareer and face everyday racism and discrimination (Eno et al, 2010; Hill, 2010).

Many interviewees described a combination of violence, generalized insecurity, a lack of livelihood opportunities and water shortage in rural areas as primary reasons for their move to Mogadishu. Reference to violence included clashes between AMISOM, Somali government forces and Al Shabaab, violent harassment and repression by the latter, or, in one case, clashes between clan militia. Four of the interviewees in Mogadishu fled primarily in reaction to, or out of fear of, physical violence, while most others identified drought as a main reason. Interviewees described how the lack of rain caused the death of livestock, made farming impossible, deprived them of their means for subsistence and eventually caused the death of family members, friends and neighbours. As Wiilo, a 38-year-old woman who fled from a village in Lower Shabelle five years prior to the interview, explained: "The rivers dried and there was no water and there was a bad drought. Through Jilaal, Gu and Deyr [seasons] the water did not come back. At no time did water come back. We were without water. It was hard when my children died" (Mogadishu, January 2018). Wiilo had given birth to ten children and decided to leave for Mogadishu after three of them had died. Many other interviewees referred to droughts, water shortages and famine as causes for their flight, but additionally referred to insecurity and violence as exacerbating factors. Shoobta, for example, fled conflict and water shortages in the Lower Shabelle region:

'There was fighting there, and our farms had no water and there was no rain. This made us come to Mogadishu. […]. There is no water up to now. People who migrated from there [and joined us in Mogadishu] told us there is still no water in the place. And these fighters called Al Shabaab still control the place. You cannot enter the place now and there is nowhere you can work. And the men are forced to stay in the Masjids [mosques], and we don't have someone to work for us. And the children will die of hunger. […] The government is not there, just Al Shabaab fighters. And the river is drying up. […] There was a lot of drought and no rain. […] And there was also fighting that we used to run away from, and [we had to] live the whole day in the forest. […] It was between Al Shabaab and AMISOM […] We ran away mostly from these two problems.' (Mogadishu, January 2018)

When talking about their journeys to Mogadishu, many interviewees outlined the problems they faced while on the move. People often experienced theft and robbery, and some lost the few belongings they carried with them. Most lacked the financial means to pay for transport. Some people tried to catch a free lift on the way, and for some parts of the journey found support from relatives or begging from strangers. Shankaroon, a young woman displaced from the Jowhar area around 2013 explained:

'The roads were not good, it was hard for us. I was pregnant at that time with my daughter, and I was with my other three kids. But with the help of some people, we managed. My children and I faced hardships but we made it. […] We had no water to drink or food, but at least we got help from some families. And a vehicle came with food and helped us and also gave us tea and water. And that's how we came to Xamar [Mogadishu].' (Mogadishu, January 2018)

Many reported losing loved ones to sickness and exhaustion along the way. Barwaaqo, who had arrived in Mogadishu from Lower Shabelle region shortly before the interview, talked about the loss she experienced:

Barwaaqo:	The journey took us seven days and we spent nights in different places. We were walking. The night that was supposed to be our eighth night, we were accompanied by my grandmother, my father's mother, and she was too old. It rained that night and we spent the night in the cold, below a tree. So she felt cold and after sleeping that night she didn't wake up the next morning, and we found her dead […] It was a road in the jungle, a hilly place away from villages and towns.

Interviewer:	Was your grandmother sick?
Barwaaqo:	No, she felt cold in that night and beside her old age she was not suffering from any other illness.
I:	So, was she walking on that journey before that night?
Barwaaqo:	Yes, she was walking [...] We were passing villages on our way, and we asked for water and help from village to village, and it was really tough. [...] We were accompanied by other people who were our neighbours. So, we were not alone. And when the old lady passed away there was a lorry that was passing nearby, and we waved a piece of bed sheet to them to signal them [to stop]. They stopped and the men in that lorry helped us to dig a grave for her and they buried her. (Mogadishu, January 2018)

Other interviewees described how family members got separated on the way and the emotional distress of not knowing where loved ones were – whether they were still alive and healthy, or what had happened to people left behind in the area from which they had fled.

People arriving in Mogadishu have often settled on unused plots in the city centre. In earlier phases of inward migration, makeshift huts were frequently set up within the conflict-damaged shells of former state or institutional buildings, such as destroyed hospitals, government offices (Figure 2.2), the

Figure 2.2: Photograph of the 'Ex-Health Ministry Camp' in downtown Mogadishu

Source: Photograph by Peter Chonka (2012).

National Theatre and schools. These settlements often took the names of the former premises and some of Mogadishu's most iconic colonial-era buildings – such as its ruined cathedral – were occupied in this way by displaced people.

Since 2012, with changes in the city's overall security situation enabling economic growth and urban reconstruction, many of these inner-city makeshift settlements have been demolished. In-migrants who were living in more central parts of the city have been pushed to the periphery where they have often reassembled huts from materials they brought with them or managed to obtain anew, again forming camp-like settlements. New arrivals to the city usually join relatives in already established camps or set up new ones. These contribute to growing clusters of camps on the city's edge, particularly in northern neighbourhoods such as Daynile and Kahda. Such camps are often built adjacent to main roads: in the case of the former two examples, the road that runs from Mogadishu to Afgoye and connects onwards to Lower Shabelle and the central regions. In Chapter 3 we return to the specific ways in which people arrive and settle in the city and the political economy of this humanitarian urbanism that involves settlements, evictions and nascent forms of post-war urban gentrification.

Baidoa

Located in the south-central inland Bay region between the Jubba and Shabelle rivers, Baidoa is the main centre of Somalia's rain-fed agricultural production. It has also been another hotspot for conflict since the collapse of the state in 1991. The Bay region was subject to the predations of militias hailing from clan factions associated with Siad Barre's deposed regime in the early 1990s, before these were countered by USC militias, which had also taken over Mogadishu. People from the Digil and Mirifle clans who predominate in the region formed their own resistance force, the Somali Democratic Movement (SDM), but lacked military capacity and equipment. After initially allying with the USC against forces loyal to Barre, the SDM was unable to stop the USC militias' violence against people living in the region. Widespread violence combined with looting of food stocks and farm products aggravated the effects of a drought and led to the devastating famine of 1991–1992. Baidoa – dubbed the 'city of death' by international aid workers – became an epicentre of suffering, with large numbers of displaced and exhausted people arriving in search of aid. The first UN humanitarian intervention was, therefore, welcomed in Baidoa, also because the arriving forces empowered Digil and Mirifle leaders to self-govern the region, for the first time in postcolonial Somali history (Bakonyi, 2013).

However, following the withdrawal of international forces in 1995, the USC reclaimed the region. This subsequently led to the mobilization of the local and Digil and Mirifle-led Rahanweyn Resistance Army (RRA).[5] The conflict simmered in the region until 1999 when the RRA captured Baidoa and began to consolidate a regional administration. Previously displaced people began returning from 1995 onwards, but intra-RRA disputes erupted into violence in the early 2000s, leading to the collapse of its embryonic administration headquartered in Baidoa. Remnants of the RRA, in cooperation with businesspeople and elders, established localized forms of rule, but Baidoa remained a centre of tension between the RRA factions. After 2005, Baidoa served for a short period as the provisional capital of the newly formed Transitional Federal Government (TFG). Ethiopia intervened on the side of the TFG when the Islamic Courts Union expanded towards Baidoa. In 2009, Baidoa was taken by Al Shabaab, which governed the city for three years until TFG troops, backed by the Ethiopian military, recaptured the city in 2012.

Since 2014, Baidoa has been the de facto capital of the new South West Federal Member State (FMS) of Somalia, encompassing the regions of Bay, Bakool and Lower Shabelle. At the time of writing (2022) the FMS government is aligned with the FGS in Mogadishu, and Baidoa is secured by AMISOM forces and forces of the South West State administration. However, Al Shabaab maintains a significant presence in the rural areas of the wider region. Large parts of the road linking Baidoa to Mogadishu are controlled by the group, allowing it to tax trade and transport to and from the city. When Al Shabaab lost control of the port city of Kismayo, and its main revenue base from taxation of charcoal exports and maritime trade, the group increased taxation on pastoralists and farmers. Along with sporadic violent conflicts and regular droughts, this heavy taxation became an important driver of displacement of people from rural areas to Baidoa. Similar to Mogadishu, the UN and other international relief organizations have a presence in the city, which also attracts in-migration of displaced people. Again similar to Mogadishu, a period of relative urban stability since 2012 has created favourable conditions for business investment and the city's economy is growing.

Although makeshift settlements established by impoverished urban in-migrants surround the city, there is a particularly high concentration of camps on its northern side, in which many of the people whose testimonies and pictures we present in this book lived. Satellite imagery of this area since 2010 shows the demarcation of plots of land, influxes of displaced people in the wake of the 2011 famine, the extension of infrastructure, especially road links, to these settlements, and the growth of camps apparently within the boundaries of the previously marked plots.

Compared to people's routes to the three other cities discussed in the book, the places where people had been displaced from tended to be closer to Baidoa, with shorter distances being covered before their arrival in the city. Most urban in-migrants have been displaced from rural areas of Bay and the neighbouring Bakool region. All interviewees identified as belonging to clans from the broader Mirifle group. Many people have clan links with Baidoa's existing urban population, and speak the Af Maay language that is predominant in the city. Most interviewees in Baidoa had been displaced within two years prior to interview, which distinguishes them from interviewees in Mogadishu and Bosaso who, on average, had lived much longer in the cities. Many people in Baidoa, however, had had previous experiences of displacement. Comparing the interview sample of Mogadishu with Baidoa, interviewees in both cities had been displaced from rural areas, although two interviewees in Baidoa first moved to Kenya and later participated in return programmes. Even before their displacement most interviewees faced livelihood difficulties. Of the Mogadishu interviewees, only a few had their own land, and many worked as tenant farmers or as day farm labourers. Although most of the farmers who fled to Baidoa owned land, their farms were often very small and hardly sufficient for more than basic subsistence. Farming was often complemented by sale of firewood or charcoal. Given the shorter distances of the flight to Baidoa, several interviewees reported periodic movement back and forth between the villages and new urban settlements, and people tended to stay in frequent contact with family members who remained in rural areas.

Interviewees generally reported conflict, economic and ecological reasons for their migration. In Baidoa, insecurity was most often identified as a driver of movement to Baidoa. Al Shabaab continues to exert influence in rural areas and fighting between AMISOM/Somali government-aligned forces and the Islamist militia regularly forces people to leave their home areas to seek shelter and safety in cities. Idow, a father of six who had arrived in Baidoa the previous year, explained why his family had left his rural home in the vicinity of Qansax Dheere:

> 'It is said a grain can't survive in between two molars. We were in between two fighting giants [...]. One was Al Shabaab and the other was the Federal Government of Somalia [...]. You are a citizen who is a farmer and pastoralist, and you don't have a gun. What can you do? So, you must move aside, to the side where you can find peace.'
> (Idow, Baidoa, January 2018)

Increased levels of taxation by Al Shabaab, such as imposing new 'pre-planting' levies on farms, as well as taxes on production and 'hut taxes', were mentioned by several interviewees as having a particularly damaging impact on their livelihoods. Al Shabaab's loss of control of urban strongholds, subsequent loss of resources, and increased military pressure, meant that the group was extracting ever more onerous sums from rural producers – whether religiously defined zakat or other fees. The group was described as being indifferent toward the hardship these taxes imposed on people under their rule:

> 'We have experienced a prolonged drought [in Qansax Dheere] with serious hunger and starvation. The livestock has gone with the drought. Apart from that, whenever you grow crops, Al Shabaab wants to charge for the farming on certain terms known as *Tabarucaad* [donation]. They ask for this money. [...] Even before you start planting, at the time of preparation, they charge a fixed amount that you need to pay to be allowed to do the farming [...] Whatever small amount you have been saving and you wanted to spend on sorting the miscellaneous expenses, will be spent on paying what they demand. [...] Some will go to work on other people's farms to be able to pay Al Shabaab. [...] They don't consider whether you have it or not [...] We can't afford it. People are poor with no wealth [...], with no jobs. And then others go and work on other people's farms [...] when the children are crying of hunger.' (Haji, Baidoa, January 2018)

Since Baidoa is under the control of South West Federal Member State and AMISOM forces, international organizations have established a significant presence in the city and populate an area around the airport that resembles the Mogadishu international airport zone, hosting UN agencies and private security and logistic companies (Bakonyi, 2022a). International presence was identified by several interviewees as a pull factor for rural-to-urban migration. For example, Idow explained that he had heard that humanitarian assistance was available in Baidoa, along with newly constructed Quranic schools where he hoped his children could study.

Many in-migrants left rural areas in groups, but they rarely remained together throughout the journey. Some stayed for a time with relatives in villages or cities they were passing through, while others continued on different routes towards various destinations. Few interviewees could afford to pay for transport, but usually walked, some for days, facing thirst and hunger and surviving mainly on support from people on the way:

> 'It took five days and nights. We had been carrying children on top of the cart [...] God is Great – we reached safely a small village called Koronbood. There lived a clan known as Yantaar. It was a small village where our Muslim brothers helped us a lot. Because of their hospitality we have survived. Nobody could tolerate [...] the situation we were in at that time. Like the woman you saw waking up right over there [pointing] no one thought she would make [survive] the journey to Baidoa.' (Haji, Baidoa, January 2018)

Despite the proximity of Al-Shabaab, and the ever more frequent reoccurrence of drought, Baidoa has been declared secure by international organizations involved in the repatriation of Somali refugees from camps in Kenya, prominently Dadaab. Since 2014 over 70,000 refugees have been returned to Somalia, with a significant proportion deciding to settle in Baidoa (Amnesty International, 2017; Sturridge et al, 2018). Such repatriations are an additional factor in wider processes of camp urbanization. Repatriated refugees have often been supported with food or cash aid on their arrival in Baidoa, but not formally provided with accommodation. Many, including two interviewees in our research project, ended up settling in the camps established by rural-urban migrants. Some received a home later on, in a resettlement area near the city that has been described by its international donors as part of 'durable solutions' for internally displaced (IOM, 2021; see Chapter 6). This shows once more how categorical distinctions between internally and internationally displaced/returned people become blurred and obfuscate wider dynamics of urbanization influenced by international agencies. People may have returned to Somalia, and those who selected Baidoa may have had previous links with the city or the broader region, but often originally fled from rural areas. Repatriation becomes another form of urban in-migration that melds into the flows and settlement patterns analysed in this book. The extent to which repatriations from Kenya have been voluntary remains disputed (Amnesty International, 2017). The level of compulsion in peoples' decisions to move is difficult to determine as reasons for flight are multiple and often overlap, especially in a complex and unpredictable security environment. Although returnees expressed in interviews that they had asked to be repatriated, the fluidity of the wider security situation to which they were returning was highlighted in Warsame's description of the bus journey, facilitated by the United Nations High Commissioner for Refugees (UNHCR), from Kenya into Somalia and, eventually, Baidoa: "The journey was good and peaceful. All Somalis were helpful on our way. Even Al-Shabaab were nice to us, and they talked to us and told us refugees from Kenya are innocent. But they warned us not to join any group" (Baidoa, November 2019). For all arrivals in Baidoa – whether internally displaced people or refugee returnees – the role of camp leaders (or gatekeepers) was reported as being important in finding a piece of land to settle on. Although few reported paying regular rents, registration fees or ad hoc contributions of external support are paid in some cases. We return to the political economy of marginalized settlements and urban construction in the following chapter, with a particular focus on forms of humanitarian entrepreneurship in Baidoa and Mogadishu. However, it is important to note here that because displaced people in Baidoa tend to share family and clan links with the groups that dominate the city, relations between new arrivals and long-term city residents have a different dynamic compared to

Mogadishu and Bosaso, the cities where the label of 'displaced person' often connotes a clan or racialized distinction vis-à-vis the 'local' population. Differences between the cities in this regard are particularly important in understanding how displacement relates to political questions of belonging and citizenship across a fragmented Somalia, a topic we address in the last chapter (6) of this book.

Bosaso

Bosaso is a port city on the north-east coast and serves as the commercial capital of the Puntland State of Somalia. The foundations for the city's rapid post-1991 growth were laid in the 1980s when Siad Barre's government allowed the city to operate as a duty-free port and rehabilitated its road link to Gaalkacyo (Marchal, 2010, 19). These steps were taken, in part, to placate resistance to his rule in the region, and enabled Bosaso to become a key hub for international trade linking the north-east with south-central Somalia. The escalation of violence in the mid to late 1980s in the north-west of the country, in what would become Somaliland, contributed to the diversion of international livestock shipment from Berbera towards the more stable Bosaso.

From the civil war of the 1980s onwards – and aside from a relatively short-lived conflict between the Islamist al-Itihaad al-Islaamiya and the SSDF in the early 1990s for control of the city and port – Bosaso was largely spared from the scale of violence that shattered the three other cities. The formation of the Puntland State of Somalia in 1998 contributed to the further relatively peaceful development of the region. The creation of this de facto autonomous (but unlike Somaliland, non-secessionist) administration was dominated by the three major Darood/Majeerteen subclans of the region. The establishment of Puntland attracted increasing levels of diaspora investment and facilitated the development of a business class.

Migration to Bosaso has a long history, but after 1991 it became a prime destination for people displaced from across Somalia. Initially, many former government officials in the military regime under Siad Barre who hailed from Daarood clans moved to the north-east where they transitioned into private enterprise. They were joined by more internationally (and often Islamist) orientated businesspeople (mostly men) from around 1998 onwards (Marchal, 2010, 20). Other population groups from south-central regions have fled recurrent conflict and have journeyed to Bosaso.

For a variety of reasons, Bosaso has become a relatively attractive destination for people fleeing from other parts of Somalia since the 1990s. Its growing trade economy draws in those seeking work in the city, particularly as casual labourers in the port itself, in the construction industry, or in domestic labour. Bosaso is the terminus of a paved road link and important economic corridor leading from the south-central regions through Gaalkacyo, a city divided administratively between Puntland and Galmudug Federal Member States. Many people from southern regions arrived in Bosaso with the intention of taking advantage of the port's maritime connections across the Gulf of Aden to Yemen and economic opportunities in the Arabian Peninsula or potential onward routes towards Europe.

In comparison with the other three cities, Bosaso has experienced the most prolonged inward flow of displaced people and, in general, has been settled in by people who have travelled the longest distances. Some interviewees and photovoice participants in Bosaso had fled from Mogadishu, Lower Shabelle, Bay and Bakool, as well as central areas such as Galgaduud. Most hailed from Digil and Mirifle clan groups, as well as Jareer (such as the Reer Shabelle) and caste groups, such as the Madhibaan. The interviewees also included individuals identifying as Darood/Marehan, Hawiye/Gaaljecel, Dir and Isaaq. This book focuses on people who have settled in marginalized, makeshift settlements that sprang up in and around the city, and thus on migrants with a particular clan and class background. City residents conveyed their perception that many prominent traders in the city also hail from southern Digil and Mirifle lineages, many of them originally displaced but not usually described as IDPs, a label that has become synonymous with residence in camp-like settlements.

A significant proportion of the interviewees had travelled along the main road link from the south: following the road up the Shabelle river to Beledweyne and from there into Puntland via Gaalkacyo. Some interviewees travelled via the Somali Region of Ethiopia. The majority of interviewees had lived in the city for one or two decades. Most had fled from the south in the early to mid 1990s when the civil war and general insecurity were at their initial peak. In particular, people who had fled from Mogadishu or the Bay region had directly experienced violence, either in the city or the rural hinterlands in the aftermath of the collapse of military regime in 1991. Famino, a female leader (gatekeeper) of one of the neighbourhoods we studied in Bosaso, for example, left Mogadishu in the early 1990s, just before Siad Barre was overthrown. She described some of her experiences of the conflict:

'I was looking around to identify the source of the gunfire and wanted to stand on a small mound of sand. When I stood up on the mound, I saw that this was a grave of a dead woman and that I was standing on her body. She was buried in this mound of sand. The shock I felt at that moment repeats in my mind all the time. I was shocked and I became like a mad person. Some scholars read the Quran over me to recover from this shock. Now I am good, and I am safe in Bosaso. Although I still see those bad dreams of those events. I remember the dead woman that I stood on, and my uncle who was dead and we left him there without taking and burying him.' (Bosaso, December 2017)

Cawo, now a 35-year-old woman, had left Mogadishu as a teenager in the late 1990s:

> 'The last day I took the decision to move from Mogadishu was the day that my brother was killed. My brother was killed after gunmen came and entered into our house and they killed him because he was protecting me. That day, the day I lost my brother [...] The people who killed my brother were interested in me. My brother was living with us. Our house consisted of six rooms and we owned the house.' (Bosaso, December 2017)

Others had left more recently, particularly in the fighting generated by the Ethiopian invasion to oust the Islamic Courts Union in Mogadishu. Some interviewees from the Somali region of Ethiopia (particularly the area around Qalaafe) referred to economic hardships, such as a lack of jobs and services, as reasons for their move north. One interviewee from the Ethiopia/Somaliland border areas had been seriously affected by drought and the death of her family's livestock in recent years.

People had experienced multiple difficulties and incidents of violence on their long and often multistaged journeys to Bosaso via the central regions of Somalia or through Ethiopia. Robbery and extortion of passenger vehicles as well as sexual violence against women was frequently mentioned, particularly regarding migration in the early 1990s and early 2000s. Bilan, a woman who left Mogadishu in the early 1990s described her journey through central Somalia:

> 'We were on our vehicle, and we were stopped by gunmen. We were told to get down from the vehicle and all our belongings were taken by those gunmen. We were then separated: females apart from the males. Young girls from old women [...] and some girls were taken to the bush. After sometime, while we were suffering with our children in this place, the young ladies – after they were raped and their belongings were taken – they were brought back to us. They were holding our vehicle and not allowing us to leave. Allah saved us from them eventually and we left them.' (Bosaso, December 2017)

Another interviewee, Edna, had left Mogadishu in the early 1990s as a child, fleeing with her family to the Somali region of Ethiopia. She stayed there until around 2009 when she was displaced again by fighting between Ethiopian forces and Oromo National Liberation Front (ONLF) rebels, which claimed the life of her brother, a civilian. She described her journey back into Somalia towards Puntland:

'I was in Ethiopia, and I experienced a miscarriage after six months due to the gunfire and the harsh situation we encountered, you know? I lost my other son due to diarrhoea and vomiting on our journey and he was buried somewhere in the desert. There were no doctors or drugs nearby. So, I remember all these problems now. [Sighs deeply]. When I reached Garowe [now capital of Puntland], I also lost another child. Alhamdulillah [Praise to God].' (Bosaso, December 2017)

Amid violence and uncertainty, however, interviewees also experienced solidarity and received assistance, often from strangers. Many interviewees emphasized that these types of support ultimately helped them to survive. Famino, in this respect, described her experiences of forced mobility as a pregnant woman:

'During my journey, my time to deliver the baby came, and I started suffering from labour pain. I was in a place where we had no relatives, no doctors, and I did not have any midwife around. I had only the clothes that I was wearing. We used to beg the people around us to get our food. Some women in that place came to me and asked about my situation and I told them I was about to give birth and that I didn't know anyone there. The location was some place around [...] some small village near Degehabur [Ethiopia] and they helped me with grass and wood to build a small place to give birth. Those ladies helped at that critical time and assisted me to deliver. I gave birth to a boy, and I named him Bashir.' (Bosaso, December 2017)

On arrival in Bosaso, some interviewees were able to stay with family or friends that they had known from their places of origin. However, most people erected makeshift shelters on vacant pieces of land within or around the edge of the city. Some of these squatter settlements would merge into larger camps, often being eventually dismantled by landowners. Interviewees reported moving from makeshift settlement to settlement after arrival and continued to be on the move owing to insecure housing arrangements and persistent danger of evictions.

Over the years, many urban in-migrants have been moved out of the main city. Currently, only one major squatter settlement in a central city area remains in Bosaso, the long-standing neighbourhood known as Boqol Buush (Hundred Tents). A somewhat greater level of tenure security has been obtained by some of the interviewees through their allocation of semi-permanent housing as part of the city's strategic resettlement plans. This internationally backed scheme has created a new cluster of neighbourhoods to the south-east of Bosaso and is examined in Chapter 6 in relation to its residents' perspectives on 'incremental tenancy agreements' and their relocation into distinct settlements for non-local or displaced people on the edge of the city.

Hargeisa

Hargeisa is the capital city of the unrecognized, but de facto independent Republic of Somaliland. Formerly the administrative centre of the British Protectorate of Somaliland, the city experienced limited growth following the union with the formerly Italian-colonized south in 1960. Being politically marginalized, Hargeisa became a locus of activism against the Mogadishu-based military regime in the 1980s. The state responded to this with the militarization of the north-western region: house searches, curfews and mass arrests, often speedily followed by mass convictions, became common features of urban life in Hargeisa in the mid 1980s. As the SNM opposition movement expanded its armed campaign in the 1980s, the military regime responded with extreme and indiscriminate violence, which peaked in aerial and artillery bombardment of the two largest cities in the north-west, Burao and Hargeisa, in 1988 (Adam, 1995). The air raids killed thousands of civilians, destroyed the cities' built environment and initiated the flight of almost all of both cities' residents, many of whom fled to refugee camps across the border in Ethiopia (Africa Watch, 1990).

Shortly after the military regime was defeated, Somaliland declared its independence in May 1991 and since then has undergone infrastructural and political reconstruction (Bradbury, 2008; Renders, 2012; Hoehne, 2013; Walls, 2014) albeit punctuated by periods of violence in the early to mid 1990s (Balthasar, 2013). Hargeisa has benefited economically from its relative stability post-1991 and has received significant investment from the diaspora. It became a booming regional economic hub whose population has grown both through the return of previous refugees and subsequent rural to urban migration.

Following Somaliland's declaration of independence, a steady stream of people returned from Ethiopia, and the last refugee camps were closed there in the early 2000s. Although they are not classified as internally displaced people but returnees or former refugees, many have settled in urban locations that have been referred to as 'camps' for the 'displaced'. They have here been joined by people fleeing further violent conflicts and environmental shocks both in Somaliland and Somalia. Among the most prominent and central of these inner-city settlements is Statehouse, named after the ruin of the former British Colonial administrative headquarters that still stands there. People settled in the ruin, but the state house is also surrounded by tightly packed makeshift tents and corrugated iron dwellings (Figure 2.3). In neighbourhoods like Statehouse or Stadium (also known as Cakaara), people

Figure 2.3: Photograph of the Statehouse neighbourhood in Hargeisa

Note: The eponymous colonial ruin is visible in the background.
Source: Photograph taken by Hodo.

displaced by recent droughts or conflicts in the wider region intermingle with other newcomers who move in because they cannot afford rising rents elsewhere in the city.

Several squatter settlements exist within and on the outskirts of the city. Furthermore, international humanitarian actors have been involved since in the resettlement of a significant number of displaced people from inside the city to resettlement areas beyond the escarpment that rises on Hargeisa's southern side. Among these resettlement areas is Digaale, a neighbourhood that we describe in more detail and analyse in Chapter 6. If similar land is donated or can be appropriated by the Somaliland state, then these settlements are intended to serve as a model for the large-scale relocation of people from dilapidated inner-city neighbourhoods. The tremendous growth of the city since the 1990s has, in effect, shifted the position of Statehouse from the periphery to the centre of the city. It now occupies valuable real estate close to the main road leading to the commercial centre of the city and is located adjacent to the governmental district that hosts several ministries and the presidential palace.

A significant proportion of interviewees from the Statehouse neighbourhood of Hargeisa had been displaced by the bombardment and destruction of the city in the late 1980s and had fled to Ethiopia to settle in camps across the border. Somaliland refugees in Ethiopia were officially repatriated in the early

2000s in a process supported by the Ethiopian and Somaliland governments in cooperation with international actors. Participants reported the bus and truck journeys back from Ethiopia as being quick and relatively smooth. Many people without access to their own land established makeshift tents in places such as Statehouse and the Stadium because the land was known to be government-owned. Some interviewees explained that family members had returned prior to the formal repatriation and that they then joined their settlements in the course of mass returns in the early 2000s. Quresha, a woman now in her mid 50s who returned to Hargeisa around 2000, described how social contacts enabled her settlement on return to the city:

> 'We had prior information about it, since there were others who relocated to Statehouse before us. They told us that there is a place for settlement. Initially, we have been told that there will be land given to us. However, few people who came before us were given land next to the northern part. Then we moved here, and we have been told then that no land will be issued, however, you will reside in a place called Statehouse in which several families are living, then we moved there. I sent my son to look for a portion of land and we found a place close to a family whom we lived together with in Dulcad [Ethiopia] and they told me to settle here. […] We don't pay rent or tax. There was a time some conmen came to us demanding tax but we chased them away.' (Hargeisa, December 2017)

Ahmed, a young man who had been a baby when his family returned from Ethiopia, described his understanding of access to different types of land for the settlement of returnees:

> 'Actually, lands are in two categories, some land belongs to the government while some is owned by individuals. However, this place [Statehouse] belongs to the government and it is the one which has [been] given out for the resettlement. […] Nobody is allowed to construct any brick buildings, [but] you can construct movable houses or corrugated steel huts. So, people were told that the government will provide you better resettlement. However, it wasn't forthcoming.' (Ahmed, Hargeisa, December 2017)

The areas filled up as more people arrived and staked claims to this 'free' land. Statehouse, for example, has remained within its original boundaries but has experienced a rapidly increasing population density. As Ahmed explained in the interview, over time, many of the tents were replaced by semi-permanent corrugated metal shacks. More recently, people saw residence on a plot here as a potential route to the official allocation of land elsewhere through expected and allegedly promised relocation schemes, which mostly have failed to materialize. The evolution of property markets based on resettlement speculation and wider city real estate trends are discussed in the following chapter. Overall, however, these processes have meant that settlement on government land, like the Statehouse, has evolved from a transitory camp made up of refugees moving back to the city into a semi-permanent slum-like settlement housing a mix of people who could be categorized as returnees, refugees or foreign migrants (like Ethiopian Oromos), rural-urban migrants and city dwellers who, unable to afford rents elsewhere in town, have also moved in. In local parlance, however, the residents are mainly referred to as IDPs. Various other urban settlements in Hargeisa are associated with displaced people, a label that reflects the marginality and precarious situations of the inhabitants but obscures significant diversity in their social make-up. For example, the Daami neighbourhood is said to be home to large numbers of displaced people but is also frequently associated with members from the marginalized and often impoverished Gabooye caste groups who may not have been displaced at all. This is just one example of what Bourdieu (2001, 306) described as the 'power of denotation' referring to practices of 'categorization' and thus the 'allocation of an identity' (Bourdieu 2001, 307) that always essentializes the social while defining and distributing values to people. This also makes people visible in certain ways as different, in need of humanitarian support, while simultaneously rendering individual experiences and differential positions of power invisible.

There are also informal settlements on the periphery of the city which tend to be inhabited by more recent arrivals from rural parts of Somaliland. Nasra, who resides in an outskirt settlement, had arrived in Hargeisa in 2017, displaced by drought and loss of livestock:

> 'I don't expect to go back home now, but it could be in the future if the situation goes back to normal. We lost what we were looking after in the rural area [livestock] [...] The difference [between current and previous droughts] is when droughts used to happen, we would lack water in some places, but it still could be found in some far areas. But in this [drought] there was no grass and there was no water anywhere in the area at all. There is no life then – without water and food.'
> (Hargeisa, July 2018)

People from southern Somalia also live across these different neighbourhoods. Some had fled from southern cities, often from Mogadishu in the early years of the war. The testimonies of these interviewees about their journeys to Hargeisa resembled those of the people in Bosaso who fled at that time, including experiences of (clan-based) violence, rape and robbery. People fleeing from the south to Hargeisa usually had pre-existing connections with the city or with Somaliland, whether being born there or hailing from a major clan in the newly established country.

Of the cities we discuss in this book, Hargeisa presents the most varied picture in terms of the profiles of people who came to settle in neighbourhoods that are frequently associated with displacement in humanitarian, government and media discourse. Many interviewees in Hargeisa, particularly those with family histories of return to the city, did not consider themselves to be displaced. Often these people were from Isaaq lineages while other interviewees were from the Dir/Gadabuursi clan and from the historically marginalized Gabooye caste group. Residents in these neighbourhoods often shared genealogical links with the major clan groups in Hargeisa. Unlike the other cities, Hargeisa is also characterized by a significant and often long-term presence of non-Somalis, particularly people from the Oromo ethnic group from Ethiopia. Despite periodic deportations by the Somaliland authorities, and other social experiences of discrimination, Oromo in-migrants have established their presence in the city. They have become a crucial part of the manual labour force, alongside Somalis who live in neighbourhoods associated with internal displacement.

Conclusion: Labelling and categorizing mobilities

Decades of conflict-linked migration have profoundly shaped processes of urbanization and de-urbanization and left their imprint on the built environment of cities such as Mogadishu, Baidoa, Bosaso and Hargeisa. This chapter has presented a historical backdrop to these processes, emphasizing how the cities are linked within the broader trajectory of the civil war that led to the collapse of the state apparatus and subsequent periods of violence and conflict-exacerbated ecological shocks that continue to the present. The reasons for individual and group migrations are complex and overlapping, often underpinned by a range of interlinked motivations relating to physical security, economic necessity, and hopes for new opportunities. Mobilities along different routes and through different timescales shaped the evolution of the four cities and the relations between them. Many of the people who participated in the research had spent a large part of their life on the move, experiencing various types and frequencies of displacement over decades within the wider Horn of Africa, and often within particular cities through recurring patterns of eviction and resettlement. We discuss the patterns and structures of inner-city displacement in more detail in the following chapter on the political economy of displacement and urban (re)construction.

Beyond providing the historical context of precarious urban lives and experiences at the margins of Somali cities, this chapter has drawn attention to the inherently essentializing denotation of people as 'the displaced'. This labelling is already complicated by the multiple, criss-crossing mobilities within and across state borders as well as within and across the cities. Perhaps even more jarring and reductive in its acronymized form, the discursive trope of the IDP blurs the complexity of people's individual stories and circumstances. These make a mockery of clear categorizations of 'forced' or 'economic' migration, and the life stories and narratives we present throughout the book demonstrate that practices of labelling are as reductive, power-laden and contested in the context of internal displacement as they are in international migration (Crawley and Skleparis, 2018; Sturridge et al, 2018). Nonetheless, internal displacement and IDPs have become a prominent part of the political, humanitarian and popular lexicon. In some cases, such labels are used by mobile populations themselves, to emphasize acute needs for humanitarian assistance. In other contexts it is resisted, particularly by those considered as non-local urban residents, even if they have lived in the cities for decades. In many cases, the label simply serves as shorthand to distinguish historically dominant population groups of the city from newcomers.

In short, the IDP label is inherently political. We approach it critically and with caution, considering as much what the term 'displaced person' elides and obfuscates, as what it reveals about histories of conflict, population movement and social belonging in cities in Somalia and Somaliland. We also show how a flattening humanitarian discourse rendering urban in-migration solely as a problem to be solved provides opportunities for different groups to use this label to access economic, political and symbolic resources. As we outline in the following chapters, categorizations of displacement are frequently operationalized by actors engaged in the political economy of urban reconstruction, and different forms of humanitarian entrepreneurship that play a key role here.

3

Camp Urbanization and Humanitarian Entrepreneurship

'So, we came to Mogadishu. Two of my brothers and I were living in a place owned by the government […] that I now forget the name of. After some time, we were told to vacate the camp because the land belonged to the government. We then moved to Maslah camp and lived there for one or two years. We then moved and settled at Shabelle University [another camp] and that is where we stayed for a while. We worked for ourselves. We woke up early in the morning to go into Xamar [Mogadishu] to look for work, like laundry, when it was available. Someone came in the camp one day and wrote something on a red painted area. I didn't understand it because I cannot read. I can just write my name. Some of the elders came and read it for us and said that it was a notice for us to vacate the camp. We would have a month before we would be kicked out. "The man who warns you is not responsible for killing you"! [Proverb: *Nin kuu digay kuma dilin*]. My father told us before the notice time ends, he will go and look for a place for us to move to. My brothers were living in Maslah camp, and we then moved there and lived there for about a year. Then we came here to my current camp where I have lived for three years. So, I came to Mogadishu five years ago.' (Wiilo, Mogadishu, January 2018)

Wiilo – whose experiences of rural to urban migration were introduced in the previous chapter – speaks about how her forced mobility continued after her arrival in Mogadishu from Lower Shabelle region. Over a period of five years, Wiilo lived in four camps, and had been evicted from three as the land was reclaimed by its purported owners. This chapter explores urbanization processes through the lens of settlement experiences of people like Wiilo, who have arrived in cities, some of them decades ago, and others only a few weeks before they were interviewed. We examine different types of urban settlements, namely urban camps established at the outskirts of the city, and squatter settlements in core city areas. Displaced people have developed various strategies to settle and obtain necessary physical protections. Some of this protection is provided by actors involved in negotiating and establishing these settlements, including landowners, so-called gatekeepers or camp leaders, humanitarian organizations and city-governments. Displaced people who are moving to cities navigate complex webs of power when negotiating access to the urban environment.

We develop here the central argument of the book: displaced people, despite occupying a subordinate position in the urban set-up, influence how cities are evolving and shape their morphologies and patterns of growth. Their agency is embedded in a political economy of urban rent-seeking that is intertwined with international aid. Practices of extraversion – rent-seeking based on international aid (Bayart, 2000; Hagmann, 2016) – have a long history in Somalia and include rents generated through mass-scale displacement and migration into (especially 1978–88) and out of the country (1988 to date) (Bakonyi, 2011). These practices, however, are currently exacerbated by and take new forms in the context of war-induced appropriation of urban land and its subsequent commodification within efforts towards urban reconstruction across Somalia and Somaliland (World Bank, 2021). Urban and infrastructural developments across Africa are often enabled by foreign aid and investment and constitute a distinctive form of financial penetration (Goodfellow, 2020, 257). The ongoing reconstruction, expansion and infrastructural development of many Somali cities is also primarily facilitated by international aid and finance. Our focus, however, is on the marginalized edges of cities, where the political economy of rent-seeking has become part of wider attempts to attract international aid to mitigate effects of forced displacement and in support of the urban settlement of in-migrants. Adapting Roy's (2010) notion of 'poverty capital', this political economy could be conceptualized as 'poverty rentierism' – initiatives that aim to extract a surplus (rent) at the receiving end of international chains of aid distribution using practices that we analyse below as petty humanitarian entrepreneurship. Urban landowners and intermediaries seek to attract impoverished in-migrants and facilitate their settlement to gain access to and retrieve a share of international aid. Displaced people enter clientelist networks in which physical protection and access to needed resources, in particular shelter and infrastructure, is exchanged for a share of aid. While rents are always embedded in relations of distribution (as distinguished from relations of production) and constitute forms of 'value grabbing' (Andreucci et al, 2017, 29), humanitarian rent-seeking renders particularly visible the inequality of global relations of distribution and the ways they are grounded in specific locations.

This chapter outlines the multiple facets and ambiguities of the clientelistic networks that underpin these rent-seeking practices, and demonstrates how the urban newcomers act within and through these networks to secure their survival. The reciprocal and (with respect to power) clearly lopsided arrangements between four actor groups – city newcomers, gatekeepers, landowners and humanitarian actors – are temporary and attest to the liminality of displacement-related urbanization and the generalized uncertainty that structures precarious lives at the urban margins. We further highlight how the creation of these settlements can increase the value ascribed to land. This contributes to the 'real-estatization of domestic urban capital' that Goodfellow (2020, 258) identifies as being primarily driven by local and diasporic investors, and which accompanies the infrastructural focus of global capital penetration in contemporary African cities. Such processes of real-estatization often involve evictions. In Somalia, the combination of protracted violence, urban reconstruction and mass-scale migration to cities has been accompanied by cycles of forced evictions that initiate nascent forms of urban gentrification. We understand gentrification with Smith (1996, 2002) as being an outcome of political strategies that aim at making inner-city neighbourhoods accessible to investors, and as processes, highlighted throughout the book, that are inscribing relations of class, race, clan and gender into the materialization of cityscapes.

Gentrification is in Somalia contributing to the extreme precarization of urban lives. Impoverished urban newcomers mostly find themselves on the losing side of these developments. Nonetheless, throughout the chapter we emphasize how these populations are actively shaping how urbanization unfolds in Somalia and Somaliland. Although they are acting from a subaltern position and in a context of deep precarity, urban in-migrants nonetheless influence the trajectories of urbanization and the shape of the city to come. This assertion contributes to the growing literature on subaltern agency (Bayat, 2000, 2010; Roy, 2011) that is complementing and correcting the powerful – but often rather sweeping – discussions of camps as political technologies used to administer unwanted migration. Agamben's (1998) highly influential work identified camps as an insignia of sovereignty and as a 'hidden matrix' for organizing modern political space. Accordingly, camps are used to organize and sort populations, as they constitute and maintain spaces of exception in which unwanted populations are reduced to bare life. The ongoing 'politicization of bare life' was thus conceptualized by Agamben (1998, 4) as the distinctive signature of modernity. Blurring the boundaries between biopolitics and thanatopolitics, the camp epitomizes the gradual expansion of biopower beyond the 'decision on bare life, in the state of exception, in which sovereignty consisted' (Agamben, 1998, 122). Departing from Agamben's philosophical intervention, empirically driven scholarship on migration, camps and humanitarian governance has come to explore the nuances of different forms of encampment including those of documented and undocumented migration. These authors point to the multiple and multifaceted ways of living at the margins and in camp spaces, identifying attempts to resist abjection and minimize destitution. In short, these studies continue to emphasize the agency of people even if they are politically and socially excluded and rendered disposable (Lemke, 2005; Turner, 2005; Martin, 2015; Jansen, 2018). We use this chapter to show how diverse forms of power and agency operate in day-to-day camp life, and point to relations *within* urban camp spaces, between camps and the wider city, and with the humanitarian regimes that structure, if not entirely control, these settlements.

The chapter first focuses on Mogadishu as a case study where these dynamics are particularly pronounced. Here, the lack of formal political authority and continued insecurity has created the conditions and incentives for a form of humanitarian entrepreneurship that manages and extracts resources through the support it provides to arriving migrants. This is also visible in Baidoa, albeit with important differences that relate to the profile of displaced people and their existing connections with the city. Bosaso has a longer history of conflict-related in-migration, and although cycles of encampment, eviction and gentrification continue, initiatives towards more permanent resettlement have been undertaken. Finally, we discuss historical dynamics of camp settlement in Hargeisa to illustrate how different contexts, political decisions and types of in-migration have set in motion the establishment, growth and densification of certain prominent inner-city squatter settlements, which (as yet) have not been demolished.

Humanitarian entrepreneurship and camp urbanization in Mogadishu

The road running north-west out of Mogadishu has long been a major artery for the movement of goods and people. This route connects Mogadishu with Afgoye, an agricultural hub and the next significant town to the west of the capital. From Afgoye there are onward road links north up the Shabelle river or south-west through the fertile Lower Shabelle region. Up until 2012, the visible urban edge of the capital reached the Somali National University campus and a major intersection leading out along this route. The two satellite images in Figure 3.1 show that within five years these outer limits had been significantly expanded. New settlements surround and lead off from the nine kilometres of main road that runs to Ceelasha Biyaha. This mid-point between Mogadishu and Afgoye was regularly mentioned by interviewees as an area to escape to in periods of urban fighting as, for example, during the battle between AMISOM and Al Shabaab in 2011.

With the bird's-eye view afforded by Google Earth, some of the new settlements are visible as distinct built structures: blocks of rectangles in plots divided by criss-crossing dirt roads. In these images, filling spaces around

Figure 3.1: Satellite images of the north-western outskirts of Mogadishu in 2012 and 2017

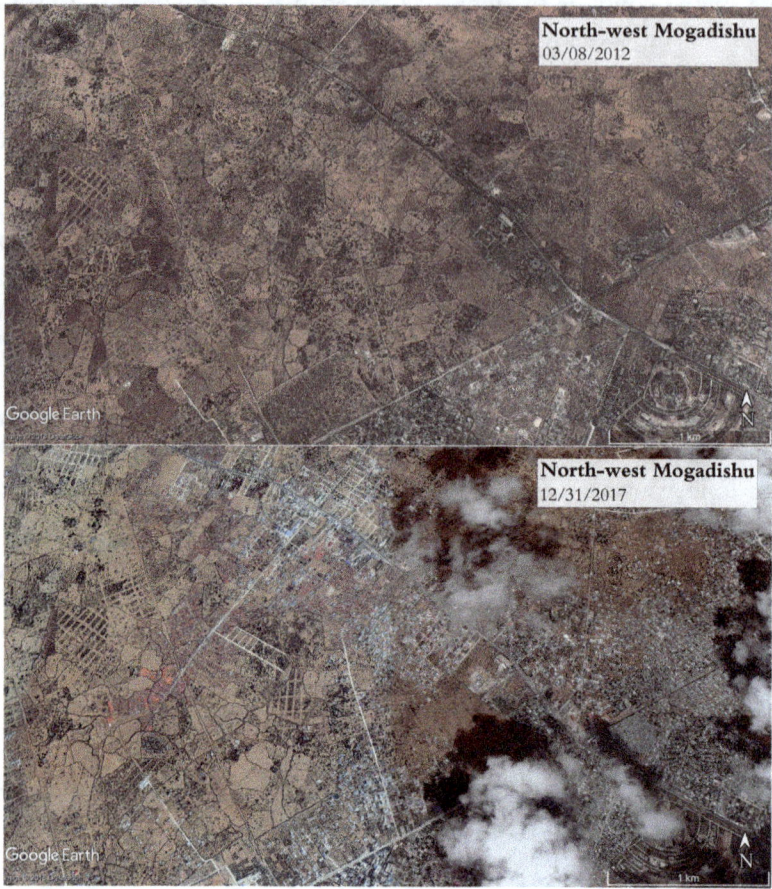

Note: Visible in the bottom right corner of both images is the Somali National University compound. The comparative view shows the expansion of city along the road to Afgoye and what we describe as a form of camp urbanization.
Source: Google Earth.

and between these roads leading from the main highway are dense splotches of orange. One has to zoom in much further to recognize these for what they are: densely packed clusters of makeshift huts, constructed with sticks, pieces of scrap metal and cloths, covered with ubiquitous orange tarpaulins delivered by humanitarian organizations or bought from markets. These are the *buul,* huts erected by mobile populations, many of whom were arriving from southern and western regions during the devasting famine of 2011. New arrivals in the large camps at this north-west part of the capital are often joined by people who were previously living in more central settlements before they were pushed to these outskirts.

Figure 3.2: Photograph of camp urbanization in north-west Mogadishu

Source: Photograph taken by Asha.

This top-down view of the expansion of the city gives the impression of disorganized urban sprawl. The patterns of settlement by city in-migrants are, however, tightly governed and structured by a range of factors. Camps hardly ever form spontaneously but emerge through initiatives of humanitarian entrepreneurs, and relationships and negotiations between these individuals, groups who formally own or have customary access to unused land, and (prospective) camp residents. Landowners are usually from locally dominant clan groups, able to provide security through their clan affiliation and often also their links with formal district authorities.

Many interviewees described their moments of arrival in cities like Mogadishu and how they were first able to find or construct some form of shelter in an already existing camp (Figure 3.2). In general, people do not simply settle on unused land or vacant plots and set up shelter. Instead, various contacts need to be made with those who manage existing camps in and around the city. Many interviewees described how they already had contacts with relatives or former neighbours who migrated before and helped to find places to settle, either sharing shelter or identifying a free space to build a hut in the settlement they themselves were living in.

However, many people arrived in the city without such contacts. Kheyrta described her experience:

'When I came [to the city] I did not come directly to the camp. We were brought to the main highway, and we stayed there for two days under a big tree. Then a lady came for us and took us to a big field. Then we built small makeshift huts. We were given a kilo of sugar, and mattresses, food and clothes by the people. The good lady also distributed $100 to each family to build houses. We bought plastic sheets and covered the house with it.' (Mogadishu, January 2018)

The "good lady" who Kheyrta is speaking about would be described by humanitarian organizations as a gatekeeper – someone who established control over entry into camps. Camp residents mostly refer to these gatekeepers as leaders (sing, *guddoomiye*) a term that encompasses a wider set of functions and responsibilities than simply control over access.

Who are these gatekeepers/leaders who reach out to new and stranded arrivals in the city, helping them settle in their camps, and even providing cash or building materials? Such individuals are better described as humanitarian entrepreneurs, as they aim to generate rents from the humanitarian support that they try to attract through the organization of camps. Humanitarian entrepreneurship is not necessarily devoid of humanitarian motives, and the interviewees often highlighted their ambiguous feelings towards these practices. After all, such entrepreneurs invest their time, social capital and often also money to enable displaced people to erect huts and form camps. Largely, their relations with camp residents are determined by their performance of an intermediary role between camp dwellers, formal or customary landowners, local district authorities and (international) organizations involved in providing humanitarian and other support to displacement affected populations. The entrepreneurs establish and manage camps under their own initiative. If displaced in-migrants can be gathered in identifiable and sizeable concentrations, then the camps are likely to attract the attention of aid organizations. The process of gatekeeping is thus predicated on the possibility of accessing humanitarian assistance and diverting part of this to the pockets of the camp leaders and landowners.

Some camp leaders, especially those in Baidoa, have themselves experienced displacement but over time have built up contacts and skills to manage a camp. Crucially, humanitarian entrepreneurs need the capacity to negotiate with owners of land, or the clan groups that hold customary entitlements to the unused and undeveloped land (*goof*) at the edge of the city. *Goof* lands are usually owned by individuals or families and are inherited paternally. Although unregistered, their boundaries are usually known (albeit often contested), and families may use these areas for grazing, farming or residence (RVI/HIPS, 2017, 38). The extracts that follow are taken from an interview with a camp leader at Mogadishu's north-western outskirts. Zahi hailed from the Hawiye/Murusade, a major clan in Mogadishu, whose members claim ancestral rights to *goof* land at the city edges that are now rented out to large numbers of displaced people (RVI/HIPS, 2017, 82). He outlined in detail how he became a camp leader, how he came to live in these camps himself, and the relationships that he maintains with various stakeholders in the process of camp settlements and, later, also evictions:

Zahi: I used to live in Mogadishu. When people were being displaced to Mogadishu, I started organizing and mobilizing camps for them. And camps are also cheaper for us. I became a leader for the camp as well as escaping [my own] payment of rents […] [But] It is not only about the rent. Some humanitarian agencies come and help the displaced people. […] There was no camp there previously. There were some camps near to the area. I settled there and welcomed the displaced people to where I was living. Some people are very vulnerable. Since I am not a displaced person, I started helping them and the land turned into a camp. The displaced people built small huts inside the camp. There are some people who are able to go into the city and work. Others are unable to make their living, like orphans and women. Some can build iron sheet houses, but most of them don't do that.

Interviewer: Who owns the land?
Zahi: It is *goof* land. We rented the land from the *goof* owners.
I: So the displaced people pay rent?
Zahi: No. They don't. We, the camp leaders, pay some money to the *goof* owners. When humanitarian aid comes, we deduct some percentage from the settlers with their consent. We pay this money to the *goof* owner.
I: What if nothing is distributed?
Zahi: In that case, the *goof* owners have to wait and be patient. And sometimes they evict IDPs. We were evicted from the camp where we were living [earlier] this month. The owners refused to allow us to stay in that camp until the end of Ramadan. We settled in a new place near to the *goof* we were evicted from. We asked the [previous] settlers. They gave us the contact of the *goof* owners. We contacted them and agreed.
I: Did you sign an agreement?
Zahi: It was a verbal agreement. There are some camps that sign agreements. Other *goof* owners don't want to sign an agreement because there is a possibility that the land is owned and purchased by different people, who want to rent it to you without the knowledge of the [real] owners. An owner of a piece of land in the middle of the camp

	may come and ask it to be vacated. Therefore, they don't want to sign an agreement.
I:	Who witnesses agreements?
Zahi:	You go to the district administration to [get them to] witness the agreement.
I:	What benefit do the *goof* owners get from the deal?
Zahi:	At the beginning, the *goof* owner requires $1,000 from you. That money is called *bowd-jebin* ['fence break', an introductory payment]. After that, the *goof* owner receives a certain percentage of the food or cash distributed to the camp. *Goof* owners receive 10 per cent of the humanitarian aid.
I:	What about the leaders and camp committee?
Zahi:	The leaders collect some percentage when the displaced people receive humanitarian assistance. Whatever the displaced people get, a certain percentage is deducted for the *goof* owner, for the leader and for security. [...] The [administration of the] district in which the camp is located in, is responsible for the security, and when aid is distributed, they take 5 per cent of it from each person. (Mogadishu, May 2019)

Zahi's detailed account attests to the complexity of social relations of land ownership and the humanitarian entrepreneurship that enables the establishment of settlements for displaced people across Mogadishu. The camp leaders and landowners provide opportunities for settlement as they speculate on future rents from aid. In Mogadishu, displaced people do not usually pay regular rents for the use of the land, although humanitarian entrepreneurs, such as Zahi, often have to make a down payment to the landowners for access. Often, these entrepreneurs narrated a combination of humanitarian motives and hopes around attracting aid, the former also visible in the initial support that some provide to newcomers. This assistance was much appreciated by interviewees across Mogadishu, and it aims to convince people to join the particular camp. Once leaders manage to receive a relatively regular flow of aid, more people are pulled towards the camp and may even compete for a place to settle. In that case, prospective settlers may have to make a down payment for a space in the camp.

In return for the services provided – the initial support, the ongoing effort to attract humanitarian distributions, and the daily camp management – residents are obliged to hand over a significant proportion of the received aid to the gatekeepers. Here, interviewees gave figures ranging from 20 to 50 per cent. The form in which the aid arrives does not matter; whether food or non-food items, cash or mobile money, gatekeepers collect a share. The case of Zahi was partly exceptional, as he was also looking to live rent-free in the camp. Most camp leaders in Mogadishu resided outside the camp, delegating daily affairs to committees. In Baidoa, leaders could emerge from among the displaced people and often managed to establish better housing structures in the camps' vicinity, for example in the form of iron sheet huts provided by international organizations.

Camp residents didn't usually complain openly about their obligations to share aid with those who enabled settlement and managed the camp. They often described this practice as a reasonable price to pay for the support they received, the time the leader invests in "running after agencies" and the opportunity to establish shelter without having to pay rent. Many spoke about the leaders' efforts, responsibilities and costs. Many of the leaders establish committees, selecting residents from the camps who take on important roles in governing the camp space and its people. Interviewees described, for example, how the leaders and/or committee members oversee a camp's cleanliness, advocate for hygiene, mediate disputes and provide rules for proper behaviour. Camp leaders are also responsible for providing basic security, either through their membership of a locally dominant clan group and/or through their payment of watchmen or district security forces. The leaders' daily efforts were often more visible to the residents than activities of aid organizations, which were regularly criticized for their perceived lack of support. As Sokorey put it: "In fact, they [the leaders] help us by building pit latrines, they were cooking food for us in the beginning, and because we were new, they welcomed us very nicely. I've never seen an organization in Mogadishu help us" (Mogadishu, January 2018).

These practices and relationships highlight how displacement and urban resettlements can be conceived of as an asset, a draw for humanitarian resources provided by UN agencies, international governmental and nongovernmental organizations and their civil society partners. In the context of mass-scale displacement, humanitarian engagement endows unused land with potential value and contributes to the emergence of property regimes that define modalities of land use and distribute entitlements for incoming aid. Beyond the camp leaders themselves, the people in the vicinity of such settlements and camps can also potentially benefit, for instance from the shares of humanitarian payments, but also from the services some organizations establish such as schools, health centres or water points.

Interviewees also described multiple ways in which humanitarian entrepreneurs maximize the amount of aid that can be attracted to a camp, for instance through inflating the numbers of camp inhabitants. Interviewees spoke about such practices, particularly the construction of what they call "rice huts" (*buush bariis*). This practice involves city residents building shelters in a camp in which they do not live in order to receive a share of humanitarian aid. These people are informed by the leader or committee members when organizations will arrive, for them to contribute to an increased presence in the camp. Some interviewees described the owners of these huts as spending time during daylight hours in and around the camp, particularly when humanitarian staff were present, or when headcounts were being done, but then returning home elsewhere in the city at night.

Very few people who participated in the research were explicitly critical of these ostensibly deceptive diversions of aid. Instead, they often acknowledged that not only displaced people were in need of support, and that many city residents were also poor. In the absence of any form of state-provided or otherwise regularly organized welfare, international aid – especially in the form of humanitarian aid that has a focus on alleviating acute suffering – filters through to wider swathes of society who may or may not live in conditions of acute precarity. It is difficult to ascertain the profiles of those who set up such rice huts, or the extent to which they represent the urban poor or more affluent groups. Regardless, these practices partly reflect deeply engrained views of international aid in Somalia as a public good potentially belonging to everybody who manages to access it through different strategies.

This redistribution of aid, and the ways in which it relates to the construction of camps, resembles forms of humanitarian urbanism described in other contexts. Examining Goma in the Democratic Republic of Congo, Büscher and Vlassenroot (2010), for example, highlight the impact of humanitarian 'presence' in reinforcing competition over urban political and socio-economic space. This, they argue, occurs through economic opportunities that are created by the arrival of a massive humanitarian industry, impacting job markets, land values, and encouraging a boom in NGOs, which provide an avenue for gaining international resources (also Büscher et al, 2018). We complement these studies through foregrounding the micro-level practices of petty humanitarian entrepreneurship and the clientelistic-affective ties these generate between residents and self-appointed camp managers. Looking at the everyday practices of gatekeeping, we draw attention to the specific ways in which private entrepreneurs seek to gain access to resources that are associated with displacement and poverty. Humanitarian entrepreneurship is widespread and occurs in multiple ways across Somalia. The petty entrepreneurship that characterizes the engagement with displacement was not considered overly problematic by most interviewees. This acceptance may be caused by the clientelistic relations in which urban newcomers enter with gatekeepers and landowners (Bakonyi, 2021). It can also be explained by the long history of humanitarian entrepreneurship in Somalia, where a broad repertoire of actions and strategies to capture rents from aid have been developed over decades and are regularly adapted to new contexts (Bakonyi, 2011, 200-228).

Nonetheless, some interviewees did complain about excessive and extortive obligations for payments, especially when gatekeepers didn't manage to attract donors or failed to administer the camp. Generally, however, interviewees paid more attention to the potential enrichment of landowners and the increased risk of evictions. They often described how they added value to previously unused *goof* land, as they had cleared away bushes and rubble or dug latrines, thereby making the land habitable or developable. Interviewees also pointed out that their settlement stimulated economic and social development. For instance, their labour and the attraction of humanitarian resources might lead to the construction of access roads, the digging of boreholes, the establishment of water points, connections to electricity networks, and the development of small retail markets in the form of kiosks and shops. International aid sometimes supported the establishment of schools, maternal and child health centres (MCHs) and organized the provision of services that not only attracted displaced people but also other town residents to settle in the camp or its vicinity.

The integration of the camp into wider commercial, aid, and trade infrastructures and networks, adds further value to the land. At this point landowners, who have often hitherto been absent, see opportunities to develop the plot or to sell it to private investors, initiating the rounds of evictions that at the time of our research were being executed on a large scale in Mogadishu, but also regularly affected Baidoa and Bosaso. Two interviewees, Shoobta and Hawa, explained these dynamics of land development and evictions that became part of ongoing processes of camp urbanization in Somalia:

'[The land] becomes valuable because it was a forest and we made it a land to live on after cutting unwanted trees and cleaning the area. And then, when so many people demand to buy it, they make us move, claiming that it does not belong to us but that it belongs to them […]. After some time, they come with a taxi and they look at the land all around, and they say this land is wanted, you must move.' (Shoobta, Mogadishu, January 2018)

Hawa, who took the photo of the newly built house (Figure 3.3), explained:

'This house was built only recently. It is located between the camps and the tarmac road. Such new houses were built mostly recently, by the people from the town who are now building for themselves. These people told us to migrate from this camp because they want to build houses. […] Before [the IDPs settled], the land was just bush, but we cleared it. Everyone from the town now wants his land back. […] Initially the land was not a place you could stay on, it was us who made it valuable. They [the house owners] now have neighbours like us, but others will follow [and build here too] like this person from the town did […].

'I don't know their clans [the house owners'], but it all depends on the money they have. [The mosques] also came recently, like the new houses. People who bought the land cheaply a long time ago now build on one side a mosque and a madrasa where kids learn the Holy Quran, and then on the other side their house [...]

For me the development is a good thing, but when the displaced are told to move from the place from where they were staying because of the value of the land, it is also painful. It is hard to move to another place when you don't have the resources, and we feel bad. [...] When you are told to move, they also tell you to settle on another land where the owner is yet to arrive. As an IDP, you can now settle there, or you can go and move to another area.' (Mogadishu, July 2018)

Hawa's narrative clearly points to the downsides of urban development and reconstruction. Evictions have become an important part of broader land and property dynamics in the four cities. Of course, it is not only the labour of urban in-migrants that has made these neighbourhoods accessible for investment. The formal withdrawal of Al Shabaab from Mogadishu around 2011, modest improvements in the general security situation, the rapid increase of aid in the context of international peace- and state-building and a massive international counter-insurgency campaign, have all contributed to increased interest of Somali's political leaders and businesspeople in urban reconstruction and land development. Private investment in construction, real estate, and social and physical infrastructures are often said to be driven by the Somali diaspora

Figure 3.3: Photograph of a newly built house in the vicinity of a camp in Mogadishu

Source: Photograph taken by Hawa.

and by returnees who accumulated capital while abroad.[1] Also important are local and diasporic business initiatives, prominently the remittance transfer, mobile banking and telecommunication companies that we examine in more detail in Chapter 5 (Jaspers et al, 2019, 10; SPA 2019, 2; Hagmann et al, 2022, 21), along with emerging real estate companies and up-market property developers. The Somali urban context corresponds closely with Goodfellow's (2020, 264) assertion that much land and housing development and speculation in Africa is driven by domestic investments (including diasporic capital) and that the growing commodification of urban land is linked to international infrastructure developments. Foreign donors, are funding the rebuilding of public buildings and support infrastructure development in Somalia. For example, Turkish state and commercial actors have been particularly active and visible in Mogadishu in the (re-)construction of transport infrastructures including roads, the airport and seaport (SPA, 2022).

Together, these multiple forms of investment have precipitated a building boom and have led to increases in land and real estate prices both in the city centre and outskirts locations (AFP, 2016). This, in turn, has drawn the attention of government and private investors to the large numbers of displaced people squatting on private or previously state-owned land and in conflict-damaged buildings. The result is recurrent cycles of violent mass evictions of people from increasingly valuable camp locations, both within the city centre and more peripheral areas. For instance, in December 2017 around 35,000 people were evicted from the Mogadishu districts of Kahda and Daynile (NRC, 2018). Many of the evicted families had already lived for several years in settlements such as the now rather ironically named 'Protect Rights' (*Xaq Dhowr*) camp. Images of these residents following the destruction of their settlements, picking through the detritus of their homes, provide a stark view of human lives rendered bare and disposable. They also attest to the violence intrinsic to assertions of property and the commodification of land (Blomley, 2003).

Such evictions additionally involve the destruction of certain forms of infrastructure – shelters, schools, health centres, latrines – often established by the settlers themselves, sometimes with the assistance of international aid. Evictions break up social networks and livelihood opportunities. People whose lives have already been characterized by enforced mobility once again lose their few belongings and become displaced again. Many interviewees in Mogadishu had been evicted from their initial settlement and moved between different camps in the years or months that they had lived in the city. Follow up interviews with participants in 2022 (as this book was going to press) indicated that the frequency of these repeated evictions had not diminished over the previous three years. Given the ongoing commodification of land in the inner-city neighbourhoods and redeveloped residential areas, urban poor are often pushed further and further to cities outskirts. Taken together, investments in the built environment of cities, the gentrification of city centres and residential neighbourhoods, and camp-based peri-urbanization and urban sprawl are imprinting themselves in the rapidly changing cityscape of Mogadishu. These developments are stratifying the living conditions and life chances of the city's inhabitants. The claims to property and the commodification of land increase the precarity of the most vulnerable urban residents, forcing them to continue to be on the move even after they arrive seeking refuge in the city.

Comparisons with Baidoa, Bosaso and Hargeisa

The political economy of camp urbanization that is embedded in humanitarian entrepreneurship and contestations over property in Mogadishu finds many parallels in experiences of displaced populations arriving and living in Baidoa, Bosaso and Hargeisa. Nonetheless, there are also important differences that are grounded in the cities' varying histories of violence; related phases of large-scale outward and inward mobilities; the demographic profile of arrivals; and wider security dynamics. The factors that make the cycles of evictions and camp (re)settlement in Mogadishu particularly acute relate to the status of the city as capital, the presence of donors, multinational and international organizations, the city's size – all of which influence the scale of investments in real estate and businesses. Also important is the city's historical and contemporary heterogeneity in terms of clan composition, which is reflected in both contestations over land and political power (RVI/HIPS, 2017). Mogadishu also has the most febrile and contested security environment of the cities we examine here. It experiences the greatest frequency of urban violence and attacks by Al Shabaab, and the group maintains parallel and shadow governance structures in the city. The nature and significance of these factors can be understood by looking at differing forms of camp urbanization in Baidoa, Bosaso and Hargeisa.

Since the expulsion of Al Shabaab from the city in 2012, Baidoa has become an important destination for people displaced from the surrounding villages and, albeit in smaller numbers, for people moving back to Somalia from refugee camps in Kenya. Unlike Mogadishu, most of the incoming migrants hail from the same region and often Baidoa's immediate hinterlands. Therefore, they tend to travel shorter distances and often belong to locally dominant clan groups or are closely affiliated with them. Displaced populations settling in camps on the edge of the city often share extended family links with city dwellers, who predominantly belong to the wider Mirifle clan family. By contrast, in Mogadishu most displaced people who settle in camps or squatter settlements do not share clan and family links with politically and economically dominant Hawiye and (to a lesser extent, Darood) subclans. In the case of the large numbers of Mogadishu in-migrants who come from the Somali Bantu Jareer clans, these divisions are also racialized, as we discuss in more detail in Chapter 6, which deals with contestations over urban belonging and citizenship.

Regardless of clan links in Baidoa, living conditions in camps for in-migrants are similar to those in Mogadishu, and are characterized by material dilapidation and extreme precarity. The petty humanitarian entrepreneurship of camp establishment and management also works in Baidoa, although gatekeepers appear to be more often part of the displaced populations themselves. Ahmed, a camp leader in Baidoa, explained how he tries to attract in-migrants and how he works with a committee to gain access to aid and manage the camp. Showing a photo of a sign with a telephone number, Ahmed explained that "this number belongs to my friend. This is the camp where I am the head, and he is the deputy. It is the deputy's number that is there, as we run the camp together" (Ahmed, Baidoa, July 2018). The telephone number is given on the sign to allow new arrivals in Baidoa to contact the camp leaders who will then help them to find a plot of land to settle on within a camp. Although few interviewees reported paying regular rents, registration fees or ad hoc contributions of external aid were reported to be paid in some cases.

Often, interviewees stated that they did not have a clear idea of exactly who owned the land they settled on, or the exact relationship between the camp leader and the landowner. Again similar to Mogadishu, some interviewees expressed their gratitude for receiving material and social support from camp leaders. Interviewees repeatedly stated that a large part of a gatekeeper's role involved going into town to secure international aid. Cash-based assistance was commonly reported, although people complained that this had not been sustained. If cash payments arrive, camp leaders are responsible for compiling lists of residents who then receive the SIM cards and, at times, also mobile phones allowing them to receive cash assistance, which is paid through mobile money accounts (see Chapter 5). Some interviewees complained that the camp leaders were inactive or unsuccessful in securing aid. Others also described the construction of "rice huts" for non-camp residents who aim at gaining access to aid. Compared to Mogadishu, interviewees reported fewer instances of evictions and forced moves between different camps, although large-scale evictions have also taken place in Baidoa. Generally, the wider perception of closer family and ethno-linguistic links between long-term residents and city newcomers was perceived as providing a less hostile environment for camp dwellers. Many interviewees referred to Baidoa as "their" town (Salman, Baidoa, January 2018). Nonetheless, international actors have recognized the increasing risk of evictions and, at the time of the research, were starting to plan the relocation of people from camps in acute risk of evictions to a planned resettlement area further north of the main clusters of camp settlements on the outskirts of Baidoa. Coordinated resettlement had not been undertaken in Mogadishu, primarily because of ongoing disputes over peripheral land and the wider urban security situation. In contrast, such schemes have a longer history in Bosaso and Hargeisa.

As explained in the previous chapter, the northern port city of Bosaso was spared from the widespread urban destructions that characterized the other three cities. It was also neither held by nor openly fought over by Al Shabaab. Due to this relative peace, migration from southern regions and from parts of Somaliland has been ongoing for several decades. A large proportion of forced migrants who are living in inner-city squatter settlements or camps are aligned to the same Digil/Mirifle and Jareer clan groups that predominate among displaced populations in both Baidoa and Mogadishu. Bosaso, however, is politically claimed by people from the Darood clan family, with Majeerteen clans forming a majority in the city and wider region. They are politically dominant in both the Puntland Federal Member State and Bosaso city.

Although most interviewees in Bosaso had been settled in the city for several years, some for decades, other aspects of camp settlement patterns in Bosaso resembled those of Baidoa and Mogadishu. For example, many also described multiple experiences of eviction and the need to move between various temporary camps in negotiation with local landowners. However, unlike in Baidoa and Mogadishu, at the time of the research, significant effort in Bosaso had already been put into resettling large numbers of people from their inner-city camps to a new cluster of settlements further outside the main city. Like Mogadishu, the edge of Bosaso is therefore largely inhabited by people labelled as displaced. The crucial difference with the capital, however, is that these settlements in Bosaso have not been solely established through a fluid and formally unregulated process of private humanitarian entrepreneurship and land clearances. Rather, their morphology, to a significant extent, has been defined by a degree of joint urban planning by municipal and international actors. These spaces also evolved in more unplanned ways, but we return to a detailed analysis of the implications of resettlement schemes – yet another form of camp urbanization and humanitarian urbanism – in Chapter 6. A small number of inner-city camp settlements – both in the form of squats and private arrangements – do remain in Bosaso, most prominent among them the Boqol Buush (Hundred Huts) neighbourhood close to the port.

Hargeisa's distinctive experience of urban destruction, large-scale (often cross-border) population flight, and subsequent returns have initiated different dynamics of camp urbanization in the wider context of the reconstruction of Somaliland's capital. As described in the previous chapter, the inner-city squatter settlements we studied in Hargeisa were mostly established by people who returned from refugee camps in Ethiopia. These settlements transformed over time as makeshift huts have been replaced by more solid corrugated metal shacks. People here have been joined over the years by

Figure 3.4: Satellite images of Statehouse in Hargeisa (2002 and 2017)

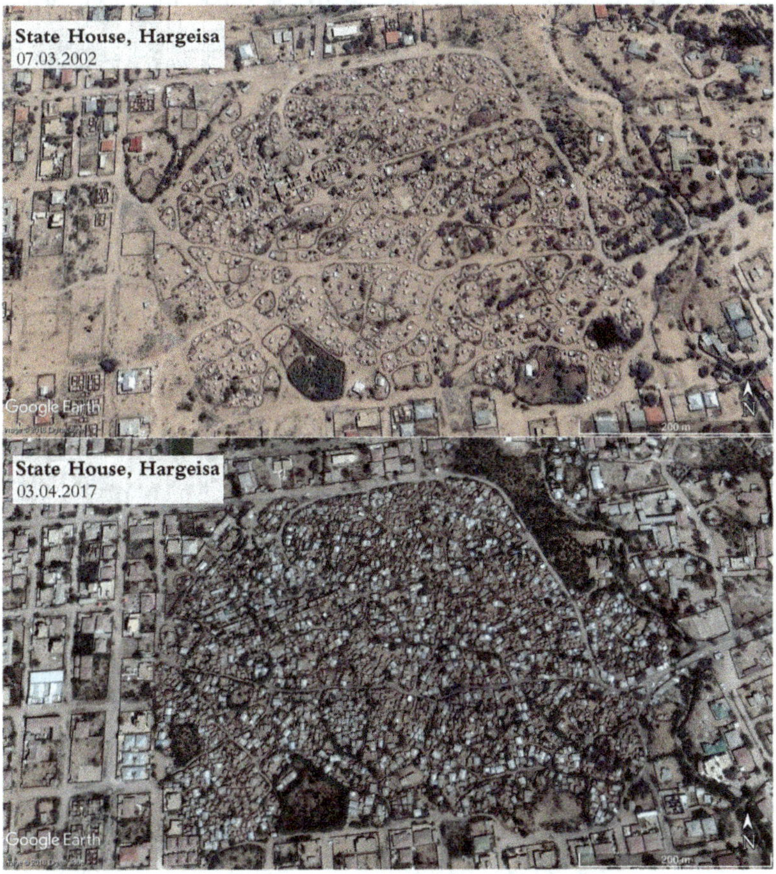

Note: Images show significant densification of settlement and shifts from tent to metal shack housing.
Source: Google Earth.

new arrivals from elsewhere in Somaliland and beyond, and increasingly also by people who either cannot afford to pay the ever-rising rents in the city or speculate on relocation. The satellite images in Figure 3.4 show the striking densification of settlement, but also the changing morphology of Statehouse between 2002 and 2017.

The forms of humanitarian entrepreneurship and gatekeeping observed in Mogadishu and Baidoa are less relevant in these neighbourhoods within Hargeisa. Instead, new forms of land ownership, 'propertying' and leasing have developed, which also reflect broader patterns of urban reconstruction and gentrification. Prominent settlements such as Statehouse were formed on what was known to be government-owned and thus public land. Interviewed residents acknowledged the government's ownership of the land, but this has not prevented the emergence of a petty property market as buying and selling of plots is ongoing. This amounts to the subletting of government properties. As no legal claim of ownership is conferred in this process and insecurity of tenure persists, prices are much more affordable than on the formal property market in Hargeisa.

We conceptualize propertying here simply as the practice of laying claim to land, whether through formal procedures and deeds, or the establishment of 'facts on the ground' through the erection of material structures. This is immediately visible in a neighbourhood like Statehouse, where fencing separates different plots with huts and metal shacks from each other. These properties are characteristically shared with relatives or parcelled out and rented/sold to new arrivals, often people displaced from within Somaliland, Somalia or elsewhere, including non-Somali migrants, such as people from the Oromo ethnic group from Ethiopia. Different practices of propertying are visible in the photos in the form of thorn fences or metal sheets used to enclose land and reflect emergent ideas and relations of property. Whereas in the early days of these settlements people could simply lay claim to an unused plot, construct shelter and fence-off a piece of land, newcomers now (usually) pay rent or buy plots from those who had earlier claimed property. Aadil comes from an Isaaq subclan that is well represented in the city but was displaced across the border by the bombardment and destruction of Hargeisa in the late 1980s, when he was a small child. He returned with his family in 2000 and described property dynamics in Statehouse, where he now lives:

Aadil: A place to settle!? There is no empty space to settle in the neighbourhood. If an empty space is found, it is owned by someone, so anyone who wants to settle should buy it from the owner. That is the only way you can join this neighbourhood. [...] If a poor person comes from the other neighbourhoods of the city, he can join us, with the condition of buying or renting the land (on) which he will settle, because it is owned by someone.

Interviewer: So, how will someone find an empty space in the neighbourhood?

Aadil: People came here one by one, those who came here from the beginning have fenced a land, that land belongs to them now. Most of them brought their relatives, but if he or she wants to sell, he can do that. So, if a poor person, who could not afford the expenses of the other neighbourhoods, if he comes here and finds someone who is selling a plot of land, he can buy it and then he can settle on it.

I: But originally who owns the land of this neighbourhood?

Aadil:	The government.
I:	If the government owns the land, how can the residents sell it to another individual?
Aadil:	It is a temporary sale, for example if the land in the other neighbourhood costs around 30,000 USD, you can buy a plot of land here for 1,000 USD, and it is for temporary settlement. The person selling it is selling part of the land where he was settling. (Hageisa, December 2017)

The transformation of squats into properties is familiar in other urban contexts where slums and informal settlements have witnessed the emergence of 'shanty town real estate' markets (Amis, 1984). Ugbaad, a mother of nine, had left Hargeisa for Ethiopia and had been back in the city for 14 years. She had found a plot in Hargeisa through a friend she had previously known in Ethiopia. She explains subsequent property dynamics in Statehouse:

> 'There is no empty land now at all, but if you are willing to pay rents, you can find a small "Somali House" [hut] available for rent, and also if you have families, relatives or friends you can also reside with them. You can also buy land if you can afford it. A sufficient plot of land can be around $800 inside the neighbourhood [...] When poor people become tired from paying frequent rent fees, they sometimes look for the support of their extended families and save money and when it becomes enough, they buy a land, because they also understand the future of this place will not affect only them, but their situation will be similar to the thousands of households who live in this area. I don't think Somaliland government will drop all these citizens out without any proper plan.' (Hargeisa, December 2017)

In this context, land ownership remains temporary and precarious. In spite of its vibrant property market, a dominant feature of Statehouse is its fragile impermanence. For example, the construction of more durable and permanent brick houses is forbidden to prevent people from developing permanent claims to land ownership. This speaks to other studies that focus on the materiality of camps, drawing attention to the 'tension between the temporary and the permanent, return and the built' (Abourahme, 2015, 200) and the ways in which these tensions shape refugee subjectivities. Drawing on Latour, Abourahme's account of refugee camps shows how human actions are mediated by things: for instance, how access to cement allows for building 'up', a vertical expansion that further affects urban density. Factoring in the materials of the camp as actants problematizes one-directional and one-dimensional readings of refugee agency within the production of camp spaces. The material differences of dwellings, sanitation and water infrastructures highlight everyday negotiations and imaginations of lives in the settlements, structure their temporality and determine different rhythms of urban lives.

In our case, the photovoice method helped to make visible the interweaving of social, spatial, material and technological means in the lived everyday at the urban margins. While people in Hargeisa's inner-city squatter settlements can buy and rent land, and construct shelters, the material they are allowed to use highlights the transitory character of the settlement. The potential to gain some legal recognition of occupancy does exist but requires engaging with the local government and paying for their services. This presents obstacles for the urban poor, and even if some documentation of ownership can be obtained this usually remains temporary. Benefits for households may potentially be realized in case the Somaliland government relocates people to resettlement areas. The documentation may then be used to make claims for compensation in case of evictions, or to take up the provision of new property in a resettlement area outside or on the current edge of the city. Like in Bosaso, such resettlement areas have been created in recent years by the municipal authorities in collaboration with international organizations. Distinctive to Hargeisa, however, is the fact that prominent urban settlements on government land, such as Statehouse, have not yet been evicted or redeveloped. The trust Ugbaad puts in the Somaliland government not to evict people without providing solutions for their relocation stands in stark contrast to Mogadishu, where no faith in governing institutions was expressed by interviewees. In Bosaso, the higher number of evictions and camp clearances was undoubtedly eased by the fact that displaced people were considered outsiders with fewer connections to local social and political networks. In Hargeisa the property relations and land ownership are to some degree protected as many of the people who live in them hail from locally powerful clan groups and can therefore muster some support against evictions.

Conclusion: The camp becomes the city?

The 'camp that is becoming a city' has become a prominent trope in journalistic accounts of displacement (Fahim, 2021). Examples have been identified across the globe (Milko and Hammond, 2019; Wernick, 2019) and academic accounts often focus particularly on the transformation of geographically isolated refugee camps into towns, cities and regional hubs (Pérouse de Montclos and Kagwanja, 2000; Agier, 2002a, 2002b; Oka, 2011; Herz, 2012; Turner, 2012; Agier and Lecadet, 2014; Dalal, 2015; Picker and Pasquetti, 2015). As with camps in Kenya such as Dadaab and Kakuma – established in the 1990s to accommodate people fleeing conflict in Somalia, Sudan and elsewhere in east and central Africa – such sites have often been established in remote corners of host states, near to the border over which refugees have fled. Their location indicates that these camps were considered by their planners and administrators to be temporary solutions until a crisis is resolved and people are able to return. Such camps may exist for years, if not decades, and start to urbanize (Pérouse de Montclos and Kagwanja, 2000; Oka, 2011; Jansen, 2018). Less research engages with camp-type settlements that evolve in and around cities. These camps often come to rub up against or become enmeshed with the wider city where they often sharpen dynamics of urban inclusion and exclusion, while bringing to light emergent ideas and relations of property in which in/exclusion is embedded. Drawing from Appadurai (1996), Martin (2015), uses the term 'campscape' to describe how Palestinian refugee camps in Beirut merged into informal settlements, becoming part the wider urban fabric. Her work draws attention to the question of how these new settlements are related to the urban environment and the ways in which urban dynamics come to penetrate them. In other contexts, settlements established at the edge of or within existing cities have also acquired a sense of permanence and have (quite literally) concretized (Agier, 2002a, 2002b; Abourahme, 2015; Martin, 2015; Totah, 2020).

Although we have drawn from this literature in our analysis, we can identify significant differences when comparing the situations of refugee populations with the experiences of internally displaced people in the Somali cities. These differences have shaped our argument about the nature and significance of displacement-induced urbanization in various ways. Despite the fluid and permeable boundaries of the Palestinian camps, their longevity speaks to a protracted spatial fixity, or at least a 'frozen transience' (Bauman, 2002, 345), that differs from the fragile impermanence and constant fluid improvisation characteristic of the urban settlements discussed in this book. Our conception of camp urbanization, therefore, does not so much capture the transformation of temporary settlements of displaced in-migrants into more permanent neighbourhoods. Instead, we point to more fluid and mobile processes by which camps and associated practices of small-scale humanitarian entrepreneurship are interwoven into the wider urban fabric through repeated land clearances, infrastructural connections, evictions, informal re-encampment (whereby these processes continue) or, in some of the cities, state/international organization-sponsored local resettlement programmes.

Campscapes on the edge of Mogadishu, for instance, have comprised continuously shifting and seemingly ever-moving patchworks of spatial and material arrangements. We argue that this transience – manifest in the forced mobility of so many interviewees from camp to camp in the city – is central to the way urbanization unfolds across Somalia. In these processes, relations of property are constituted, maintained and again transformed as gentrification is put into motion. Evictions have tended to be particularly widespread and violent in Mogadishu. This reflects the limited social and economic capital that in-migrant populations are able to accumulate and use in a context characterized by non-formalized and clan-based forms of political regulation, and booming urban land markets. In the inner-city settlements in Hargeisa, the last case discussed above, camp urbanization may come close to manifesting as relatively bounded and increasingly densely populated urban space within the wider city. This is visible in Statehouse's changing architecture and its enclosure by streets and fences that demarcate its outer limits. The fragile permanence that characterizes this neighbourhood is feeding into the property market, because among the reasons for investing in land or houses is the potential to benefit from either resettlement or compensation when (or if) the Somaliland state reclaims the land. Such speculations on land reclamations are linked to another distinctive form of camp urbanization – the development of resettlement schemes for inner-city camp dwellers. These schemes have been implemented in Bosaso and Hargeisa (and now also Baidoa), creating new centres of gravity for in-migration and constituting yet another type of humanitarian urbanism that we return to in Chapter 6.

Another important difference with much of the global literature on protracted encampment relates to the legal status of refugees. Although Martin's (2015, 12) discussion of Palestinian settlements in Beirut emphasizes how wider sectarian structures in Lebanon draw multiple lines of exclusion and inclusion for citizens, the urban camps of refugees are still legally differentiated from the city's slums. In Oesch's research on Palestinian refugees in Jordan, the emergence of the dual status for some as 'refugee citizens' produces ambiguity but does not eliminate the importance of the legal categorization as refugee in that context (Oesch, 2017). Similarly, Jansen's ethnographic account of Kenya's Kakuma refugee camp presents the space as an 'entitlement arena'. Access to these entitlements hinge on complex and multilateral negotiations within and beyond the camp about rights that are tied to refugee status, the provisions of international humanitarian law, and state-signed refugee conventions. The UNHCR, as both a rights guarantor and a humanitarian implementer, plays an important but bifurcated – and therefore problematic – governance role in this arena (Jansen, 2018, 42).

However, the situation for internally displaced people is (even) more ambiguous. In Somalia, despite the federal government's ratification of the African Union (AU) Convention for the Protection and Assistance of Internally Displaced People in Africa, the legal or citizenship status of urban in-migrants within Somalia is ill-defined across the politically fragmented territory. In consequence, entitlements to humanitarian protection or assistance are not uniformly applied. This does not mean that aid is unimportant, or that displaced people are not subject to humanitarian governance. However, it does contribute to ambiguous forms of exclusion or, drawing from Agamben (1998, 9), forms of 'inclusive exclusion' that are enacted through multiple informal practices of encampment. Again, this is a topic to which we return in Chapter 6 as we look to the longer-term politics of internal displacement, race/ethnicity and the territorialization of stigma and citizenship in the Somali context.

Camp urbanization in Somalia is also closely related to the 'humanitarian urbanism' conceptualized by Potvin (2013, 3) as 'the production of space through humanitarian action'. Critiquing overemphasis on the distinct and separate spatial figure of the camp, even if described as being urbanized, Potvin draws attention to the wider spatial practices of humanitarian governance, involving architects, urban planners and geographers. For example, in post-2001 Afghanistan, urban space has been shaped by encounters of humanitarian, military, state and private actors, all engaging and negotiating their interests in the potentially profitable reconstruction of cities. However, we also showed that the presence of international humanitarian actors has a somewhat different appearance than in many other settings where the sudden arrivals of international organizations can quickly create 'aid towns' whose economic growth is rapidly and significantly skewed towards this highly visible international presence and investment (Büscher and Vlassenroot, 2010; Büscher et al, 2018). International actors are also heavily engaged in Somali cities. However, they are mostly clustered in tightly secured and segregated enclaves, often around airports, such as in Mogadishu and Baidoa (Bakonyi, 2022a). Although these zones sustain international mobilities of staff and goods, and contribute to the emergence of aid-based economies, security threats against international aid workers make their presence in these cities much less visible. Gentrification is related to international presence, but it is also driven by a wider range of investments in real estate, banking, telecom and retail from the large Somali diaspora and through local or transnational business conglomerates. These urbanizing and gentrifying dynamics are thus embedded in activities that are sometimes enabled by, and at other times indirectly related to (but often also transcend) aid interventions. While investments are contributing to the economic growth of cities, not everybody benefits equally from the new economy, which drives up land prices and increased evictions of squatters.

While the wider literature on how humanitarian action shapes space has often focused on the activities, organizational structures, formal protocols and bubbles created within 'Aidland' (Apthorpe, 2005; Mosse 2011; Smirl, 2015), our account of camp urbanization and humanitarian urbanism has focused on micro-level dynamics that relate to expectations of access to aid by petty humanitarian entrepreneurs. These are the individuals who set up and manage camps as a potential resource. The promise of access to support is among the draws for impoverished and displaced people moving into cities. This chapter has demonstrated various ways in which small-scale activities and investments focused on the *possibility* of accessing humanitarian resources are contributing to the making of cities. The testimonies and photos speak to how this type of humanitarian urbanism is experienced by some of the cities' poorest inhabitants. This takes place through their interactions with gatekeepers: their negotiation within clientelist networks in which petty-humanitarian entrepreneurship is embedded. The navigation of the emergent relations between in-migrants, gatekeepers, landowners and humanitarians is materializing in socio-spatial assemblages that shape the morphology of Somali campscapes and the wider cities.

Less visible, these assemblages are connected to recent forms of financial penetration of African economies through international infrastructural investments and aligned 'local' investments in real estate aimed at generating income from rents. Rents are always generated through the appropriation of value from networks of distribution (Andreucci et al, 2017). The humanitarian rents that emerge at the marginalized edges of cities prepare the ground – often literally – for more ordinary processes of real-estatization. Our analysis steers clear of passing moral judgements on such practices, albeit recognizing that humanitarian entrepreneurs divert (some) aid from the intended recipients and thus generate rents from poverty. By and large, however, the interviewed camp dwellers expressed ambivalent or even, at times, positive interpretations of their camp managers' initiatives.

Our empirical examination of camp urbanization also pointed to the need to differentiate between camp forms. Although all are constituted as temporary, the socio-materiality of camp spaces differs within and across the cities we studied. These differences affect lives at the margins. Perhaps more importantly, from a theoretical point of view, these differences also show the difficulty – if not impossibility – of rendering life entirely 'bare'. If we follow Butler (1990) who has challenged the differentiation between the political (or social) and physical (or natural) body, a reduction to a bare biological existence is never fully possible as the biological is always already socially mediated, leaving some room for manoeuvring and resistance (also Wilcox 2019, 309). Instead, empirical studies can explore how the boundaries between political, social and physical lives are made, challenged, refuted, confirmed and remade. In our case, this occurs through the daily actions of people who are establishing, managing, maintaining and living in camps, and of those who are evicting, taking over and gentrifying campscapes and wider urban spaces.

Urban in-migrants, despite occupying subordinate positions, influence how cities are developing and shape their morphologies and patterns of growth. This occurs both in terms of spatial expansion and densification of cities. Although this influence is not necessarily exerted to their own advantage, how people experience their place and role in these patterns of urbanization is not solely defined by their relationship with a plot of land, or the need to create and move between camps. Experiences of the city are also mediated by the infrastructures that people create through improvisations within clientelistic relations, and the development of social solidarities. The ways in which these infrastructural improvisations come to embody experiences of displacement and city-making is where the next chapter now turns.

4

Improvising Infrastructure: The Micropolitics of Camp Life

Universal access to infrastructure is one of the core ideals of modernity and is viewed as a symbol of development and progress. Infrastructures evoke imaginaries of material connectivity and uniformity (Lawhon et al, 2017, 725) and are supposed to provide the 'closely choreographed intersection between technology, space and society' that characterizes the 'archetypical modern city' (Gandy, 2004, 366). The identification of infrastructural 'gaps' across Africa and an expectation of potentially lucrative returns for capital (Goodfellow, 2020, 264) has driven international investments in both mega and smaller-scale infrastructure over the last decade. In Somalia and Somaliland, bilateral, multilateral and private organizations are currently investing in transport infrastructure, prominently seaports, airports and roads. These investments demonstrate the close intertwinement of geo-economic and geo-political interests, and, together with the rapidly growing emphasis on the management of global flows, are driven by the integration of capitalist production and circulation (Danyluk, 2017, 630–1). The rise of logistics, along with a global focus on supply chain management and security, further contributes to investment in transport infrastructure across the globe. This also materializes in specific forms in the context of protracted insecurity across the Horn of Africa and international humanitarian and state-building interventions in Somalia (Bakonyi, 2022a).

Infrastructural gaps have been identified across Africa, where they are predominantly framed as a development problem (World Bank, 2010). Infrastructural development therefore features prominently in several of the United Nations' sustainable development goals (SDGs), including SDG11 for the promotion of sustainable cities and communities. SDG11 sets out that infrastructure development should be promoted in ways that increase inclusivity and justice. Infrastructural development also plays an important role within the 'durable solutions' initiative, launched in 2016 as a comprehensive international attempt to deal with rapid, displacement-related urbanization in the Horn of Africa. Centrally planned and uniformly delivered infrastructure remains the dominant idea and aspiration within 'durable' urban planning.

The SDGs, 'durable solutions' and related schemes acknowledge that infrastructural development is neither necessarily inclusive nor automatically increases equality. Nonetheless, in their often technical (and thus depoliticizing) language, these initiatives appear to underestimate how tightly infrastructures are entangled with relations of power and shaped by struggles for rights and citizenship. Related to conflicts of land and property, infrastructures are, as this chapter shows, at the centre of everyday contestations over the 'right to the city' (Lefebvre, 1996). These contestations take place in multiple daily practices and negotiations that shape how cities are made, unmade and remade.

Ahmed is a skilled construction worker who lives in the Boqol Buush (Hundred Tents) settlement close to the city centre of Bosaso. Originally from the Somali region of Ethiopia, he had been resident in Mogadishu but fled fighting there around 2009 and moved north to Puntland. Boqol Buush is one of the oldest settlements of displaced people within Bosaso city and is one of the few in the urban centre that has not (yet) been cleared for the resettlement of its inhabitants to new areas to the east of the main city. In what follows, Ahmed gives a detailed explanation of the infrastructure and services available in this neighbourhood:

> 'Among the services here there is some basic health care. We have one MCH [mother and child health centre] in the camp and another one in a nearby neighbourhood […]. These centres provide health services to the pregnant women who might have anaemia, although the medical drugs and other materials are limited. But some basic services are available. Medicine that is not available in the MCH, we buy from the market in town. The public hospital does not provide any medical drugs to the patients and the MCH is better than the hospital in this respect.
>
> As for electricity availability: the power sector is private or is owned by the government and this is a paid service; those people who can afford it install power in their houses. […] Water is brought by a water tank on a vehicle and stored in a water tank which is fixed on the ground. Twenty litres of water costs about SoSh 3,000 [approximately 0.15 USD]. Businessmen own these water tanks and sell water to the people. For education, there is a school constructed by UNICEF called Daryeel. This school provides intermediate level education, and my children are studying in the school. This boy is my son, and he studies in that school. We pay three dollars for each student per month.

Our biggest issue in this camp is housing. When a person secures a prominent house for his family, it is tremendous progress. Food availability varies, sometimes it is difficult to get food. But if you miss a mealtime, you will be able to get the second one. The most important aspect of human life is housing security. If the displaced people are supported with land or some people donate to buy us a land, maybe after some time, somebody will claim that he owns the land […].

When I came to this camp […] there was no electricity, water or school. At that time, the living situation was very difficult, and the people were ignorant. There were no toilets available in the camp, which was the biggest problem. The people used to go to the seashore for urination. A private [commercial] toilet was created that charges SoSh 3,000 each time. Our family is composed of nine members. And if we use the commercial toilet, it will cost us about SoSh 27,000 [approximately 1.35 USD] for one use, or 54,000 for twice a day. Building a private toilet in your house is not allowed. It is refused by the landowners. They say that this is their business.' (Bosaso, June 2019)

Ahmed's explanation shows how people's lives in marginalized urban settlements are embedded neither in centrally provided nor closely choreographed infrastructures. Instead, infrastructures are dispersed, variegated and non-uniform. Services are generally privatized, and access is commodified. This accentuates and reproduces social differences and hierarchies. As in many cities across the globe, a broad range of actors are engaged in the uneven establishment, maintenance and repair of multiple 'heterogenous infrastructure configurations' (Lawhon et al, 2017; also Blundo and Le Meur, 2008, 15). These configurations are undertaken by large businesses or small-scale entrepreneurs, multilateral and international agencies, grassroots and community-based organizations, religious congregations and self-help groups.

This chapter comparatively examines how in-migrants to Somali cities, like Ahmed, described and photographed infrastructure, and how struggles for access shape their everyday lives. Looking at life at the urban margins through infrastructure, we follow the direction of Lawhon et al (2014, 512) to study the 'everyday modalities' of urban materiality, and Desai et al (2015, 2) in focusing on certain aspects of the mundane and 'lived worlds of urban infrastructures'. Ahmed has shown that accessing basic infrastructure – sanitation, water, healthcare, education – is quite complicated for people living in camps or settlements associated with displaced populations. Residents here negotiate, cobble together, assemble, organize, assess and improvise with basic infrastructure. They thereby produce the socio-materiality of places and configure urban morphologies. These, in turn, shape their everyday bodily experiences in and of the city.

We use this chapter to zoom into the intersection of social and material aspects of urban lives and to discuss how infrastructures mediate and differentiate urban practices. Following the approach of Swyngedouw (1996, 67), albeit focusing on the urban margins, we use examples of sanitation, water, health and education as analytical entry points to highlight some of the 'interrelated tales of city: the story of its people, and the socio-ecological processes that produce the urban and its spaces of privilege and exclusion'. The chapter builds on the previous analyses of the political economy of urban in-migration and settlement, notably humanitarian entrepreneurship and poverty rentierism. It further expands on this account by demonstrating how infrastructural struggles are conditioned through relations of property that intersect with arrangements for security. We also emphasize again how people at the margins are active agents of urbanization, even if they themselves do not usually benefit from these contributions to city-making.

Toilet technologies: embodied infrastructure

The previous chapter outlined how impoverished urban in-migrants across Somali cities negotiate the relations that allow them to use seemingly empty and unused land in city centres and on their outskirts. Through the mediation of camp leaders, city newcomers obtain permission from landowners to erect makeshift huts. These are often barely able to shelter the occupiers from the elements, especially in the wet season. In many of the larger camps at the outskirts of the cities, humanitarian organizations have supported the establishment of pit latrines. These latrines often have solid concrete foundations and use iron sheets to protect the privacy of users. The materials of these toilets, as well as their arrangement in straight lines, frequently stand in visible contrast to the tight and irregular clustering of fabric, tarpaulin and cardboard huts that fill the rest of the camp.

Ahmed's account confirms the deep-seated locational insecurity that was also described in the last chapter. Mass evictions of such marginalized settlements are part and parcel of cities' reconstruction, economic development and nascent gentrification. Evictions are often executed without or on very short notice and regularly involve physical violence. While not entirely discounting humanitarian motives, landowners or camp managers generally allow and facilitate the establishment of camps to extract aid-related rents. Complementing the 'payment made to landlords for the right to use land', rents are often also charged for the use of the land's 'appurtenances' (Harvey, 1982, 330). This became apparent in Ahmed's account of the landowner's monopolization of water and sanitation infrastructures:

'The owners of the land refused [to allow] us to build private toilets. They said they have built commercial toilets in the camp and the displaced people need to use these. The water tanks also belong to them, and we pay the rent for the land. Everything here is owned by the landlord. We just own these small houses.' (Bosaso, June 2019)

Beyond the attempt to make money, the provision of toilet infrastructures and services also allows the owners of the Boqol Buush land to micromanage their properties and to assert and maintain control over the space and the people residing there. The ability to meet basic needs is, therefore, not detached from the locational insecurity people experience when they squat on land owned by others, even in those cases where they regularly pay rents. How this uncertainty stretches to the commodification of toilet technologies was outlined by Yasmin, a woman in her early 30s and mother of eight, who fled to Bosaso together with her husband thirteen years previously. She now lives in a resettlement area at the city's outskirts, but emphasized that in the past "using toilets [was] a problem, a real problem" once she "became a refugee":

Yasmin:	We moved from there [her first camp in Bosaso] because the owner said he needed his land. Then we moved to another place where we had no latrines. In that place, we stayed for five months, but the owners of that land were two brothers who had different ideas: one dug latrines and people were paying him for 2,000 SoSh [0.1 USD] per use, and everyone is charged that amount regardless of age – children or old people or young women. So, people used to go elsewhere, and the place was very dirty. So, we asked around about somewhere else […] Everyone was charged that amount, for a jerrycan of water to use [for the toilet]. He used to make around 4 to 5 million [SoSh].
Interviewer:	Even if you have diarrhoea and have to go many times?
Yasmin:	Yes, we had to pay every time we used it […]. We were not allowed [to build latrines elsewhere]. There was an agency that wanted to build [latrines] for us, but this was refused. After that we looked for other land. Fortunately, we got this land. Now here, it is good. We have cards [from humanitarian agencies], we are given rice, milk weekly, sometimes. Here it is a blessing. (Yasmin, Bosaso, December 2017)

Many interviewees in the Boqol Buush settlement emphasized their challenges in paying for sanitary needs and how they had to improvise. Hadhira outlined that she could not afford "to use them [the toilets] every time as sometimes you cannot pay the money. Sometimes you are forced to use a metal box or tin for urination and for others, and then throw the box away, to manage this issue" (Bosaso, June 2019). Improvisation characterizes every aspect of life at the margins of Somali cities, where the provision of infrastructures, particularly water and sanitation, has become an additional component of the political economy of displacement and the demarcation and enforcement of property in which this economy is embedded (also Bakonyi et al, 2019; Bakonyi, 2021). However, commercial toilets were not the most common form of facilities across marginalized urban settlements. More often – and likely also more lucrative – was the provision of contracts with international organizations for constructing such facilities, which allowed camp managers and landowners to skim off resources. During one of the photovoice discussions in Baidoa, Ismail showed a picture of a small camp which had only a few huts but numerous latrines (Figure 4.1). According to Ismail, the leader of this camp was very successful in attracting contracts and compared it with his own camp nearby where "we only have two toilets, not enough for us. But in this neighbouring camp, these latrines are more than forty-seven, although there are no people here in that camp, maybe only ten to fifteen people" (Baidoa, July 2018).

Obtaining contracts for the establishment of water points, toilets, schools or health centres requires social capital. Relevant social connections and networks that include landowners and gatekeepers are reflective of the localized power of particular clan groups, and this was emphasized by Ismail as a primary factor in the toilet example he described.

Sanitation technologies become an important part of the political and economic struggles that shape cityscapes at the margins, while simultaneously

Figure 4.1: Photograph of toilets established before the growth of an outskirts camp in Baidoa

Source: Photograph taken by Ismail.

facilitating bodily experiences of urban life. However, Ahmed's earlier answer about the Boqol Buush settlement in Bosaso alludes to an additional layer of meaning imbricated in the establishment and use of sanitation infrastructure. Asked about how life has changed over his years in the camp, Ahmed embeds the availability of infrastructure within a narrative of progress. He recalls times when neither electricity nor education or toilets were available, a lack he associates with *jaahilnimo*, an ignorance etymologically associated with pre-Islamic societies. His memory of how people used to urinate at the nearby beach indicates a sense of shame about the failure or inability to deal with bodily excretions in the privacy provided by (adequate) sanitation facilities. While Ahmed does not mention defecation, Yasmin explained how the "dirt" forced them to leave a camp, while Quresha (December 2017), a woman living in the Statehouse neighbourhood in Hargeisa, explained that her family's "embarrassment will emerge" soon, as their toilet was filled up and would not be usable much longer. The provision and use of sanitation infrastructure is not only central within imaginaries of modernity but transports with these images ideas about dignity and emotive responses of shame or disgust (Jewitt, 2011, 610; Desai et al, 2015, 7). Bodily waste carries symbolic significance (Douglas, 1970). In the region, toilet practices are anchored in Islamic beliefs that associate human urine and faeces with impurity and uncleanliness and require a strict toilet etiquette which interviewees could not always fulfil. Open defecation is not considered as unclean per se, as long as the required washing rituals are observed. However, the density of the city, the gaze of others and the sensorial disturbances associated with inadequate toilets caused physical and emotional distress in many settlements.

Toilets were a regular topic in the photovoice discussions and in interviews across settlements in the cities. Many people provided photos of what they described as inadequate or too few toilets. Ibrahim presented a photo of a self-dug toilet in Mogadishu (Figure 4.2) and explained: "this is a toilet with no iron sheets, just some rugs put around it for privacy. And it has a lot of rubbish around it. So, there is a lack of proper sanitation and hygiene" (Mogadishu, July 2018). The iron sheets, fabric and/or stones placed around shared toilets separate the private from the public realm. If materials to enable some privacy are not available or affordable for residents, they once more rely on improvisation (Gandy, 2004; Desai et al, 2015, 2, 4). The interviews and photos emphasize the intersection of biophysical and social processes and show how infrastructures mediate (gendered) corporeal experiences of the city and shape the everyday rhythm of camp and urban lives.

Residents without access to toilets were trying to regulate their bodily functions in ways that allowed them to protect their privacy and dignity. For example, they used designated places at selected times. As Idris, who lived in Hargeisa's Mohamed Moge settlement, described it: "Everybody,

Figure 4.2: Photograph of toilet in a camp at Mogadishu's outskirts

Source: Photograph taken by Ibrahim.

including children and adults, goes to the bush [for] toilets" (July 2018). He also explained how adults wait till sunset to compensate for the lack of privacy, as the place people use is "an open area, there is not a single tree there." Similarly, Nunay in Baidoa explained how camp residents only "go to the bush in the evening" (January 2018). Gedi, a 70-year-old resident of a camp in Baidoa found the lack of toilets to be particularly challenging "during daytime" as the surrounding area is not shielded from view of others. Waiting until sunset, however, increases security risks for women. Hadhira from the Boqol Buush camp in Bosaso, for example, explained that the commercial toilets are closed at night, but that women cannot use alternative places as they "cannot go out there as they fear something bad may happen to them" (Bosaso, June 2019).

The maintenance of sanitation facilities differed across the settlements. Toilets established by international organizations were usually free of charge, and a system in which families share designated toilets was often established. Female users sometimes developed a rotational cleaning system. However, in most camps latrines were too few to allow for their controlled use or cleaning. A male camp leader in Mogadishu, for example, outlined how the 75 households in his camp shared 13 toilets, most of them "hand-dug by us". The challenge of keeping overcrowded latrines clean was emphasized by many residents. To address this, one of the camp leaders in Baidoa resorted to locking the toilets. Manur showed a photo of a row of pit latrines locked with padlocks and explained: "The [camp] leader holds the key [...] If you want to use it you have to go to his place and take the key. [He does this] to control the cleanliness in them, because if left open, the people will misuse them and they will be unclean" (Baidoa, July 2018). Asked if the leader charges for the use of toilets, Manur answered that "he gets nothing, but he keeps the cleanliness of the latrines and knows who makes it unclean, and he or she is [then] ordered to clean it." She also noted that sometimes the key was unavailable and people then "have to use [the place] behind the latrines and go there, or they go to the bush". Overall, the decision to lock the toilets to avoid improper use was appreciated by Manur. The example is nonetheless revealing of facets of micropolitical control in the camp setting, where a self-entitled keyholder determines sanitation needs and can 'force' people to adhere to proper standards of cleanliness. S/he also holds the power to discipline those who do not adhere to these standards by refusing the key for the toilet and thus forcing people to relieve themselves outside.

Camp residents often lack the means to empty filled-up latrines. If space is available, they tend to abandon filled latrines and instead dig new ones. This was also sometimes the case for brick toilet blocks built by humanitarian organizations in planned resettlement neighbourhoods in Bosaso. Yasin, a young man living in this area, took a photo to illustrate this (Figure 4.3)

Figure 4.3: Photograph of dilapidated toilets in resettlement neighbourhood on the edge of Bosaso

Source: Photograph taken by Yasin.

and call into the question the sustainability of humanitarian infrastructure that had quickly deteriorated.

Furthermore, not all settlements have the space for new latrines. Quresha from Hargeisa's densely populated Statehouse explained:

> 'We have challenges with toilets. We don't even have roads to transport a body in case someone dies in the camp. That's not good, is it? There is a narrow road which passes in front of my house, but it does not go beyond my house [...]. If your toilet is filled up, there is nowhere to go [to build a new toilet] because the compound is made up of your house and the toilet and nothing more. If we stay in this situation beyond this year, I am certain of our embarrassment [...]. It is bad for our lives. And there is nowhere to dump the garbage. Since morning I have been collecting rubbish like plastic bags, but there is nowhere to dump them, there are no vehicles to transport the garbage. So I burnt it.' (Hargeisa, December 2017)

Quresha's description of the difficulties of vehicular access to the overcrowded Statehouse highlights the networked character of infrastructural configurations, even if they are heterogenous and dispersed. The failure of one facility – in her case, roads – leads to the disruption and misfunctioning of others, such as sanitation, garbage disposal or even the burial of the deceased. Mundane biophysical activities – eating, drinking, excreting – are embedded in an ever-changing assemblage of situated and power-laden social practices. These, in turn, continuously weave together humans with materials and technologies. They constitute fragments of more or less networked configurations that cobble together 'socio-ecological and techno-natural processes' (Swyngedouw, 2006, 106) while enabling urban circulation and growth. Disruption of one configuration nearly always has effects on others.

The leftover materials, rubble and debris used in infrastructural ensembles reflect the value attributed to the lives of people at the margins who often must wait for handouts from humanitarian organizations, and need permission from local power holders (landowners) to establish even rudimentary infrastructures. The provision and maintenance of these facilities, along with regulation of access to them, are determining the form and rhythm of intimate bodily practices. MacFarlane (2019, 1245) emphasizes that the urban environment profoundly shapes how metabolic bodily functions are experienced and how physical and social bodily risks are distributed. While directing the rhythms and forms of biophysiological routines, these infrastructural arrangements contribute to the making of precarious places and materialize layers of social differentiation within and beyond the urban margins. While infrastructures shape and foster experiences of inequality, they also show how these experiences become expressed in feelings of inadequacy, shame or even disgust. In this way, infrastructure holds a crucial place in the production of subject positions. The gendered nature of this link between infrastructure and subject-making appears most obviously in water practices, and the assemblage and management of water technologies in marginalized urban settlements is where the analysis now turns.

Water technologies: differentiating and gendering urban life

The accessibility of water is closely linked to the heterogeneous assemblages of sanitation infrastructure. While charging for toilet facilities was not too commonly practiced (with aforementioned exceptions such as in inner-city Bosaso), water provision is entirely commercialized across cities in Somalia and Somaliland. Access to water is a struggle. Even relatively affluent or central neighbourhoods lack access to a singularly networked grid of piped water – despite slow but ongoing private efforts towards this in some cities. In general, those able to buy and store water in larger quantities assemble a storage system in their compounds. Water trucking is now less common in central Mogadishu, but prevalent in its outskirts. In all other cities, water is regularly delivered by trucks to households, transferred to ground level tanks, and from there pumped up to smaller tanks on rooftops. Without the space or means for trucking and large-scale storage, access to water for people in marginalized urban settlements is a demanding daily chore.

Although facing different everyday challenges, for almost all urban dwellers water access is embedded in localized, often overlapping and loosely interconnected infrastructural configurations. While city-wide pipe networks barely exist, classifying Somali cities as 'off-grid' overlooks the multiple ways in which people compensate and make up for gaps or absence of technostructures. Simone (2004) addressed this misconception in his theorization of 'people as infrastructure'. People living at urban margins are, in daily and seemingly disjointed activities, weaving together technologies, animals and materials to compensate for missing, disrupted or malfunctioning infrastructures and services. They use their labour, mobility, skills and voices to assemble water circuits, as they are continuously cobbling together water sources (wells, catchments), pumps, trucks, tanks, pipes, containers, jerry-cans, telephone networks, mobile phones and money services. Their activities connect camp residents with those who own, manage and operate water sources; those who drive and maintain water trucks, water motorbikes and water donkey carts; and those who carry jerrycans of water from water kiosks to their homes. People are also forming and engaging in water committees, or are assembling and maintaining tanks on their own land, aiming to generate rents on land owned by others. People eventually consume this water and send money in the opposite direction to the water flows – from the consumer to the managers and owners of water sources. Social and monetary power intersect, and both are materialized in infrastructural arrangements. Commercialization characterizes every juncture of these dispersed systems, except for the human transport from water kiosks to household homes, an activity undertaken by women as part of their unpaid reproductive duties. The logic of the market – considering its multiple layers of commercialization and the fact that consumers in marginalized settlements can only afford (and hence consume) small quantities of water – drives up water prices in city outskirts while amplifying existing inequalities (see also World Bank, 2021).

Types and modes of household water consumption and the infrastructural assemblages that enable them are closely tied to the ownership of land. In most settlements on cities' peripheries, water is provided at water-tap kiosks. Humanitarian organizations or landowners establish water tanks at the edges of these settlements. While the first rounds of water provided by humanitarian organizations may be free of charge, sooner or later people take over the responsibility to organize, maintain and manage water supplies. Hodan, who lives in a settlement at Bosaso's outskirts explained:

> 'There are several water tanks built in the camp; these water tanks are filled, and the people buy water with SoSh 2000 [USD 0.1 per 20 l canister]. There is someone who is responsible for the management of the water tanks, who collects money and makes sure the tanks are filled by water trucks. At the beginning, we used to use the water freely, but now we pay.' (Bosaso, December 2017)

Arrangements for tank management differed across the cities and settlements. In some cases, landowners provided water, and camp residents were usually not allowed to establish their own tanks or to find alternative water sources. In other places, such as at the outskirt resettlement areas of Bosaso, residents self-organized and took over the management of tanks (Figure 4.4), as described by Hodan. Cosoble, a committee chairman in one of these settlements, explained that the tank "takes two trucks to fill and she [the camp leader] pays 600,000 SoSh, each is 300,000 SoSh, [which] she sells back to us" (Bosaso, December 2017). Yasir, a vice chairman of another camp in Bosaso, recalled that a water company had tried to provide piped water to the camp's outskirts but could not sustain the service as it was more expensive than the trucked water. "The displaced people could not cover the water expenses," he explained. "they [therefore] prefer to use the water in the tanks that is brought by a tanker" (Bosaso, December 2017). Also, according to Yasir, "the tank water tastes good, compared to the tap water". However, Afan from the inner-city Boqol Buush settlement explained health concerns related to tank-stored water:

'We sometimes get sick because of the water, which is stored in unhygienic water tanks. Nobody is cleaning the water tanks and [water is] stored there all the time and you don't have other water source. The children get sick always because of that and it is difficult for the IDPs to buy smaller water tanks to avoid the contaminated water.' (Bosaso, June 2019)

The difference between the two locations is a potential factor here. At the outskirts, tanks are maintained by residents who also drink the same water. However, the tanks in the Boqol Buush are maintained by landowners who live elsewhere and may pay less attention to hygiene standards.

In some settlements, residents received their water from taps linked to locally available water sources, wells or catchments. These are localized infrastructural systems often constructed either by humanitarian organizations or businesspeople and managed by those who control the water source. Piped water, however, is generally unreliable. The water level in wells and catchments that provide piped water are often too low to serve the whole city. Increased density and expansion of cities puts water sources under enormous pressure. Ladan who lives in the Stadium/Cakaara area in Hargeisa, explained how water is no longer sufficient for the population:

'It is very hard to get enough water here. We have challenges of accessing water here […] We usually have to buy from water trucks. There are no pipelines which bring us water here. For such a long time,

Figure 4.4: Photograph of a water point at the outskirts of Bosaso

Source: Photograph taken by Nuurow.

we haven't had free water, we were being charged for a barrel, around 15,000 SolSh [approximately 2 USD].' (Hargeisa, December 2017)

Water trucking, too, is affected by severe water shortages, and people in marginalized settlements often need to search for alternatives, most of them more expensive and time-consuming. Gabow, who lives in one of the camps at Baidoa's outskirts outlined how residents in the dry season:

'go and fetch water from wells where 20 litres of water are sold for 2,000 SoSh [double the usual amount]. There is no free water. The water is from a well with no water pumps. It is fetched by hand, and it is very dirty. The only clean water we get is from the tankers.' (Baidoa, January 2018)

Gabow also the outlined health implications of contaminated water, as "children got cholera and diarrhoea and vomiting. There are agencies who give us ORS [diarrhoea treatment] and pills to add to the water. [But] we still don't have clean water." Later in the interview he explains how international organizations advocate for health and hygiene, but that "no one is taking it [seriously]. Because if the only water you can get is dirty water, then you should use it, you will drink that dirty water because it is all that is available."

Gabow's statement reveals how access to infrastructures can become 'a matter of life and death' (Swyngedouw, 2006, 106; Chant and McIlwaine, 2016, 113). Infrastructural disconnections and omissions can have harmful bodily effects resembling those of direct physical violence (Rodgers and O'Neill, 2012). Dirty water and inadequate sanitation already cause severe health problems, among them acute watery diarrhoea (AWD), cholera and polio. These contribute to high mortality and morbidity rates, especially among children and the elderly across Somalia and Somaliland. While Simone (2004) emphasizes that people compensate for infrastructural gaps and failures, his account also reminds us that infrastructural arrangements are embedded in webs of social relations that reproduce embodied practices and experiences, and display social difference and power. At the margins of Somali cities, these dynamics are accentuated in vital but deficient water arrangements. Here, people become the 'central means through which materials flow' (Lawhon et al, 2014, 507) but are directly exposed to the risks carried by inadequate, unclean and insufficient materials.

The social webs that produce, connect, make work or compensate for infrastructural gaps are gendered and gendering, and the literature has often used urban water technologies to highlight these dynamics (Sultana, 2009; O'Reilly, 2010; Truelove, 2011; Neves Alves, 2019; Kundu and Chatterjee, 2020; Truelove and Cornea, 2020). Water practices in Somali cities are no exception, as fetching, carrying and storing water is generally considered

Figure 4.5: Photograph of girl/young woman fetching water in a Mogadishu camp

Source: Photograph taken by Hawa.

the task of women and adolescent girls. Water is usually collected in 20-litre jerrycans, and women tend to go in the early morning hours before the rest of their household wakes up. They fetch at least one or, if they can afford or manage, two jerrycans of water. They carry these back home, with one on their back, and the other in their hand. In fewer cases, younger children (independent of their gender) are asked to fetch water. Lacking the strength to carry 20 litres, they may use smaller containers and go in pairs or groups to jointly pull and push them to their homes (Figure 4.5). Many female interviewees noted that they try to go at least twice daily to the water point, the first time early in the morning, the second time on their way back from their day's labour.

In case of water shortages, women can spend most of their day searching. Aamal, who lives in a camp in Baidoa that was experiencing severe water shortages at the time of the interview, described the situation:

'The well we go to fetch water from is overcrowded and one takes hours of long queuing to get the water […] two to three hours. But sometimes the yield of the well may go down and there is less water that comes out. So that day there will be so much overcrowding and one may come back home without water. […] Yes, because of too much overcrowding, you sometimes find the well closed and the owner fenced it off, so you will only go back when it has been opened and the crowd is smaller.' (Baidoa, January 2018)

Searching for and fetching water, along with waiting and queuing, are crucial parts of ordinary spatial and temporal practices that produce women's bodily experiences at the urban margins. Access to water requires considerable improvisation and efforts, and this is grounded in uncertainty. "Sometimes we get water and sometimes we don't" is how Shankaroon in Mogadishu summarized it (Mogadishu, January 2018). Asked what she does if she can't get water, Shankaroon explained how women try to obtain it "from the community who have water pipes in their homes, and if we can't get the water from them, we go far outside the camp to get it from the neighbours". Improvisation costs time and energy and people have no guarantee that their effort will lead to results.

Waiting is time spent on an uncertain outcome. It is an 'indicator for social inequality' (Paris, 2001, 711) and differentiation even within the urban margins. For example, people who have managed to lay claim to property – such as in the Stadium and Statehouse in Hargeisa or in some of the resettlement areas on the outskirts of Bosaso – may establish private water tanks in their compounds and mitigate periods of shortage. The differentiation of class and status is manifested in the ownership of land. Even if this ownership is informal and transitional, as in the Hargeisa squatter settlements, it can determine possibilities for infrastructural assemblage. These range from the type of housing to water and sanitation facilities. Dhubow from Bosaso explains this process of social differentiation: "The people are [composed of] two groups; some of them have built their own water tanks and use it as source for water and the other group still uses the donated water tank as source of water. They buy water" (Bosaso, January 2018). In fact, both groups buy water, but the ability to store at least some water in a private tank increases security and minimizes effort, time and (female) labour. Social and economic status materialize in infrastructural arrangements that become part of gendered bodily experiences and, as such, shape and differentiate how men and women navigate the city. Beyond gendered bodily experiences, however, the lived female body is used to express social and cultural distance. This was demonstrated in a statement from Dhuhulow, an elder from a dominant clan group that lives in the camp's vicinity in Mogadishu. When asked about the relation between displaced city newcomers and those who have resided longer in the city, Dhuhulow maintained that there was no discrimination against the former, even if they were from minority clans or outcaste groups. However, he went on to explain that intermarriage is very rare, because of what he understood as cultural differences:

> 'The displaced girls do not want to marry the local boys and the local girls do not want to marry displaced people. They have different characters, so they do not want to marry each other. The local girl will not agree to living in a traditional Somali hut. The displaced boy does not want a wife that will not carry water on her back for the family. It is common for their girls to carry water on their backs. They have

different cultures and will not see eye to eye. Our girls do not carry anything on their backs. Their 5-year-old girls carry 5-litre jerrycans, and their six-year-old girls carry a 10-litre jerrycan on their backs. My wife, who gave birth to my children, never carried water on her back and she cannot carry in the future either. She can carry the water by hand to the house. People are equal. However, they have different cultures and capabilities. The [displaced] women bring water on their backs and grind grains manually. Our women take their grains to the grain mill. Because of the different cultures, it is not possible for us to marry from one another. However, we live alongside each other. They live on our lands. They make a fence for the area we give them. They can bring a hundred people to the camp and they are accountable for their actions. The locals have to go through the camp leader for anything that [concerns camp residents] and he mediates between the two parties on everything. If they need something, they can come and ask us, and vice versa.' (Mogadishu, January 2018)

Dhuhulow's explanations show how everyday water practices generate and reproduce social differences and inequality. The female body and its comportment are mediated by water infrastructures and shaped by material constraints. This is used by Dhuhulow to describe cultural boundaries, to explain difference, and to assert incompatibilities between 'the host community' (in humanitarian parlance) and city newcomers. Such rationalizations are masking deeply entrenched social hierarchies and determine privileges as well as monetary and material benefits. For decades, feminists have been discussing the different ways in which social norms inscribe themselves and shape gendered bodily practices, differentiate bodily experiences and constitute (binary) gendered identities (Young, 1980; Lennon, 2019). Dhuhulow, however, additionally shows that experiences and perceptions of embodiment are closely linked to infrastructure and technology. Access to proper housing, availability of water facilities in the home, or the affordability of mills are shaping the bodily conduct of women, which, in Dhuhulow's explanation, are then identified as markers of poverty, social status and belonging. For Simone (2004) people can be considered *as* infrastructure, but compensation for gaps and malfunctions is not only unequally spread across human bodies but also codifies the intersection of gender and class. Here, it also generates the bodily comportment of women as culturally specific. Infrastructurally mediated somatic registers are used to sort people into discrete collective identities. This corresponds with Rodger and O'Neill's (2012, 406) findings that corporal suffering caused by exclusion from urban infrastructures (physically) marks bodies and facilitates social exclusion. Such embodied differentiation also contradicts the myth of cultural homogeneity and classless social organization that is a rhetorical feature of popular and nationalist-inflected discourses in Somalia and continues to influence studies of Somalia. This is a theme we return to in Chapter 6, which provides an analysis of wider discourses that foster differentiations of 'IDPs' from 'locals', and how resettlement schemes shape narratives of belonging in Somali cities.

Health practices and infrastructures

Compared to the attention given to water and sanitation, intra-urban health differences – and particularly health practices in marginalized settlements – have gained surprisingly scant academic attention (Ezeh et al, 2017, 550; see also Chant and McIlwaine, 2016, 113, 116).[1] Throughout Somalia and Somaliland, most available health services are privatized and require payment. Working against extremely high child and maternal mortality rates[2] and acknowledging gendered inequalities in health care (Chant and McIlwaine, 2016), international organizations have supported the establishment of maternal and child health (MCH) centres across Somalia and Somaliland (Figure 4.6). In marginalized settlements, MCHs have become the primary access point for basic healthcare for the residents and often also wider communities. MCHs provide a range of free health services, with some working throughout the week, others (especially those at the cities' outskirts) opening only on one or two days. Some interviewees explained that due to funding issues, MCHs in some of the new settlements were only functional for an initial period when they assisted newly arriving people who had acute health needs.

Each of the four cities has at least one general hospital, but people in marginalized settlements could often not afford their services. Instead, they went to MCHs for medical advice on all types of sickness. Abdihakim, a vice chairman of a neighbourhood in a resettlement area in Bosaso where an MCH operates, explained that:

Abdihakim: There are two facilities for health services: one is the MCH, and the other is a private hospital. The MCH has many services including provision of good medications from Europe, to men and women. The MCH has no laboratory and surgical service, but other services are available. For women's delivery, apart from the displaced people, women are brought even from the town to give birth in this MCH. It is open day and night.

Interviewer: Why are women from the town brought here?

Abdihakim: Because the private hospitals will charge money, about $50, while the MCH will charge nothing for a woman to give birth. That is why. And it is open day and night.

Figure 4.6: Photograph of a maternal and child health centre (MCH) in Bosaso

Source: Photograph taken by Dheeraad.

> The aim of this MCH is to facilitate women's deliveries. The MCH also tests for malaria and gives vaccination against measles and dresses wounds. The service that cannot be provided by the MCH can be taken to the private hospital which charges for them. (Boasao, December 2017)

Other interviewees were more critical of the functionality of MCHs in Bosaso, complaining about their limited capacities for both diagnosis and treatment, even with respect to paediatric care. Abdilaahi, for example, explained that the MCH in the centre-city Boqol Buush camp mainly provides: "ORS [oral rehydration salt] for treatment of the diarrhoea and maybe some tablets. They do not have drugs and they cannot perform medical tests including for faecal samples and blood samples. They can just detect malaria and provide ORS" (Bosaso, June 2019). Notwithstanding differences between MCHs and general limitations, most interviewees attended MCHs when they or their family members got sick. Aala from the Boqol Buush settlement in Bosaso, for example, complained that MCHs often run short of medication but acknowledged that they are at least able to give "some basic treatment like tablets and syrup if you are sick" (June 2019). Alternatively, health workers can advise on medication, which then needs to be bought in one of the many pharmacies in the city. Kheyrta, who lives in an outskirt camp in Mogadishu, explains that children are usually taken to the MCH, as "you can get some medicine from a woman there. In the hot season, sometimes there is a diarrhoea outbreak and agencies give out things for that. People can find it there. There is also vaccination" (January 2018). Access to close-by services is important, as many residents in marginalized neighbourhoods neither have the financial means for public transport nor the time available to access hospitals in city centres. The problem of access is compounded in health emergencies as ambulance services are often unavailable and interviewees generally lacked the means to rent a car.

Some settlements in Mogadishu and Baidoa were served by mobile health teams. These are often funded and equipped by international aid organizations and implemented by local NGOs. Salman explained that a team arrives "after every two weeks. [...] Whoever is sick will then see the medical team and receive their respective treatments" (Baidoa, January 2018). Neither diagnosis nor advice or medication are consistently accessible or affordable for people living at the urban margins. Waiting – in this case for the mobile health team to arrive – goes hand in hand with the continuous need to improvise, weaving together relations and things while building up networks for survival. Many interviewees reported underlying health issues that severely impeded their ability to make a living. Waris, a middle-aged woman in the Daami neighbourhood in Hargeisa, was among the many people who outlined how the inability to afford proper treatment affected their daily lives:

Waris: One of the girls [a nurse] who helps the village people gave us medical support. And I take the medicine that girl gave us regularly, as long as it lasts. I've been to the doctor and was diagnosed. Gastritis is worse for me than the diabetes and [high] blood pressure. The gastritis caused me regular vomiting but it's *Alhamdulilah* […] [implying unpredictability]. But the treatment abroad would cost lots of money – who could pay? And is not available here.

Interviewer: And for the high blood pressure and diabetes, you take small pills like painkillers every day?

Waris: Yes, the pills are 1000 SolSh, and I take them at night. But the treatment for diabetes is 7 [US] dollars. And at night I am affected by gastritis […] and it is difficult to sleep. I haven't slept for three nights. There is no God but Allah. (Hargeisa, December 2017)

Poor health impedes people's ability to improvise – to daily mobilize the social, economic and material resources needed for survival (Chant and McIlwaine, 2016, 114). Many interviewees could no longer go out to work due to sickness, while others had to endure constant or recurring severe pain. Sick people often had to rely on the support and goodwill of family members or neighbours who tried to share their food and water or to support them in daily chores. For more complex cases where expensive hospital treatment is needed, residents within a settlement often collect money to pay for medical advice and, if sufficient, treatment. However, even if such networks of mutual support are established and function, they rarely seem to suffice, at least not in the long run. Amaal clearly pointed out the vicious cycle of precarious living conditions and health challenges: "The problem is, even if you go to the hospital many times, we are living in makeshift structures with no bed inside and we spend [nights] on the ground with lots of dust. How can such a person stay healthy and free from colds and fever?" (Baidoa, January 2018). Deprivation and associated health risks are significantly influenced by infrastructural assemblages, while intra-urban spatial differences shape patterns and experiences of health, morbidity and mortality. Inadequate and overcrowded housing, lack of water and sanitation, insufficient health care and malnutrition cause significantly higher disease and mortality rates in deprived urban neighbourhoods (Chant and McIlwaine, 2016, 116). The health infrastructure gaps are filled as effectively as possible within the neighbourhood through social solidarity that animates financial collections and the (often gendered) work of care.

For instance, younger or adolescent girls are often tasked to stay home to take care of the sick or elderly or their siblings. Poverty requires people to make tough choices as to which activity or service to prioritize. Olad in Baidoa explained that three of his children were sick, but that he and his wife neither had the time to take them to hospital, "because we are looking for our daily livelihood" nor did they have the "money to buy them the medicine" that they would likely need (January 2018). Guuleed, the chairman of a resettlement area in Bosaso explained that sick adults often are reluctant to go to hospitals, asking themselves if they really "should be treated if [this means that] the children do not get food that day" (December 2017). The social relations in which people are embedded provide for some protection, but they also trap people, constraining their abilities to move out of the situation of poverty. People at the margins – and especially female carers – are providing for and making use of the social mechanisms that enable their family's survival, but simultaneously reinforce their material poverty (Simone, 2018, 111). Another area where the choices people are forced to make become pronounced are with respect to education, a topic we draw attention to in the next section.

Investing (and improvising) for the future: schooling

The establishment of schools for urban in-migrants and others living at the urban margins can be undertaken by international organizations, at least if a settlement exists over a substantial period of time and the landowner allows for the construction of facilities. These schools are often not sustained, as the vice chairman of one of the resettlement neighbourhoods in Bosaso explained:

> 'There are two schools constructed for the IDPs near to the camp. The land of the schools was donated by [anonymized individual]. The school is managed by a teacher who is from the same clan [as the person who donated the land]. Both schools supported the students and provided education to the students. An [international] NGO [...] used to support the students with uniforms, fees, books and pens. The displaced people were relieved with this support and the young children learnt something. But [the INGO] stopped funding the students and the manager told us that nobody supports the school to sustain its service, and you need to contribute so that we can sustain the education provided to your children. So, when they were requested to contribute and pay the fee for the school, most children of the displaced people left the school as they were not able to pay the fee. So, those who were able to do the payment continued their education. The schools are there, but the displaced people cannot afford the fee and other cost of

providing education to their children. So, that support was crucial for them and we need that.' (Yasir, December 2017)

Guuleed, the chairman of the settlement, confirmed:

'We used to get support for education from [...], but now this support stopped, and [the INGO] relocated to southern regions of Somalia, so I'm told. Now education depends on the family and their ability to pay the school fee. Many IDP children who used to study left the schools and they do shoe polish to secure their family's needs. [...] Yes, very few [children] remained in the schools, maybe 20 per cent. They need to study, but they [parents] cannot cover the school fee.' (Bosaso, December 2017)

Later in the interview, Guuleed narrates similar problems in other resettlement areas in Bosaso where "[most] education support services have been stopped".

The narratives of Guuleed and the vice chairman were confirmed by many people living at the urban margins. International organizations provide the necessary physical infrastructure for education and regularly also train teachers. As long as teaching is free of charge, parents try to provide their children with school education, even if they struggle to pay for uniforms and learning equipment, and even if this means that they lose income from their children's labour. However, the moment international funding stops, and parents have to pay school fees to sustain the school and teachers, school dropouts increase.

Many settlements at the urban outskirts of Mogadishu and Baidoa have no formal educational infrastructure – or the type of permanent schools usually referred to as *iskuul*. Here, the only alternative is provided by madrasas, often locally known as *dugsi*, that operate across urban areas in both Somalia and Somaliland. These Quranic schools are run as private enterprises by individual teachers, who are themselves often residing in the same neighbourhood. Children are taught the Quran, and the social norms and practices of Islam, and people who can afford it try to provide their children with both religious and secular education. *Dugsi* are often conducted in open air spaces with equipment limited to wooden *looh* writing boards, traditionally used in Islamic teaching (Figure 4.7). Therefore, fees are often lower and teachers were regularly described to be less strict with payment, tolerating delays. Fees for both formal primary schools and *dugsi* differed across the settlements but were reported as between $2 and $20 per student per month. Only very few people who have settled for a longer time in Bosaso or Hargeisa were able to afford secondary education for (some of) their children.

Figure 4.7: Photograph of a Quranic school (*dugsi*) in Mogadishu

Source: Photograph taken by Muktar.

In general, interviewees identified educational benefits and referred to these when they outlined how hard they tried to provide their children with at least some basic education. Aala for example, explained that she pays $8 for each of her three children per month, "for the Quran school $3 and for the [formal/secular] school $5 monthly" (Bosaso, June 2019). Asked how she managed to afford this, she emphasized that, if necessary "the food will be reduced to cover the expenses of the study, because the education is more important for us." Others decide to send only some of their children to school, hoping that their education will later help support the whole family. Most parents, however, struggled to regularly pay school fees. When asked if he sends his children to the *dugsi* or a secular school, Borow in Baidoa responded: "No, where would I get that fee from? I have taken them to a *dugsi*, and I was told each student is 60,000 SoSh. I could not afford that and left. I have not thought about taking them to school [since]" (Baidoa, January 2018). Some people try to send their children to school at least for the period they can afford to pay, but then take them out again when money is short. Others pay for some of their children to attend the more expensive formal schools, and try to at least provide religious education to the others. Guuleed, for example, sends five of his ten children to secular schools and five to religious schools. In some places, *dugsis* have reacted to payment problems and offer different prices for daily, weekly or monthly teaching. Yasmin, who is also unable to send all of her children to a *dugsi*, complained that teachers in Bosaso "are demanding too much" and that they tend "to chase kids [away]" (December 2017). She therefore planned to send her children back to her mother who lives in Baidoa, where they can find cheaper education. This, she outlines, would have the additional advantage that she can work more and then "send [the] little money I get to them". Many people described how they try to negotiate late payments with teachers but do not always succeed.

This brief section on educational infrastructure emphasized that parental aspiration for children's education is high across the settlements. The gap in public educational infrastructures is partly compensated by the rise of commercially orientated schools, some of which provide for some flexibility in terms of payment and attendance. However, socio-economic precarity means that parents are often forced to make tough choices, deciding, for example, which of their children they can afford to send to school, to which type of school, and, at times, between paying school fees and foregoing other basic daily expenditure, even food.

Conclusion: Lived infrastructures – disruptions and the commodification of connections

Infrastructure mediates human experiences as it underpins social interactions and frequently determines how humans relate to each other and their environment. Infrastructures also demonstrate the intersection of human bodies with technologies, materials and nature. They shape and differentiate corporeal experiences of and corporeal conduct within cities. Building on Simone's (2004) 'people as infrastructure' we have emphasized that infrastructures are not merely technical or material but are generated by, enacted through, and embedded within social relations, and are shaped by daily practices. In short, infrastructures are lived.

This becomes particularly pronounced at the urban margins, where people are compensating for infrastructural gaps and improvising to make infrastructures work. Here, humans become a visible part of material conduits as they facilitate connections and adapt these to ever-changing circumstances, shortfalls and risks. Infrastructures at the margins of Somali cities are flexible and often only loosely conjoined techno-social-human-material-ecological assemblages. These enable multiple flows and circulations while they are producing an urban form that is fluid and uncertain.

Heterogeneous infrastructural assemblages are produced by, and are themselves productive of, socio-spatial relations and power differences. As Furlong (2014, 142) puts it, the stabilization of such socio-technical systems 'is produced with the social context; it is not dependent upon the existence of a particular social context a priori' (see also Barnes and Alatout, 2012). The multiple entanglements of biophysical, social, material and technological processes are particularly pronounced in practices dealing with bodily waste and the sanitation and water infrastructures that mediate them. Analysis of these intimate infrastructural ensembles highlights the centrality of the human body and shows how intimately bodily practices are 'tied to the experience of urban space and rights' (Truelove, 2011, 147). Water practices – particularly people's varying abilities to assemble facilities for storage and use – also shed light on the ways infrastructures are embedded in intersectional relations of power while (re)producing gendered and classed social bodies (Truelove, 2011, 147–8).

The field of science and technology studies focuses on the intertwinement of 'modern' (usually digitally networked) infrastructure with society, along with the technical systems that facilitate contemporary lifestyles and the ways they are linked to operations of power and capital. However, in this chapter, we have drawn attention to the complexities of (ostensibly) basic and mundane infrastructure on the urban margins of regions that are not often engaged with by this field (Furlong, 2014). Using an infrastructural lens to view experiences of (and in) the urban margins, we show how precarious lives are embedded in deep-seated contingency and uncertainty which requires continuous improvisations. Improvisation, therefore, constitutes a central feature of precarious urbanism and defines how precarious lives unfold (see also Simone, 2018). The mode of improvisation, however, is in Somalia and Somaliland increasingly determined by commodification, including the commodification of materials and service provisions, their management and administration, transport and distribution. Commercial actors are working at every level, layer and juncture of infrastructural flows. Both improvisation and commercialization at the urban margins develop their own temporality composed of rapidly shifting rhythms and speeds. The fast pace needed when searching for solutions – for access to water, education, health, a job opportunity, money and credit – is regularly superseded by the slow rhythm of waiting, often for prolonged periods of time. People wait at queues at water points; sit at the street corner to sell their labour power (as we explore in the following chapter); wait for promised money to arrive; for medicine to be available; for neighbours to contribute for urgently needed hospital treatment; for the sun to set to be finally able to fulfil bodily functions; or for new opportunities and a better life to come. As Burale, an urban newcomer to Baidoa puts it: "We have no education, water and hospitals here. We have nothing at all, which [would fulfil] the basic requirement of human life. And we have to show tolerance and wait for what God has written [for us]" (January 2018). Improvisation and waiting go hand in hand in contexts where the ability of people to make longer term plans is severely limited. Survival itself becomes uncertain, while infrastructural assemblages and the ways they can be accessed determine survivability. Interviewees described their daily struggles in ways that resonate with Agamben's (1998) discussions of refugee populations and of camps as modern 'zones of indistinction', where political and biological lives become indistinguishable. In the marginalized urban settlements, the everyday is indeed dominated by matters of life and death, and people are seemingly reduced to their 'naked' or 'bare life'. One can sense the realities of 'bare life' in many interviews and the physical and mental exhaustion and everyday experiences of violence that shape precarious urban lives in Somalia and Somaliland. However, within this context of extreme poverty interviewees also described sociality and, at times, solidarities as prerequisites for their daily survival. People establish relations and organize themselves in ways that attempt to counter their reduction to bare life. This 'counterpolitics of sheer life' (Collier and Lakoff, 2005, 29) has many facets, including reciprocal support and cooperation. Both the politics and counterpolitics of sheer life rely on improvision and on negotiations, themselves practices that are (increasingly) commodified and themselves contributing to further commodifications.

Drawing from Swyngedouw (2006) we can also show how techno-social-human-material-ecological infrastructure assemblages constitute a kind of metabolism of the city. However, we point to the ways this metabolism works at the urban edges. Infrastructures are lived, and they blur the boundaries between the human and material, life and matter, society and nature. To fulfil biophysical bodily needs, for example, requires access to nature even if this access is mediated through infrastructural ensembles – some more simply, others rather complex. The ongoing 'urbanization of nature' (Swyngedouw, 2006, 105) is most evident in water and sanitation infrastructures and technologies, which, albeit heterogenous and dispersed, provide the material foundation through which urban residents ensure their survival and answer to their bodily demands. To look at city experiences at the margins through the lens of sanitation, water, health and educational infrastructure reveals the materiality of social differentiation, but also once more brings to the fore the political economy that undergirds social suffering and precarious living.

The chapter has also showed again that in-migrants are not only building their new urban lives but that they are thereby also building cities. They are using their bodies, knowledge and labour to establish, connect and make work the multiple materials and flows that allow their survival, often in ways that reinforce their own marginalization. The agentic interaction of displaced in-migrants, landowners, humanitarian and commercial entrepreneurs are creating systems and norms of infrastructural provision and relations of access. As argued throughout the book – and as the infrastructural lens further underscores – displacement and urban in-migration have become a central feature of the social and spatial development of cities across the Horn of Africa (and beyond). They are neither temporary nor peripheral, nor do they constitute merely a problem to be 'humanitarianized' and solved.

This chapter has explored flows, experiences and practices of urbanization primarily through analytics of infrastructural improvisation *within* marginalized settlements that are predominantly populated by displaced city newcomers. Building on this, the following chapter examines patterns of physical mobility and virtual circuits that connect people in these margins to resources and interlocutors throughout the wider city. Virtual grids provide densely choreographed structures of connectivity and mobility that stand in stark contrast to the dispersed and malfunctioning infrastructural ensembles of sanitation, water, health and schooling analysed previously. These grids nonetheless reflect and reinforce the unequal relations of power that characterize life at the urban margins, a topic we return to in the context of labour relations and their links with (virtual and physical) mobility and connectivity.

5

Techno Relief? Connectivity, Inequality and Mobile Urban Livelihoods

The previous two chapters have illustrated how the establishment of settlements at the urban margins impacts how urbanization unfolds. We have emphasized the political economy that underpins these processes of camp urbanization and elaborated its spatio-material and infrastructural dimensions. As a counterpoint to the 'people as infrastructure' experiences analysed above, this chapter provides insights into the role of information and communication technologies (ICTs) that have penetrated city margins around the globe.[1] Widespread and relatively accessible mobile communications networks might be seen in contrast to the numerous gaps or shortcomings in the infrastructures explored in the previous chapter. Gandy's (2004: 372–3) early contention that the 'digital divide' is less pronounced than the 'persistent and widening disparities in access to basic services' is confirmed in Somali cities, at least in terms of (basic) mobile telephony and related innovations such as mobile money.

Somalia has long been integrated into the seemingly ever-expanding global consumer market for information and communication services and technologies. Here, we explore how mobile phones are used by poor in-migrant populations. We discuss the effects of continuous ICT expansion, focusing on the links between ubiquitous mobile telephony, human mobility, labour and money. Experiences of migration, work and money transfers are increasingly shaped by ICTs, as these facilitate information flows, including around labour needs and access to urban labour markets (Figure 5.1). They are also increasingly enabling financial transfers. While people rely on their bodies and labour power to establish settlements and infrastructural connections, they also increasingly depend on ICTs to navigate through and around infrastructural gaps, and to access services and resources. These technologies facilitate movement into and around the city, both in

Figure 5.1: Photograph of a woman doing laundry in a camp in Mogadishu

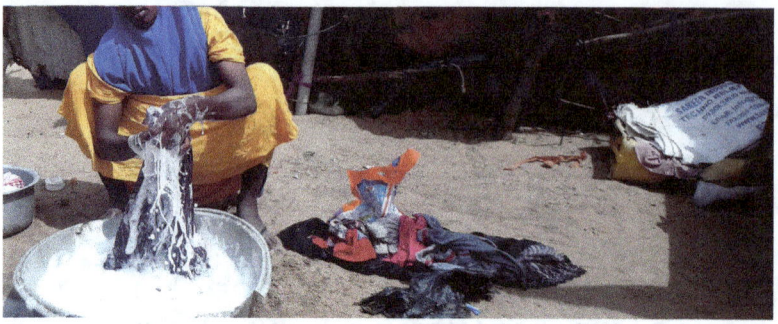

Source: Photograph taken by Hawa.

determining migration routes, and city selection and settlement. ICTs have a profound impact on people's working lives and shape the constant struggle for self-entrepreneurship and employment in urban labour markets – struggles that, as we show, continue to be structured by gender, ethnicity and race, and contribute to class dynamics, all of which intersect with 'local' versus 'outsider' differentiations.

Information about work opportunities, payments for labour or delivery of humanitarian aid are in Somalia and Somaliland often transferred through mobile technologies and networks. This development also shapes how people engage with and generate (urban) spaces, at the margins and beyond. ICT use facilitates social relations and interactions between displaced city newcomers and longer-term residents and provides new links to powerful institutional interlocutors, importantly here, humanitarian agencies and the (intertwined) telecommunications and banking sector.

The chapter examines these dynamics of livelihood-linked mobility and connectivity. It builds critically on a steadily evolving body of literature that assesses the impact of mobile technologies on the ways in which people earn a living. Since the early 2000s, a tech-optimist narrative has emerged among national and international policymakers that highlights the potential of mobile connectivity to mitigate effects of poverty, conflict and forced mobility. Here, marginalized populations – and particularly women living in patriarchal social settings – have been envisioned to leverage ICTs and tech-related 'innovation' in pursuit of entrepreneurial opportunities and socio-economic empowerment (Betts et al, 2015; Komunte, 2015; Suri and Jack, 2016; World Bank, 2016; Hendricks, 2019). Meanwhile, however, a more critical trend has developed in the broader literature questioning the egalitarian and emancipatory promises of technology for marginalized groups across different contexts. Although ICTs may enable access to long-distance resources and opportunities, this mobile connectivity does not necessarily transform existing social structures. ICTs are frequently used in ways that buttress structural and agentic constraints on gender equality, reinforce dominant power dynamics, and maintain patriarchal ties (Horst, 2006; Hahn and Kibora, 2008; Wallis, 2011, 2013; Wyche and Olson, 2018; Porter et al, 2020).

Noting the relative paucity of research on the role of ICTs for internal displacement in comparison to that on international migration, we add perspectives from Somali cities to this critical literature. Insight from these contexts brings to light aspects of socio-spatial inequality that have not so far been explored in the growing literature on mobile money – for instance, power dynamics in practices of remote payment between camp-dwelling domestic female workers and their casual employers. The chapter is divided into three main sections. The first section uses research participants' interviews and photographs to draw attention to the labour relations and forms of petty entrepreneurship that emerge within and from the marginalized settlements, emphasizing in particular their gendered character and the ways in which they constitute and sustain precarious lives. We analyse the social relations and hierarchies in which gendered labour practices are taking place and show how urban newcomers try to embed themselves into the wider political economy of the city. This section also shows that the settlements and camps constitute huge labour reservoirs and draws attention to intense competition for manual work opportunities. As with other aspects of urban in-migration discussed throughout the book, the labour power of the migrants is significantly contributing to the physical reconstruction and economic growth of cities.

The next section shifts to ICTs and draws attention to the mobile phone infrastructure that underpins and facilitates many of these labour practices. Before analysing the relationship between labour and ICTs, this section first contextualizes the significance of an ever-expanding Somali telecommunications sector. In other global contexts, market-driven investments tend to prioritize ICT infrastructure, which has much lower 'sunk costs' than, for example, roads or electricity grids, and therefore promises faster and larger returns (Gandy, 2004, 372). Communication networks also require less political regulation to become operational, which additionally explains their extremely rapid expansion in Somalia and Somaliland. By 2017, mobile phone penetration reached around 48 per cent of the Somali population (World Bank 2021, 10). Beyond investment benefits, however, we also show that the humanitarian shift to towards mobile cash transfers has additionally contributed to this expansion – and has increased the political and economic power of ICT/banking companies.

We subsequently explore the affordances and challenges of virtual connectivity and especially mobile phone use at the urban margins. We examine how ICT-enabled information and resource flows impact mobility and urban settlement patterns in Somalia and Somaliland. The main focus, however, is placed on the linkages between labour, livelihood strategies and mobile money, discussing the role of this technology in the working lives of urban in-migrants. The testimonies of interviewees emphasize challenges related to labour rights and digital literacy. We conclude by bringing the topics of labour and connectivity together by problematizing the focus on entrepreneurial innovation in imaginaries of development purported by international and national policymakers. This discourse often foregrounds dynamic digital 'inclusion' while eliding fundamental questions of labour relations and exploitation. We emphasize the ambiguous impacts of connectivity on the social and economic lives of people in marginalized urban settlements. Technologies facilitating connectivity, such as mobile phones or mobile money, do not work outside existing layers of gendered, raced and classed inequality, and, as a consequence, can accentuate and foster unequal social and spatial distributions of hardship and immiseration in the city.

Urban marginalization and gendered labour

Zamzam: My husband went to work, but nowadays he is sick and has a wound on his hand.

Interviewer: There are some clothes to be washed in the picture, who will wash them?

Zamzam: It is me, here in my house. I wash them using 20 litres of water. The clothes were so many because I have been going to work these days.

I: How do you feel when you are washing clothes as your job and then doing the house laundry as well?

Zamzam: I am happy because I am washing my clothes in my house, although I am also tired. But washing my clothes is a must. There are some places in the town where they have machines to wash the clothes. I like the machines, because they make work easier, and you just have to hang the clothes up to dry.

I: How do you feel when you wash clothes for others?

Zamzam: We don't like it, but the circumstances force us to do it. It is very exhausting, and I have so much pain in the back. But what can you do when your kids are hungry, and you don't have anything else? So, we don't have a choice. The reason we work is because our husbands don't bring enough money to the family. Sometimes they don't find a job and come back in the evening with nothing. When I work, some people also give me food to eat. Some add a packet of flour, some rice or different food. But only very few of the families we work for give us food. Some

> give us lunch, but some don't. They are eating their food and hide it from us. (Zamzam, Mogadishu, July 2018)

Zamzam's testimony alludes to a range of factors that determine the working lives of men and women at the urban margins of Somali cities. She succinctly captures the 'double burden' (Baxter et al, 1990) of women who combine domestic work with paid labour outside their household (Figure 5.1). Zamzam also emphasizes her exhaustion, the irregularity and day-to-day negotiation of employment opportunities, the treatment she receives, and the divisions and power-relations that characterize Mogadishu's stratified labour market. Like Zamzam, many female interviewees described their preferences for attending to their housework and taking care of their children but emphasized that they had to look for paid work to sustain their families. Time and time again, female interviewees talked about absent husbands, or physically or mentally incapacitated partners unable or unwilling to find regular work.

Most female interviewees actively sought work in domestic labour and were willing to take on any job that would allow them to provide for their families. Male and female interviewees often pointed to the difficulties men face in accessing the urban labour market. Combined with regular reports of male sickness, injury and/or costly addiction to khat (a leaf chewed for its narcotic effects),[2] this pushed many women into the role of being the main or even sole breadwinner, even if couples cohabit. Family conflict was also often generated by arguments over men's earnings, and this was often reported by interviewees to lead to domestic violence against women. Not unrelated to this, El-Bushra and Gardner (2016) have emphasized how, as a result of war, many men in the Somali context have experienced the sense of a loss of manhood because they have been no longer able to fulfil traditionally gendered roles of protection and provision for their families. Ugbaad in Hargeisa explained shifts in gendered labour roles:

> 'Mostly it is women who work. Some sell vegetables, some have small shops, some who offer clothes washing services like me, some who wash dishes […] everyone struggles to feed her family. We leave houses early in the morning and we come back late in the night, that is our routine. […] I am not blaming them [the men], they do their best, most of them are working at construction sites because they don't have other skills. And you know there are not many construction sites, so when they go out for work and come back empty-handed and children don't get something to eat, women cannot just watch and sit back. They are forced to go out and look for food for the children.' (Hargeisa, December 2017)

Interviewed men described how they tried, often on a daily basis, to offer their labour on building sites, where they carry stones and other materials, help to build walls and fences, dig latrines or rubbish pits. Men tend to receive a higher day rate for manual than women, who mainly undertook domestic work in clients' households. However, men had more difficulties in finding jobs on a regular basis. Those with particular skills, such as carpentry or plumbing, assembled at locations in the city where clients would hire their labour on a short-term basis (Figure 5.2). As Rooble put it, most men "just go out in the morning and see what [they] can get" (Bosaso, December 2017). Amin, a local NGO worker in Bosaso explained:

> 'For example, if you now go to Halwo Banadir [a place where men gather to sell their labour], you will see many, at least 80 IDPs looking for work and they are skilled people like construction workers, electricians, technician or painters. Everyone can recognize their profession through their clothing and tools they are holding. And four or five of these skilled workers are offered a job, and the rest gets nothing.' (Bosaso, January 2018)

Nuurow, one of these men, explained the competition for the small number of jobs:

> 'We normally come together in one place, and maybe I was called [in advance] but when somebody who wants a worker arrives, we scramble together and fight over it- "I'll work, I'll work!" – Sometimes I am given the opportunity.' (Bosaso, July 2018)

Competition for these jobs is high and increases in the context of ongoing and, at times, mass-scale in-migration. Kirish, who fled in 1995 from violence in Bardera (Gedo region), explained the difference between rural and urban job hunting: "[In Bardera] people used to beg for labourers to work for them, and now we are fighting over getting a labourer's job" (Hargeisa, December 2017). Skilled labourers like Nuurow or Kirish can make somewhere between five and ten US dollars for a day's work. These earnings are reduced by the need to hire tools and other equipment. Many men from Bosaso's margins tried to find day jobs at the city's seaport, waiting in large groups of porters for an opportunity to load or unload a ship or lorry. Those jobs are highly competitive, and the proposed expansion and modernization at the port had – at the time of our research – further reduced demands for casual labour.

People who had been settled in the city for longer may build up social connections and a pool of potential clients. Finding paid work was more difficult for newcomers, who often felt that jobs were distributed on basis of

Figure 5.2: Photograph of manual workers waiting for jobs in Bosaso

Source: Photograph taken by Nuurow.

Figure 5.3: Photographs of cow and milk container, Baidoa

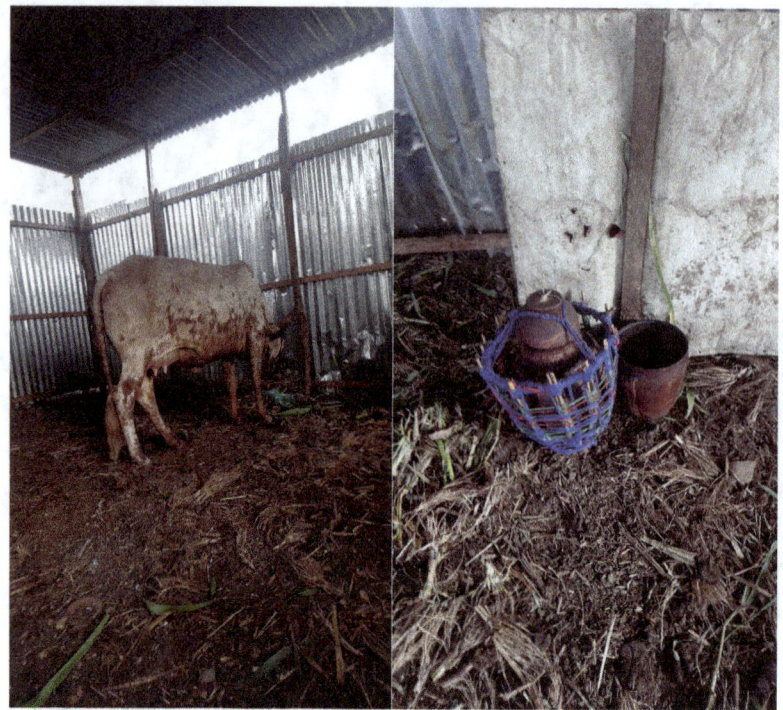

Source: Photograph taken by Abdirahman.

clan or other connections. Additionally, many employment opportunities are seasonal. During the rainy season in Mogadishu and Baidoa, or during the hottest season in Bosaso, men and women had problems finding employment. Construction, in particular, periodically slows down, as a male camp leader in Mogadishu explained: "There is no reliable full-time job for the IDPs. When it is raining, life is tough. You don't know where to go. Getting food is hard" (Mogadishu, May 2019). In the outskirts' camps of Baidoa, many men searched for work on farms near to the city in the sowing or harvest seasons. Some people managed to rescue and raise goats or cows, selling or using the animals and their products for their own subsistence. Baidoa's outskirt camps blurred the boundaries between city and countryside, urban and rural lifestyles. This was also reflected in the pictures taken by the photovoice participants, which were often of the farms or livestock at the edge of the city that helped sustaining them.

'You can see the cow, a friend of mine built the shelter for me (Figure 5.3). He is also responsible for the livestock keeping. We have the cow for our living, as the cow's milk is valuable. We get about two litres per day. I have two of them, and it is all for home consumption, unless you share a little with the neighbours for their children. I came with the cow from where I migrated, around 60–70km from Baidoa. We walked all the way. Others brought animals from Bakool [region] which is 90km away.

This is used to milk the cow, and the other is for storage, it's a milk container. Mainly women do the milking, but also whoever has a strong will to do it can do so, not just a specific individual. But for camels it is men alone who do the milking. Men also milk goats if no one else is there to do it. But mostly that's done by women.' (Abdirahman, Baidoa, July 2018)

Women across the four cities predominantly looked for employment in households, working for wealthier families, doing their laundry or other cleaning jobs (Figure 5.4). Nagan, a woman in her late 40s who arrived in Mogadishu ten months before the interview, explained her daily routine:

Nagan:	I go around, knock on doors, and ask if there is someone who needs their laundry to be washed. If the customers are pleased with my services, they take my phone number. If one of their neighbours needs someone to wash their laundry, they say we know someone who is good, and they call me. […] On my best days, I am paid four dollars for washing laundry. Rich households give me five dollars […] Normally, you agree on the price before you start working. However, I do not do that. I start washing the laundry right away. I take whatever amount my employer for that day offers me. Given my circumstances.
Interviewer:	What if you are not satisfied with the money you are given?
Nagan:	You just take it regardless. [Saying 'no' to the money] is not an option for me, getting in an argument with my employer is not one either. I take the money and I purchase food for my children with it. […] After you finish washing the laundry, some people claim that the clothes are not clean. You start all over again. If you do not, you are not paid. It is only because of my circumstances that I do it again. After I finish and I am paid my dues, I never go back to that household again. (Mogadishu, January 2018)

The distribution of power in these labour relations is clearly lopsided. Many female interviewees across the four cities identified their lack of negotiation power with employers. Shankaroon explained: "If the money is small, I have no option but to do the job because my kids need food on the table. However little the pay, I am forced to still do it for my kids" (Mogadishu, January 2018).

Figure 5.4: Photograph of laundry in Mogadishu

Source: Photograph taken by Asha.

Some women explained how they had been refused payment or received less than the agreed sum at the end of the workday. They then had no option but to accept their loss. A woman in Mogadishu explained how she was physically attacked by her female employer, and another that she was sexually assaulted by the male house owner. Accounts of (sexual) violence circulate among women and prompt them to work in groups where possible to reduce risk of physical harm. Some female interviewees emphasized that they do not enter a household if only men are present or insist that clothes are brought outside the house. Nonetheless, if women lack other employment options, they may take these risks in order to feed their children that evening. In the highly patriarchal context, women seemed more willing than men to do a wider range of odd jobs and to accept any payment. Male pride may be a factor here and is among the reasons why women often become – in practice – their families' main or sole breadwinners.

Aside from domestic labour, some women also found jobs in local markets, washing dishes in restaurants, or carrying the shopping baskets of wealthier women. Many attempted petty trade in vegetables, toothbrush sticks or firewood. Collection of the latter was another enterprise that entailed a risk of sexual violence and an associated need for women to work in groups when venturing outside of the urban settlements. Artisanal production was common too, and involved the making of ropes from recycled fibres, or sewed-up plastic sheets to be sold as waterproofing for huts in the rainy season. Others collected and broke up stones into gravel for construction sites. Maryan (Figure 5.5) highlights the latter as one of many forms of small-scale and often invisible forms of labour undertaken in (or from) peripheral settlements that contribute directly to the making of the wider city.

Figure 5.5: Photograph of woman making gravel in a Baidoa camp

Note: 'This is a woman who is breaking down big rocks to make gravel and she sells it to the people who construct buildings.'

Source: Photograph and description by Maryan (Baidoa).

Figure 5.6: Photograph of women and children searching a rubbish dump on the edge of Bosaso

Source: Photograph taken by Yasin.

Also reflecting the labour connections and material circulations between peripheral and core urban areas, many women (particularly in Bosaso) described how they went with their children to salvage scrap at rubbish pits located around and between settlements, looking for materials to use or sell, such as fabric, cardboard, metal or wood (Figure 5.6).

Some women with longer periods of residence in Bosaso had managed to build up more sustained businesses through self-organized microfinance or savings schemes, locally known as *ayuuto* or *hagbad*.[3] A treasurer of a group collects small but regular monetary contributions from members, and the pot is given to members in rotation. Referring to a photo she took, Famino describes how *hagbad* works and how it provided capital for a small-scale enterprise:

> 'This woman works selling firewood. She bought a cart for a couple of million shillings. She breaks the firewood into smaller bits, and she sells them to people for $1 a bundle. […] She got this [money] from a group saving scheme. They are usually 15, 10 or 20 people, […] they agree and trust each other. And so they gave the first collection of the money to this woman, and she bought the cart to carry the firewood with.' (Bosaso, December 2017)

Another enterprise highlighted by women in Bosaso involved the sale of second-hand clothes. Women acquire clothes on credit from wholesalers and then sell door to door in their neighbourhoods, often accepting payments in instalments from customers. This venture is known as *ha i wareerin* ('don't disturb me') referring to the frequent response from customers when the sellers try to collect payments they also need to pay back their own creditors.

Depending on available social networks, interviewees also described how they relied on a variety of small-scale loans and regularly obtained goods from shops on short-term credit. Extended chains of credit and debt are a common feature of Somali trade networks. They work without state and legal regulations in a context where trade is built on a mixture of trust and control exercised predominantly through clan affiliation. However, despite the often-praised success of these forms of trade, there is no guarantee of payment, and some interviewees' businesses failed because they could not recoup their money.

In general, women in Hargeisa and Bosaso have been able to establish longer-term businesses, albeit generally small-scale ventures. Women interviewed in the inner-city settlements or relocation areas tended to have been longer settled in these cities than those in the outskirt camps in Mogadishu and Baidoa. They had built up and extended social networks that improved their business capacities and options. Nonetheless, women across marginalized settlements in all cities had neither a permanent nor sufficient income.

For some people, begging provided the only or most viable option, either on a regular basis or only periodically when they found no other income opportunity. Begging was often the only option for people without support networks who could not or no longer manage physical labour due to disabilities, sickness or age. According to Fahmo, an elderly woman and resident of a camp in Mogadishu:

> 'I couldn't work because I was weak because of my age. I had no option but to go around people to beg and I used to be sick all the time. I have no energy or strength to work. [...] In this life, everything is money, and I don't have money or livestock. I am old and sick, at the same time I survive by begging people to help me, some give me 5 to 10 shillings. Those were the problems I was going through. I go to the shop to buy things. I ask people to help me with a place to sleep and they helped me. After ten days, I was told to leave because the owner of the place I was living in has arrived and I should either start paying rent or vacate. I don't have rent!' (Mogadishu, January 2018)

As illustrated here, many elderly and sick people without family members to take care of them rely on help from their neighbours. People often share their limited resources with those even poorer than themselves, or those who are unable to find work to feed their families at the end of the day. Children were also often required to work to contribute to the family income (Figure 5.7).

The previous chapter outlined how people mitigate infrastructural failure and malfunction using their bodies and labour power. This includes children

Figure 5.7: Photograph of shoeshine boys, Bosaso

Note: 'Those boys, they are carrying milk tins with polish. They are shoe shiners, and they work next to the port and earn for their whole family's needs. They are coming from the market and they are going home. [...] I know them, they live in the camp. Some of their fathers have died and, those two boys, their mothers are divorced. What they earn they bring it back home.'

Source: Photograph and description by Canab.

and, to a large extent, girls, who are required to take care of siblings at home while their parents leave the camp to look for work, water or to get credit from shops or neighbours. Children often contributed to domestic work, alongside their mothers who – beyond their day jobs – are responsible for the family household and to organize most of the needs of family members including food, shelter, water, energy (usually charcoal and firewood), health and education.

The jobs and entrepreneurial activities of urban in-migrants to Somali cities described previously resemble the precarious labour conditions of the seemingly ever-increasing pool of residents in marginalized urban neighbourhoods across the global South and, increasingly, also the global North. They build on 'relations of trust and care, economies of affect, networks of reciprocity encompassing both tangible and intangible resources, and material and emotional transfers that are supported by moral obligations' (Narotsky and Besnier, 2014, 6) to survive in contexts where labour power was either never (fully) absorbed or can no longer be absorbed by capitalist trades and industries. In contemporary societies worldwide, these relations, networks and (precarious) labour opportunities are increasingly structured by and facilitated through mobile ICTs. The intersection of infrastructures of connectivity and mobile, marginalized labour is where the chapter now turns.

Mobiles, mobility, and the (self)management of precarity

The snapshots above highlight strategies and improvisations of people at the cities' margins in their search for *nolol maalmeed* – their daily live(lihood)s. Many of these labour relations and practices rely on information and communication infrastructures and technologies, particularly mobile phones. Most interviewees owned a basic handset, and many described the use of these phones as an essential means of survival. Mobile connectivity allows people to mitigate certain aspects of socio-economic precarity. This includes access to crucial information about security threats, humanitarian support, entrepreneurial and labour market opportunities, the establishment and maintenance of important social relations, the use of mobile money for payment for work, and receipt of financial support from friends and families. This section traces links between the emergence of a dynamic, powerful and transnational Somali telecommunications sector, different forms and scales of livelihoods-related mobility (and displacement), and the everyday affordances of mobile phones for the gendered livelihood strategies of people at the margins of Somali cities.

Despite recurring periods of instability, a dynamic telecommunications sector has developed across the Somali territories since the 1990s. Often closely linked with the diaspora, Somali telecommunication companies have rolled out mobile infrastructures and broader ICT services across and beyond the politically fragmented territories (Feldman, 2007; Nurhussein, 2008; Collins, 2009). ICT providers learned to operate without formal regulations and protection, relying on kin and religious networks, and developing new products that quickly found local markets. Emblematic here has been the development of SMS-based mobile money systems that are now prevalent across the Horn of Africa. Telesom, Somaliland's leading provider, launched the Zaad mobile money service in 2009 (Iazzolino, 2015), a service that was soon emulated and built upon by other companies in Somalia. The systems enable users to deposit cash in mobile accounts, and then use input codes to check balances or make transfers to other users. Personal identification numbers (PINs) ensure data security, and SMS notifications inform users that money has been sent or received. Crucially, only network coverage is required for these services and not mobile internet access. Therefore, even basic handsets can be used for these financial transactions.

In a context where the vast majority of the population are formally 'unbanked', people also use mobile money accounts for savings (Hughes and Lonie, 2007). Unlike Kenya's renowned M-Pesa, Somali mobile money systems do not charge transaction fees. Generally, these systems have operated in US dollar denominations, which is well suited to the Somali context, where devalued local currencies could not be easily or securely transported, and where printed banknotes have nearly disappeared.

As part of the state apparatus, the central bank of Somalia collapsed in 1991. The Somali shilling (SoSh) has nonetheless continued to be used in southern Somalia and Puntland (Little, 2021), alongside the US dollar, which is needed for larger transactions and international businesses.[4] Since the 1990s, several politico-military leaders have printed new banknotes and contributed to steady inflation (Luther, 2012). In recent years the printing of such 'forged' banknotes came to a halt, but in turn, the availability of SoSh notes also declined (Figure 5.8). This contributed to the uptake of mobile money, which was additionally eased by the parallel price-drop and proliferation of phone handsets. Meanwhile, mobile money has been taken up extensively across economic sectors, for private as well as public monetary transactions. Usage cuts across class and gender lines and includes many of the poorest urban residents. People's daily shopping, wage payments, humanitarian or family support are conducted using mobile money. Even those begging on the street often have signs with telephone numbers for transfers as passers-by are unlikely to carry hard cash.

Although Somalia has some of the cheapest mobile data rates in the world,[5] smart- or featurephone internet access is unaffordable for most of the population, and very few interviewees spoke about use of online platforms. Nonetheless, almost all interviewees – men and women – owned a basic mobile phone, usually a Tecno or Nokia model, and used this for both

Figure 5.8: Photograph of children in a resettlement area in Bosaso playing with worthless paper currency

Source: Photograph taken by Nuurow.

communication and SMS money transfers. Only four interviewees across the cities, all elderly, did not own a phone, but used the devices of relatives or neighbours to receive money or make calls. Some interviewees reported that they had not had a phone for some time, due to breakage, theft or their need to sell it, but also described how they were trying to get a replacement device quickly and, in the meantime, used someone else's phone to call or transfer and receive money. Mobile phone sharing was common in families and among neighbours (as elsewhere in Africa) and lack of ownership does therefore not necessary equate to lack of use.

Telecom companies overlap with the vital foreign remittance business and an emerging formal banking sector. Emblematic of urban growth, their corporate HQs are dominant on the skylines of cities such as Mogadishu or Hargeisa. Hormuud is the leading telecom company in southern Somalia – with Golis and Telesom operating in Puntland and Somaliland respectively.[6] Hormuud has accumulated significant financial power and exerts its influence in the wider political economy of southern Somalia, including in relation to the country's aid sector. Globally, the spread of mobile phones has precipitated humanitarian industry moves towards cash transfers (Burton, 2020). Jaspars et al, (2019) highlight some of the wide-ranging implications of this shift in Somalia, drawing attention to the wider intertwinement of humanitarian assistance, business and armed groups. International aid agencies give out phones or SIM cards to their 'beneficiaries' and preload the cards with cash or electronic vouchers, the latter of which can only be used for essential items at registered retailers, sometimes in concert with biometric ID systems. Many of the people we interviewed in Mogadishu and Baidoa had at one time or another received such cash transfers from international organizations. The organization of these transfers requires close cooperation between aid agencies and telecom companies. Approximately 90 per cent of cash aid in Somalia flows through Hormuud, which charges aid organizations fees for new beneficiaries and for the SIM cards and phones they provide (Jaspars et al, 2019, 18). Hormuud is also a large investor in food imports and owns land used for export-orientated cash crops. According to Jaspars et al, (2019, 18, 25), both food imports and agricultural exports lead to declining food production and rising prices for agricultural land. In turn, this contributes to displacements of farmers, particularly from less powerful or marginalized (clan) groups.

Many of these dynamics unfold in rural hinterlands, including areas where Al Shabaab exerts control and wages war. This additionally pushes people off their land and towards cities. The telecommunications sector, therefore, plays a part in the wider political economy that connects humanitarian aid with agriculture, food imports and the urban land and property markets that shape the conflict-induced rural-urban migration documented across this book. The impact of increased mobile connectivity and the telecommunications industry can, therefore, not solely be understood through microanalyses of ICT use. It is, as Brinkman et al, (2017) emphasize in the case of South Sudan, also deeply entangled in the political economy of forced mobility and speculation around emerging telecommunication markets. This necessitates analytical shifts back and forth between micro and macro perspectives to show how daily ICT use connects marginalized populations to wider networks of power that influence economic development, urban reconstruction and related labour markets across the Somali territories.

At the micro level, mobile connectivity underpins many of the organizational features of the settlement of displaced populations, and the humanitarian entrepreneurship and rentierism that emerge with it. Mobile phones provide a vital techno-social tool for connecting city newcomers, camp leaders, landowners and humanitarian actors. Camps at Mogadishu and Baidoa's outskirts are, for example, marked with written and pictorial signs that include the mobile telephone numbers of camp leaders or camp committee members, allowing both people who want to settle and humanitarians to request access (Figure 5.9).

The mobile phone also heavily influences mobility patterns. Before city in-migrants even arrive at specific camps, phone connectivity may have already played a role in encouraging and facilitating their movement and choice of destination. Interviewees in the emergent urban settlements had often talked with relatives and neighbours who had previously moved and settled in a city. These contacts often directed incoming migrants to places where they were more likely to obtain support and resources, and gave advice on strategies of survival until the newcomers learned how to navigate the city. Mobile phones also allowed people to keep in contact with family members in the countryside or abroad. Ikran used an auditory simile to emphasize the importance of phones for gathering information, describing lack of access as akin to being "like a deaf person" (Bosaso, December 2017). Many interviewees spoke frequently with their relatives to receive personal information, updates on security or farming conditions, for example "whether they received rain or not" (Olad, Baidoa, January 2018). People regularly noted how the phone provided the means to access information from a distance and eliminated the need for physical mobility.

Nonetheless, these urban-rural communications may be disrupted by local conflict dynamics. Interviewees in Baidoa, for example, reported difficulties contacting family members in the hinterlands because of Al Shabaab's disruption of mobile networks. Robla, for example, outlined how Al Shabaab suspect that people "are communicating with their enemies" and therefore "end up destroying the antennae [telephone masts]" (Baidoa, January 2018). Al-Shabaab has regularly banned the use of smartphones and outlawed mobile internet (RSF, 2014). Interviewees, therefore, also talked about risks connected to mobile phone use in areas controlled by the group. Robla, for example, explained how callers in the rural area "talk in fear" of repercussions by Al Shabaab.

Phones are important for internal and international mobility patterns. While there is a burgeoning literature on the role of mobile connectivity

Figure 5.9: Photograph of camp sign at the outskirts of Mogadishu

Source: Photograph taken by Arab.

for international migrants en route to global North destinations (Schaub, 2012; Dekker and Engbersen, 2014; Frouws et al, 2016; Gillespie et al, 2016; Borkert et al, 2018) and the role of these technologies in the transnational lives of diasporic communities (Hiller and Franz, 2004; Vertovec, 2004; Diminescu, 2008; Lindley, 2009a; Komito, 2011; Madianou and Miller, 2012; Oiarzabal and Reips, 2012; Charmarkeh, 2013), there is little empirical research on how these digitally mediated connections are experienced by those who remain behind. Insight from interviewees highlighted the potential intertwinement of internal and international migration describing how phone contact presents both opportunities and risks for people in marginalized urban settlements who are connected to relatives overseas. Interviewees in Bosaso – which serves as an important onward departure point for international migration – emphasized dangers associated with the use of mobile communication by young people motivated to undertake dangerous journeys towards Europe, either using the route across the Gulf of Aden to the Arabian Peninsula or through the Sahara. Talking about her children's use of the WhatsApp messaging application, Murayo (Bosaso, December 2017) described her daughter's difficult migration to Europe. On her way, she was detained by traffickers in Libya, who then contacted Murayo. Over the phone, her daughter spoke about the violence she was enduring, and her captors submitted their demand for a several thousand dollar ransom to secure her release and onward travel across the Mediterranean. Murayo described how she pleaded her own limited financial means to negotiate the sum down to $2,600. She then raised this among family and acquaintances and transferred the money to a Mogadishu-based intermediary and onwards to members of the smuggler's network in Sudan. Ultimately, Murayo's daughter reached Europe, first Italy and later the Netherlands. Murayo outlined how her daughter now struggles to find employment and cannot send money to her mother on a regular basis. The bulk of the debt that Murayo incurred in raising the ransom was still owed to her lenders. Many similar stories circulate in the cities and the countryside of Puntland and the wider region. Several interviewees in Bosaso had tried to leave Somalia via the sea route, but often had to return as they could not manage the passage through Yemen, where they often were trapped by the civil war and Saudi-led intervention.

Murayo's account hints at the importance of the international remittance economy for financing daily household expenses. These remittances and other financial flows from the diaspora involve ICT-based connectivity. Mobile phones are used to alert recipients of receipt of funds and, increasingly, for receiving remittances directly through mobile money services. Remittance flows are not equally spread, and while city dwellers are more likely to receive international monetary flows than their rural counterparts, people living at the urban margins are not (Majid et al, 2018). Correspondingly, although people in cities in Puntland and Somaliland are said to have wider diasporic connections, only a few interviewees in Bosaso and Hargeisa mentioned receipt of remittances.[7]

The importance of phones for building up transnational social connections and networks of support has also been identified in the literature on (forced) migration in the Somali context (Horst, 2007; Lindley, 2009; Charmarkeh, 2013; Dahya and Dryden-Peterson, 2017). Interviewees, however, frequently emphasized the importance of mobile communications for contact and resource transfers between dispersed family networks within the Somali territories. Although the role of long-distance information sharing via ICTs in shaping mobility patterns is relevant to both global and more local migration dynamics, in comparison to work on international refugee movements and migration to the global North, there is much less research on mobile communications among people who were internally displaced (for an exception see Boas, 2020). There has also been limited attention paid to the way ICTs impact on labour relations and shape livelihood options and strategies for these populations, and we explore this topic in the following section.

Mobile connectivity, precarious labour and other livelihood strategies

Interviewees across the four Somali cities emphasized the importance of mobile connectivity, for the diversification of livelihood strategies. Research in African contexts has found that ICTs have 'facilitated new connections and decreased the physical and psychological distance between the city and the countryside' (Steel et al, 2017, 148), a finding that includes settings affected by recurrent instability and displacement. Dissolving spatial distinctions and blurring categories of nearness and remoteness, mobility and fixity, presence and absence (Urry, 2007: 180–1), the mobile phone enables the remote management of both family and business affairs, whether within cities or between rural and urban areas. In Somalia and Somaliland, the relatively recently established mobile money infrastructures were considered to be particularly important by interviewees. Mobile money transfers have evolved into a means of survival for the many people who live hand-to-mouth without savings and in conditions of acute precarity. Eney, for example, explained:

> 'I benefit [from the phone], for example, when I wanted something from someone, I used to go to him or her. But now, I just call them while I am at home. If I don't have something for my family to eat, [you call and say] "If you have worked today and you made some money, please bring me something. […]" Yeah, he will send me 5

dollars or 2 dollars. So, I benefit from not having to walk in the sun.' (Baidoa, January 2018)

Eney confirms how mobile phones allow people to communicate and to mobilize contacts and resources without needing to move physically. Shoobta (Mogadishu, January 2018) emphasized how her husband, even if late from work, would send the money to feed their children. Similarly, albeit over a greater distance, Megaag (Baidoa, January 2018) explained how, after his arrival in Baidoa, he had instructed his brothers in the countryside to sell his livestock and send this money to facilitate his settlement in a city camp.

Mobile money was seen to increase both economic and physical security. In Baidoa, for example, Idow highlighted how mobile money contributes to security while on the move:

'It helped me a lot. You know, when you are a traveller and you look after animals you just deposit money into the EVC [Electronic Voucher Card] service because you might encounter thieves on the way. Carrying cash is riskier [...] So, when your money is in the EVC service, no one can take it from you. Maybe someone can take your life, but can you take [money from] a SIM card? No one can.' (Baidoa, January 2018)

There is, however, a downside, as mobiles themselves have become a frequent target of robbers, and interviewees described their own experiences or fear of violent crime. Deynabo, a woman in Mogadishu, spoke about being robbed:

'There are some thieves around some of the places where I work. One day, as I was walking from work, they attacked me with a knife. They robbed me of my phone, and my money was inside it. [...] Immediately, I went to the [telephone] company and informed them that my mobile phone was stolen by thieves. And the money was returned. I was coming from work, it was late afternoon around 4pm. I was then without a phone for some months, but I later got another one.' (Mogadishu, January 2018)

Although some people described how robbers could use violence to obtain a victim's PIN to access their accounts, mobile money was perceived as being more secure than carrying cash. For Deynabo, her savings were protected and reaccessible as soon as the phone company provided her with a new SIM.

Lacking access to formal banking, mobile money effectively functions as a savings account. Yasmin in Bosaso explained: "If my husband brings ten dollars a day, we use five dollars for things like rent and keep the other five in Sahal [mobile money account]. [...] The phone helps us to save the little money we get" (December 2017). Mobile money is also increasingly used in the rotating group saving schemes described previously.

Phone connectivity was also described as central to people's navigation of cities in their search for work and receipt of payment for their labour. As women often go door-to-door in city neighbourhoods to offer laundry and cleaning services, they also give out their mobile numbers to allow clients to contact them when their labour is needed and to make payments. Once contacts are established, people can also request additional support from their regular employers in case of urgent need, as Dhahiro explained:

> 'When there is work, [customers] check on me when they don't see me around. They ask if I am sick, and they sometimes send me a dollar so that I can buy food for my kids. [...] I might say that my daughter is hungry. They would say, I will send a dollar to this poor person or two dollars so I can buy milk for my children. Thank God.' (Mogadishu, January 2018)

Aasia explained that there is "not much [paper] cash circulating" and that mobile phones are therefore a prerequisite to be paid for work (Mogadishu, January 2018).

As previously discussed, humanitarian organizations also increasingly depend upon mobile connectivity for delivering aid. Some interviewees described how they were biometrically registered by international organizations and given SIM cards; others also received phones, usually shortly after they had arrived in a settlement. Many interviewees had received some form of monetary support from international organizations, but often complained that the mobile cash transfer was irregular or had not been sustained beyond a few months. Digital cash transfers are often considered to be more discrete, giving recipients greater autonomy over their use of aid (Sossouvi, 2013). Such transfers often target women, acknowledging their crucial roles in organizing the survival of the (often extended) family while simultaneously aiming to strengthen female autonomy. Humanitarian cash transfers also aim at increasing transparency and diminishing diversion of the aid, as they are directly transferred to the intended beneficiaries and don't need a gatekeeper for access. However, information about cash transfers can hardly be organized discreetly in densely populated settings where people have established close networks for mutual support. Camp leaders were, therefore, still able to request their share in cash aid, which became an important part of the rent payments gatekeepers and landowners collected for the use of land and provision of security, as detailed in Chapter 3 (also Bakonyi, 2021).

Many of the affordances of mobile phones discussed earlier highlight their utility for people living in conditions of precarity. By and large, they

Figure 5.10: Photograph of woman holding baby and mobile phone in a Mogadishu camp

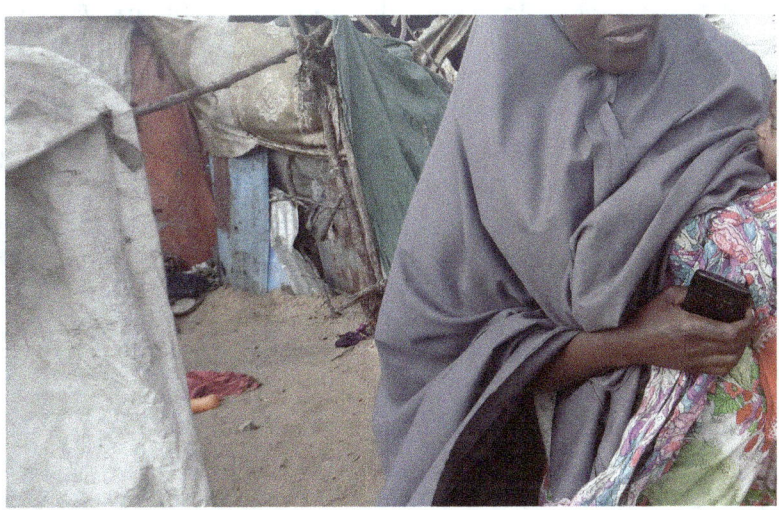

Source: Photograph taken by Hawa.

correspond with humanitarian discourses around ICT-enabled empowerment of the marginalized, especially women (Figure 5.10). However, although interviewees strongly appreciated mobile connectivity, their testimonies also illustrate how this connectivity is embedded in socio-economic hierarchies and can further foster inequalities.

Aasia (January 2018), who lives in an outskirts camp in Mogadishu, described three occasions when she was hired for housework and her employers failed to send the promised payment. Other women had similar experiences, describing how they were either paid less than the agreed amount or did not receive any payment at all. Aalima described her position in this situation – which revolved around the use of her mobile money account – and her small hope for recovering the money she believed she was owed:

> 'Sometimes they [the employers] say to us "Give your number and we will send the money to you." Then, after a while, they send you less money than what you have worked for. This happened to me one day. I went shopping and when I reached the market, I collected what I needed and then told the seller to withdraw his money from my phone. When he tried it, there was no money in my phone. Then I ran back to where I had worked. I told the sister [of my employer] "You sent me only a message – so give the money to me in cash." She said, "I already sent you the money. So, if I have not sent you the money, why did you leave here?" As we were quarrelling, some of the neighbours came and tried to calm the lady. But she insisted and forced

me out of her house. One of the ladies assisted me with one thousand shillings [$0.04] and advised me to leave. I left and went to the telecom company. But they told me that there was no money that was sent to the phone. Then I kept quiet and left.' (Mogadishu, January 2018)

Physical cash payments for day-work are immediate, open (visible) and, therefore, more directly controllable by employees. With (hard) cash payments, women like Aalima would be reluctant to leave their workplace without receiving their money. Dissolving spatial and, as a result, also temporal distinctions, the use of mobile money builds in options for abuse as it requires knowledge of technologies, literacy and (immediate) access to a network. The employer's ability to defer payment relies on the prevalence of mobile money. Aalima's employer is spatially detached and lives in a compound in a different city neighbourhood, from where they can make the remote payment. Aalima was unable to control the transfer as she does not know how to fully use her mobile account. Only after she asks the shopkeeper to withdraw money from her phone on her behalf does she realize that she has been cheated. From her subordinate position, she is unable to enforce the payment.

We received several similar stories in the interviews, and other examples demonstrating the lack of negotiation power of day labourers. Here, technological illiteracy provided new avenues for exploitation and abuse. Although most interviewees described themselves as able to use mobile money systems without assistance, many elderly people and some women of different age groups seemed to struggle with the technology. Nagan, who also washes clothes for a living, outlined that she is not fully equipped to operate the mobile money system on her phone:

'I do not know how to use it. I go to [shops] and tell them to get the money out for me. [...] I can tell how much I have left in my account. However, I do not know how to send money to others. I was taught how to check my account, but I could not understand how to send money well.' (Mogadishu, January 2018)

Shamsa confirmed: "I ask the people I trust to help me to send money to the people to whom I owe money" (Mogadishu, January 2018). Although this kind of mutual assistance is characteristic of lives in the informal settlements and wider society, individuals' inability to fully use mobile money services reduced their capacities to act independently and created spaces for abuse or control by others. None of the interviewees explicitly pointed out such risks, but their discussion of labour rights violations above are certainly exacerbated by inequalities in digital literacy. This is linked with traditional literacy, as users emphasized their inability to read text-based inputs and notifications (also Wasuge, 2019). Research from other countries has highlighted similar challenges, showing how text-based phone interfaces can hinder users' engagement with digital financial applications and services (Wyche and Steinfield, 2016).

Although Somalia and Somaliland are often described as having some of the cheapest mobile airtime rates in the world (Pénicaud and McGrath, 2013), phones and the use of ICT services do not come free of charge. The use of mobile services and the ability to be connected were by many respondents considered part of their essential living expenses. However, they also outlined how they struggled to afford the costs and only topped up airtime irregularly:

> 'I call my clients and ask if they have a job to be done. […] I spend a lot of money. The rate of calling is too high. When you call the families and the clients asking if you can come for them, you must top up each time. […] The amount I use is very high. Sometimes I miss a job and take debt from neighbours. Or we sleep hungry for some nights. But if I get a job, that night my children will have a good night.' (Dahabo, Mogadishu, January 2018)

Many interviewees were only able to top up the required minimum of ten cents of airtime to keep the line open and allowing them to 'flash' others: a missed call as a request to be called back. Charging phones requires electricity and as most households were not directly connected to a grid, people needed to pay at kiosks or shops in or near to their settlements to charge their phones.

Conclusion: Interrogating innovation

Focusing on mobile phone technologies that are ubiquitous across Somalia and Somaliland, this chapter has analysed the intertwinement of livelihood strategies and mobile connectivities. We have examined different forms and scales of mobility, and interconnections between the labour market, livelihood struggles and different forms of digital connectivity in the urban environment. The previous chapter outlined how people at the urban margins of Somali cities use their bodies and skills to compensate for infrastructural gaps. This chapter has investigated the multiple and often innovative ways in which they make a living, either selling their labour in day jobs as construction workers or porters, or attempting various forms of petty entrepreneurship ranging from waste scavenging to manual gravel production or small-scale trade. People in settlements at the urban margins provide a large pool of cheap labour, which is often exploited directly or indirectly (as in case of women's unpaid reproductive labour), in processes of urban reconstruction. The growth of Somali cities and their economies is embedded in the availability of this cheap and unprotected labour.

Governments and aid agencies have problematized the economic precarity faced by ever-growing numbers of urban poor in rapidly growing cities in Somalia. However, they also tend to frame informal settlements and camps as particular types of problems to be solved and have already started to suggest solutions, usually in the form of urban planning and resettlement initiatives. We discuss these specifically in the following chapter. However, beyond planning and developing longer-term solutions, many of the more immediate measures to mitigate human suffering are embedded in a modernist tech-optimism manifest, for example, in the 'ICT for development' (ICT4D) discourse and the beneficial and empowering role that technology is imagined playing for marginalized and impoverished households and people, often with a focus on women.

Many of our findings appear to correspond with the powerful tech-optimist discourse currently promoted globally by corporate, governmental, humanitarian and development actors, which highlights the potentials of mobile connectivity for 'frugal innovation' (Radjou and Prabhu, 2015) to solve 'challenges' of poverty, conflict and forced mobility (World Bank, 2016). In related research, marginalized populations are argued to be able to leverage ICT initiatives for entrepreneurial opportunities and socio-economic empowerment (Duale, 2011; Awotwi et al, 2011; Hounsell and Owuor, 2018; Hatayama, 2018; Hendricks, 2019; Ritchie, 2022). While undertaking initiatives such as the promotion of 'innovation hubs', policymakers tend to engage with a vibrant and youthful tech scene with many of its members connected to the diaspora and the wider Somali telecom and finance sector. Beyond fostering the development of 'home-grown' digital solutions to humanitarian issues – famine crisis-mapping would be a recent example (Dahir and Kazeem, 2017) – these initiatives are also seen as vehicles for employment generation and the promotion of small-scale entrepreneurship, including for marginalized populations (Fukui and Arderne, 2018). The development and rapid widespread uptake of mobile money systems is itself often taken as evidence for the potential of tech-orientated responses to the various humanitarian and developmental issues.

Nonetheless, this chapter has added to a growing literature that cautions against an over-optimistic or tech-solutionist orientation towards empowerment, and we have drawn attention to both the value and risks of different forms of connectivity. The time–space contractions enabled by mobile telephony, along with the more recent innovations in mobile cash transfers have become vital lifelines for many people living in acute poverty. People use their phones to exchange potentially lifesaving information about safe travel routes, places for settlement, jobs or aid. They also use it to cultivate social contacts and maintain social relations with relatives in the country or abroad as well as with (potential) employers. Equally important, they use the mobile phone to receive money, whether payment from labour, international aid, mutual self-help schemes or relatives, neighbours and friends. However, we have also shown how the use of mobile phones remains firmly embedded in already established social relations and thus rarely transcends social hierarchies and dynamics of power. Power operates through layered social relations and through intersections of gender, class, clan and race – as the following chapter will explore in greater depth.

Interviewees' testimonies have provided many examples of the ambiguous affordances of mobile communication and mobile money enabled through the steady extension and continuous modernization of ICT infrastructures and services. They also show that ICTs are engendering new options, shape new livelihood strategies, but also come with their own challenges and contradictions. On one hand, ICTs enable people at the urban margins to manage their acute socio-economic precarity. For instance, mobile money systems can be used to make microtransfers remotely, which can be particularly important where people without any savings live 'hand to mouth' and require daily access to cash to purchase essentials. However, we also outline how compulsions to use mobile platforms combined with obstacles in relation to digital literacy can create new vulnerabilities for people, such as abuses of labour rights, as well as scams, or extortion linked to migration. For certain groups – particularly elderly users and female domestic labourers – the compulsion to use increasingly ubiquitous technologies, especially mobile money, combined with only partial digital and traditional literacy created situations where connectivity contributed to increased vulnerabilities to labour abuses or financial risk. The dynamics of livelihood-linked mobility and connectivity we have examined in this chapter reflect gendered labour and power relations, and speak to wider patriarchal and economic constraints to the potential of technologically facilitated empowerment.

The control of mobile payments requires access to a network, knowledge of the phone and basic literacy. Inequalities in these prerequisites potentially invite misconduct, as relations between employers and employees are built on trust. There are no simple technological fixes to the social and economic relations that produce precarity and foster structures of inequality. In foregrounding individual agency and tech-capacitated entrepreneurial possibilities, aid programs may not only ignore – and thereby implicitly reinforce – structural inequalities, but also shift the burden of progress, of betterment and improvement, onto the shoulders of marginalized populations. These include women such as Zamzam, whose testimony opened this chapter and who is someone already multiply burdened by gendered labour relations and her marginalized status as a displaced person in the growing city.

The supposedly emancipatory potential of technology also fits into wider humanitarian and development imaginaries emphasizing adaptation and innovation for 'resilience' (Chandler and Reid, 2016). Such programming has been critiqued for its neoliberal-inspired promotion of innovative and entrepreneurial self-help, self-reliance, and self-care on the part of marginalized populations. The positioning of marginalized populations as potential entrepreneurs able to 'bootstrap' themselves out of poverty may be seen to shift responsibilities for their welfare onto their own shoulders (Skran and Easton-Calabria, 2020). 'Innovation' with new ICTs is an important component of a discourse described by some commentators as 'techno-colonial' in the way it reinforces divides between givers and receivers of aid (Madianou, 2019). For Duffield (2018, 142), the emphasis on tech-mediated, design-based responses to poverty is part of a broader 'post-humanitarian' shift away from advocacy for structural social transformations and towards acceptance of the continued inability of states to provide basic services to populations and wider global inequality (also Natile, 2020). This trend is visible in a wide range of ICT-related programming that relies on 'disaggregated biopolitical technologies', ubiquitous mobile telephony/finance, an increasingly global 'gig economy', and the digital facilitation of remote humanitarian management.

Humanitarian and development programming that emphasizes the role of digital inclusion and technological innovation often foregrounds the entrepreneurial capacity or potential of displaced or otherwise marginalized populations. By contrast, we show in this chapter that greater attention needs to be paid to the work that displaced people are already doing in cities, and the issues they face in terms of labour rights (or lack thereof). Further, we have drawn attention to various ways in which digital technologies may reinforce spatial, social and educational divides between an urban underclass, made up to a large extent by displaced populations living in marginalized settlements, and resident employers, a process of differentiation that we will further analyse in the following chapter.

Before moving on to this discussion, our focus previously on labour rights and digital connectivity additionally points to another concern, albeit one that this chapter has not directly addressed empirically. Here we refer to the 'datafication' of social relations (Mayer-Schönberger and Cukier, 2013) that is taking place in the cities we have examined and which – we argue – demands further research. Neither Somalia or Somaliland have formal state oversight or legislation that protects the data (Haji, 2019) generated and extracted from individuals at multiple levels, for instance through mobile phone/money use and the capture of biometric data in collaborations between humanitarian organizations, telecom companies and (often nascent) state actors (see Owino, 2020). Globally, the uncontrolled and unregulated generation of humanitarian (meta)data and the potentially acute risks this involves has only quite recently highlighted by certain humanitarian and advocacy actors (Privacy International/ICRC, 2018). These risks include surveillance from both foreign or national intelligence agencies or non-state armed organizations such as Al Shabaab. The risk of humanitarian data misuse for economic motivations and commercial interests is equally high. We currently know very little about how these data-related practices and dynamics are playing out in the Somali digital political economy, partly because micro-level accounts of marginalized communities' everyday use of ICTs have so far been lacking. As a step towards accounting for the growing role of data in socio-economic relations in contexts like the Somali Horn of Africa, this chapter has begun to shed some light on everyday practices of mobile telephony. It has outlined how these uses of technology are entangled with transnational networks of communications and finance, and has identified some of the risks of connectivity that are already borne by populations at the margins of rapidly growing cities.

6

Liminal Durability: Belonging in the City and Enduring Solutions

'I came to Bosaso. All Somalis are my relatives, and we named this camp Bariga Bosaso [East Bosaso]. Unlike the other camps which have clan or [origin] location-based names such as Ajuran or Shabelle, we have this name which does not show a specific clan or place. The residents of this camp are a collection of clans, even some families here are Oromo from Ethiopia.' (Guuleed, camp chairman, East Bosaso, December 2017)

Guuleed's testimony shows how displacement – along with discursive and material responses to this phenomenon – are shaping dominant understandings of belonging and citizenship across Somalia's fragmented political landscape (Figure 6.1). Building on previous analyses of improvised and iterative responses to precarity in the urban everyday, this chapter explores how people understand their place and future in the city. It is analytically inspired by the Foucauldian concept of problematization (Rabinow, 2009) and analyses 'durable solutions' initiatives to show how the challenges of displacement and urban in-migration are designated as interlinked ensembles of problems and become areas of interventions that promise remedies. This politics of problematization, we argue, has various impacts on people at the urban margins and shapes their sense and experiences of socio-political belonging.

Many urban in-migrants see their future in the cities they have moved to and are unlikely to return to the places they have fled from. The Federal Government of Somalia has, therefore, agreed with the United Nations to develop longer-term responses for displacement that move beyond humanitarian aid (Del Ministro, 2021, 26). At the time of our research, international organizations had been collaborating with municipal authorities in Bosaso and Hargeisa to move significant numbers of people from inner-city settlements into designated areas and newly established settlements on

Figure 6.1: Photograph of a woman from southern Somalia in a (re)settlement area in the northern city of Bosaso

Note: The woman's dress features the star of Somalia's flag, the five points of which symbolized aspirational unity between ethnic Somalis across the Horn of Africa in the post-independence era.
Source: Photograph taken by Sahra.

the urban periphery. These initiatives, which were also starting in Baidoa (IOM, 2021) are framed as 'durable solutions' within a global policy discourse on (forced) migration. The durable solutions vocabulary was developed by organizations dealing with refugees and from here migrated (as it were) into the reports and policy documents of institutions engaging with displacement and migration within countries.

Across the Horn of Africa, the durable solutions framework and programmes exert a significant influence on the management of urban space and contribute to the ordering of urban populations. We show that resettlement schemes designed through this framework can increase tenure security. These resettlement areas, therefore, have evolved into new centres of gravity for inward migration and provide new opportunities for speculation around city growth, future resettlement initiatives and associated land values. In these ways, resettlement schemes intertwine with the political economies that have evolved around displacement, as outlined in previous chapters. However, these initiatives also run the risk of contributing to the urban segregation of those who are summarily labelled as 'the displaced' in international as well as local parlance. As many of the resettlement areas are located at the outskirts of cities, they enable the territorialization of stigma associated with displacement.

This chapter begins by outlining the development of the durable solutions discourse on displacement and Somalia's emergence as a paradigmatic case of inter-agency collaboration and policy integration. Broadly confirming policy assumptions that large-scale returns of people to places of origin are unlikely, our analysis first focuses on how in-migrants experience, assess and understand their (new) urban lives and various forms of (potential) return mobility. We then look back at the patterns of urban growth introduced in Chapter 2 and 3, this time focusing on how local resettlement schemes in Bosaso and Hargeisa have created new clusters of peripheral settlements with varying connections to the main cities. These sections do not intend to evaluate the success of the durable solution framework or its implementation in Somali cities. Instead, we present and analyse resettled residents' different experiences of land tenure and material opportunities or constraints in what have emerged as new liminal urban spaces. We then examine categorizations and classifications that structure relations between people who have newly settled in the city and those who consider themselves indigenous residents. Here, tensions exist between co-produced narratives of pan-Somali solidarity and experiences of belonging and discrimination aligned with place, race, clan, caste and ethnicity. The discursive and spatial reordering of urban populations, in the context of the durable solutions framework, relies on and reproduces reductive labels of displacement, which, as we will discuss later, are folding themselves into locally prevalent discourses and practices of discrimination. Categories and classifications of displacement are inserted into – and co-generate – the social and moral order of society, where they are appropriated by a wide range of actors, including those who are so categorized. People tend to position themselves in relation to the ambiguous opportunities that associated policymaking can provide. The IDP label, for example, is already used as shorthand for people who are in different ways positioned as both poor and outsiders in relation to the cities (or even wider regions) they have settled in and which they may wish to call home. These tensions define, shape and differentiate peoples' right to the city (Lefebvre, 1996; Samara et al, 2013) and shape urban struggles for citizenship.

Problematizing displacement and institutionalizing durable solutions

International engagement with internal displacement has a relatively short history that reflects transformations in wider understandings of sovereignty in the post-Cold War era. It has only been over the last two decades that principles for legal and humanitarian engagement with internal displacement have emerged. The United Nations' Commission on Human Rights' 1998 Guiding Principles on Internal Displacement articulated for the first time that people who have been forced from their places of residence – but have not crossed an international border – deserve long-term solutions to problems caused by these circumstances. Similar to earlier discussions about refugees, options for 'return, resettlement and reintegration' (UNOCHA, 1998, 1) initially dominated. However, over the years, new tools and standards have been developed to expand and operationalize these guiding principles. A step to recognize and define procedures for the handling of internal displacement was provided by the African Union Convention for the Protection and Assistance of Internally Displaced Persons in Africa (2009). This has been ratified by 31 of the 55 signatory states, including Somalia in 2019. In 2010, the Inter-Agency Standing Committee (IASC) forum of UN and humanitarian partners produced the Framework on Durable Solutions for Internally Displaced Persons. This framework explains that a 'durable solution' is reached 'when internally displaced persons no longer have any specific assistance and protection needs that are linked to their displacement and can enjoy their human rights without discrimination on account of their displacement' (IASC, 2010, 3). Modifying and clarifying the Guiding Principles' options of return, resettlement and reintegration, the IASC framework explains that solutions may be achieved through reintegration of displaced people in their places of origin; local integration in places where they took refuge; or settlement and integration in another part of the country (IASC, 2010).

The importance of durable solutions for internally displaced people is further reflected in the so-called 'triple nexus' approach to programming that came out of the 2016 World Humanitarian Summit. This points to the integration of responses that appreciate the intertwinement of emergency humanitarian assistance with longer-term developmental interventions, and the imperative of peace for addressing protracted crises (Howe, 2019). In Somalia, and against a backdrop of protracted displacement and recurring challenges of humanitarian access, triple nexus approaches have been particularly influential. Displacement has here been identified as 'simultaneously, a humanitarian, development and a peacebuilding challenge' (Kälin, 2019, 6). International actors have coordinated their activities and programmes and attempted to overcome static distinctions between short-term humanitarian assistance and longer-term approaches aimed at economic growth and political stabilization (Nguya and Siddiqui, 2020).

In this respect, Somalia has been described as a 'successful example' of nexus actors' regular and consistent engagement with national or subnational authorities towards reframing national priorities and legislation aligned with the Guiding Principles and IASC Framework (Nguya and Siddiqui, 2020, 472). Accordingly, the formation and formalization of regional federal member states (FMS) in Somalia in 2016 enabled cross-regional coordination and planning. UN agencies and INGOs emphasize their successful cooperation with regional authorities in FMS such as Jubaland and South West to set up 'technical durable solutions working groups', along with a Durable Solutions Unit in Mogadishu. The Federal Government of Somalia established a Durable Solutions Secretariat in October 2019 and, supported by international actors, has published its 'National Durable Solutions Strategy 2020–2024' (FGS, 2021). The durable solutions discourse is based on an understanding that the majority of displaced people in Somali cities are unlikely to return to their places of origin. Durable solutions programming is additionally affected by ongoing conflict dynamics that continue to drive displacements, while urban reconstruction, as we outlined in preceding chapters, contributes to evictions and displacements within Somali cities.

Imagining a good future: current and future mobilities

Our findings largely confirm durable solutions policy assumptions that displacement to Somali cities is mostly long-term and that return is (currently) not an option for many people, even if they now live in acute poverty at the margins of cities. However, people's prospects are often not limited to binary choices of 'staying' or 'returning'. They try different options: some return to regions they fled from, though not necessarily to rural places of origin; some go back for periods of time to evaluate their livelihood opportunities; others split up families to diversify possibilities. Migratory patterns are often multidirectional, and mobility decisions are not necessarily permanent. Instead, they are based on continuous re-evaluations of current and future options, especially in the context of protracted insecurity involving counterinsurgency and state-building efforts, as well as recurrent environmental shocks.

Some interviewees indicated that wider insecurity prevented them from even planning a return to the southern Somali regions or to rural areas, while others were clear that even if security improved, they would not wish to return. Reasons varied. Some people explained that they had adapted to an urban lifestyle or that the city offered more economic opportunities and better access to services such as healthcare and education. Others referred to a lack of financial resources and jobs in their places of origin, or to a mixture of all of the above. Astur, who fled from drought in Buuhoodle district (on the Ethiopian border) three years prior to the interview and lives in Bosaso's outskirts, noted that:

> 'There is a big difference between that life [in the countryside] and the life here. Where we come from, life was very hard. We used to look after our livestock but all of them are dead because of drought and famine in the region. And there are no jobs in our rural areas. But in the town, you may get some little jobs like washing of clothes and cleaning of houses for our neighbours to get some money which we use to buy food for our children and support them. Though here we don't have a house like in our villages.' (Bosaso, December 2017)

Astur also explained that people in her place of origin regularly lacked access to water and had no provisions for health care. Her children did not have education opportunities but used to "just sit around". Similarly, Yasmin (Bosaso, December 2017) explained that "One can make money from work in Bosaso. Back home [a village in southern Somalia] there is no money, just farming. I don't like it there because of destruction […] and conflict." Nonetheless, she indicated her willingness to return to southern Somalia if she had enough money to restore her previous livelihood and if security improved, as she liked "both places, back home and here". However, memories of violence were reasons for several interviewees why they did not wish to return to the area they fled from, even if life there was considered easier or better.

Other people explained how mass displacement and long-term migration had dispersed villages and neighbourhoods and left people scattered across the country. War and flight destroyed social networks, and people, especially those who migrated a longer time ago, often just felt "more at home" in the cities in which they had managed to find refuge. This was emphasized by Abshir, who fled to Bosaso in 1994, but went back to Baidoa a decade later in an attempt to be closer to his relatives. He found his experience in Baidoa unsettling:

'When I got back to Baidoa, I was with my brother. He was a businessman. But I was forgotten by the locals since I had not been there [for a long time]. The young people who were in the city centre – boys of 20 or 25 years old – said to my brother, "We know you, but where did you bring this man from?" It was my town and I used to have a farm and other properties there and my people are there, but nobody knew me because I was [absent]. If I go to the town without my brother, then these young people do not know me and may start trouble. […] I was scared for my life. […] I told [my brother] I cannot live in the town by myself since I will not be recognized by the majority of the people, and they may suspect me and think I am a spy and kill me.' (Bosaso, December 2017)

Abshir's sense of security and belonging is embedded in the availability of social contacts, as he needs to be known and recognized to move safely through the town, which was at the time of his return contested by various warlords and clan militias.[1] His move to Bosaso disrupted his social connections and his fear highlights that without them he no longer felt able to navigate the city. Abshir had since built up new networks and acquired social status as chairman of a camp in Bosaso. He described how he is known there both by the people in his neighbourhood and by those he described as locals of the town. Other interviewees in Bosaso had returned to their areas of origin but found adaptation to a rural lifestyle challenging. Rooble, for example, returned to Bardera (in the southern Gedo region), partly to prevent his children from trying to embark on dangerous migration out of Somalia, a concern he shared with many parents interviewed in Bosaso. In Bardera, Rooble tried to restart farming, but soon returned to Bosaso because of "the things I missed […] the jobs I had here, and the people I knew here and the way they live, that I had gotten used to" (Bosaso, December 2017).

Comparisons made between previous and current livelihoods often shaped the decision to stay, but these varied significantly between people, and were based on multiple different considerations and individual circumstances. Shamsa, a middle-aged woman in Mogadishu, who had escaped violence and drought in El Buur in Somalia's central regions in 2014, compared the daily challenges of survival in rural and urban contexts:

'At the village we couldn't get a bit of sugar or rice because you had to go town and sell an animal and buy the food you want. But here in the camps if you don't have money you can go to the shops, ask for food on credit and get what you need then. So it is better here […] It was difficult for a poor person to live there. But a poor person can get by here in Xamar [Mogadishu]. At the village if you ask for a half or a quarter kilo of sugar or rice they wouldn't sell it to you – they even don't know what half a kilo is! They would only sell you a kilo, five kilo or twenty-five kilos. [...] Here you can get a little bit or get a bit of milk for the infant to drink. You don't have to sell livestock or rely on them. There, if someone's livestock dies then they die.' (Mogadishu, January 2018)

Shamsa's experiences confirm the finding of a recent World Bank study emphasizing the deep-rooted and multidimensional forms of poverty many people in rural Somalia experience (World Bank, 2019, XV–XVII). Related to (rural) poverty is the ownership of land or livestock, and the willingness of people to return was clearly dependent on their access to such assets. Nasir, for example, emphasized his plan to return to the countryside as "We don't have property, land or business here [in Baidoa]. What we have is a farm back there. We are here temporarily until the drought is over, we will [then] go back and start farming". Dahabo, who lives in an outskirts camp in Mogadishu, explained that return was an option

'especially [for] those who left land and farms. If you have a farm, you can cultivate and plant maize and beans, then you harvest and consume what you have farmed. But if you don't have a farm the only option is to work for other farmers and cultivate for them.' (Mogadishu, January 2018)

In the latter case, she explained, city life is the better choice. However, according to her, people who went back to their farms, often complained about the "lack of water. They are saying they would return to Mogadishu if they had the money to travel back."

Others felt that their lives were reduced to a state of waiting in the urban setting. Nafiso was an elderly woman who had fled from rural areas close to Hargeisa and now lives in the Stadium neighbourhood. She explained:

'Circumstances forced me [to settle here], but I don't have anything in this town. It's peaceful and we just stay here. But [...] there's nothing we can do and we don't have a clean place [...] Where I have lived [before] I had livestock to go with. But here, I don't have property. But there is peace. We trust in God for life.' (Hargeisa, December 2017)

Older people often had difficulty in adapting to urban life. Burale, a man in his late 60s fled from the rural surroundings to Baidoa and shared Nafiso's sentiments. While he was displaced by drought and insecurity, he also emphasized that his family expected that they would be able to access "education, clean water and better health facilities" and "to live a better life" (Baidoa, January 2018). However, he continued, "what we have seen is totally different from our expectation" and "if only the rural security would improve, I would like to resettle and become an independent person [again]. That is my plan in the future." Burale did not want to depend on aid and was likely too old to find day jobs to provide for his family. Others had lost property to armed groups or the drought and many explained that they simply lacked the resources to rebuild their rural lives. Improvement of security and climatic conditions were given as preconditions for return even by those who hoped to recover their land. Ebdow who revealed his plans "to go back to where I initially fled from because I have a farm there. I want to cultivate it, look after my livestock and become a wealthy man" (Baidoa, January 2018). Many interviewees, however, were already poor when they fled to the urban regions and did not own land. Instead, they worked as day labourers on farms belonging to others and often had only a very small numbers of animals that barely enabled them to survive.

While both men and women often imagined returning to previous lifestyles, options for return were gendered as ownership of land in many rural settings is limited to men. Shankaroon, a young woman from Jowhar district who was displaced by 2013 floods, also described how she would return to farming if given the option:

> 'My life before was much better than now. We used to have farms and grow cash crops and my ex-husband also used to help me cultivate. But here it is different. My children wait for what I get from doing laundry. Sometimes I get something, sometimes I don't. So, it isn't the same.' (Mogadishu, January 2018)

However, when Shankaroon explained why she was unable to return, the idealized picture of her past is compromised by her previous dependence on her husband's support. Men generally own land, and without her husband she has no safety net and lacks the means to provide for her children:

> 'I told my mother that I was divorced by my husband, and I would like to go back and join them back home. But she told me that if I want to go back, I should give the kids to their dad because she doesn't need that extra burden. I don't want to do that.'

Beyond the ability to secure a livelihood, concerns for children's future often influenced mobility intentions as interviewees evaluated potential opportunities in other places. Yasmin, a woman in her 30s who first moved from Baidoa to Mogadishu in the late 1990s and later to Bosaso, was struggling even to afford to pay for her eight children to attend a *dugsi* Quranic school and was considering sending them back to her mother in Baidoa, where they could find cheaper education. This, she said, would have the additional advantage that she could work more and then "send [the] little money I get to them". Splitting families and diversifying mobilities is a common strategy to deal with poverty. In Yasmin's case, her connections with Baidoa remained strong and she indicated that she would be willing to go back permanently if she could. However, she also emphasized how her family in Baidoa were also struggling and that she would stay in Bosaso.

Decisions to stay or return depend on many factors and vary across people forced to flee to cities. Return may be an option, but it may not be permanent, and people may rather decide to move forward and backward whether to better protect themselves and their families from violence and discrimination or to increase their chances to earn money and build a future. In a context where transnational livelihood strategies involve complex, circular migration patterns, 'revolving returns' or return of parts of families may allow people to hedge their bets, manage risks and access resources (Stepputat, 2004; Nyberg Sørensen, 2004; Hansen, 2007). Horst and Nur (2016) have argued that although mobility is among the main strategies of self-protection for displaced populations, approaches dealing with displacement often ignore the multiple understandings and needs of mobility of people they support. Similar concerns were raised with respect to refugees, where scholars have challenged clear differentiations between return, repatriation and integration, which they deem incompatible with mobile or migratory livelihood strategies (Long, 2012, 153). These critiques reveal the 'sedentary bias' (Bakewell, 2008b) in both migration studies and practical responses as they are based on global norms of fixed residence and conceive of displacement as temporary disruption to be resolved by either (re-)settlement or return. The validity of this critique is particularly evident in Somalia, where people often base livelihood strategies on mobility and regional or transnational connections.

So far, the bulk of mobility literature has focused on international forms of (circular) migration or the global connections of people living in and beyond Somalia. This literature also emphasizes the importance of transnational family or trade networks and remittances for local livelihoods (Ahmed, 2000; Majid et al, 2018), as well as information about various types of economic opportunity (Horst, 2007; Lindley, 2009b; Dahya and Dryden-Peterson, 2017). The dynamics of everyday livelihood-related mobility that do not (or only briefly) cross state borders have received less attention.[2] Here and throughout the book we have shown how mobility decisions can be both transnational and national. They are also often deeply intertwined, as the example of international migratory aspirations and embarkation from Bosaso demonstrates.

In this context, many interviewees clearly indicated their wish to stay in the city, to become "part of the residents in the town" (Abdihakim, Bosaso, December 2017), to "become a Mogadishu citizen [...] to get a decent work

Figure 6.2: Photograph of the resettlement area at Bosaso's outskirts

Source: Photograph taken by Nuurow.

and rent a house" (Hamid, Mogadishu, May 2019) and to "make a better future for my children and allow them study the universities and to build my own house" (Mohamoud, Bosaso, June 2019). Durable solutions initiatives for local resettlement are designed to support such wishes. Focusing on resettlement areas in Bosaso and Hargeisa, the following section engages with the ways in which people have described and experienced these schemes.

'This camp is the town': resettlement on Bosaso's urban periphery

Between 2005 and 2014, Bosaso's municipal authorities were supported by international actors to resettle around 1,700 people who were identified as displaced and predominantly hailed from clan groups not considered indigenous to the city. They were relocated from camp-like settlements in more central urban areas to land at the eastern outskirts of Bosaso (Figure 6.2). Much of this rocky and arid land was provided by landowners who were encouraged by the city government to donate plots.

Infrastructural developments promised to better connect the outskirts to the city and thus to increase the value of land and provide further incentive for voluntary donations (Internal Displacement Monitoring Centre, 2018, 4). The donated parcels of land were integrated into a grid and subdivided into small plots each with either a corrugated metal hut or brick house. A lottery system distributed plots and houses among people who had been living for a minimum of five years in identified IDP camps. Noor, a woman who had left Mogadishu in 2004 for Bosaso, was among the winners. She received a plot of land with a metal-sheet house:

'I was among the displaced people who was lucky to get a house here in the camp which was built by the local government for the IDPs. I got this one room, [an outdoor] toilet and kitchen. [...] It was a lottery and pieces of paper were put in a box and everybody picked up one piece of paper. [...] I was lucky and we were satisfied. God gave it to us. We were [previously] in tents that were vulnerable to thieves, and there was rape. I fled my house one night after an attempted rape. Because of this, I took my children elsewhere. I also fell then and injured my arm that night. There is a scar.' (Bosaso, December 2017)

The provision of houses was linked to an incremental tenure model, whereby recipients receive full property rights and ownership documentation only after they live there for fifteen consecutive years. Located east of a newly built bypass road, the area was designed to be as close to the main city as possible, with public transport giving those who could afford it access to their existing social and economic networks downtown. However, located beyond the bypass, the distinctive layout and physical separation of this cluster of new settlements reinforce the image of a separate or satellite town with its own shops and markets, a police station, health centres and a mosque. Khalid, who like Noor had received a plot in the lottery, described the area:

'Now you have visited us in the daytime, but if you visited us at night, you would say this camp is the town, the big town of Bosaso. Now you are in the centre of the displaced people's camps, and all sides are other camps. At night, the lights are on and the businesses are open till the morning.' (December 2017)

As Khalid's description indicates, planned and demarcated plots swiftly gave way to new buildings and installations that cut across the planning grid, which had aimed at disciplining the land and ordering its population. The resettlement area became a draw for new arrivals to the city, many of whom were relatives of those who received a plot.

Some of those who did not win initial lotteries bypassed municipality waiting lists and purchased or rented plots in the area. Some beneficiaries of the original resettlement scheme started to rent out their houses while others sold title documents to those who speculated on increases in the value of the land. Divorce and family break-up also impacted ownership. According to a staff member from a Somali NGO in Bosaso (August 2018), women who receive incremental tenure tend to hand over ownership documentation to their husbands. Upon divorce, the husband might sell the land and move, while ex-wives often stay in the settlement but are ineligible for alternative plots as they were already registered as beneficiaries.

Earlier settlement practices also continue as people without luck in lotteries continue to agree with landowners and put up their makeshift shelters close to the official resettlement area. Dynamic (re)use of urban spaces takes place as the permanent brick and semi-permanent metal shacks built under the auspices of the resettlement scheme become interspersed with makeshift tents of newcomers – as is starkly depicted by Nuurow's photograph on the cover of this book. The emergent morphology of the resettlement area attests to the active utilization of space in ways that circumvent its domestication into the rational order of urban planners (Bakonyi et al, 2019). The continuum of mobility and settlement, and the materiality of the shelters – makeshift huts, metal shacks and brick houses – provide a 'transitional optic' (Murphy and McDowell, 2018, 2500) to the resettlement area. Corrugated metal shacks, which constitute the bulk of housings in resettlement areas, occupy a position between the makeshift huts assembled from leftover materials (and which are made in the expectation of future movements) and the more solid and durable solution provided by brick houses. For international organizations, the corrugated metal shacks provide 'transitional shelters', which in aidspeak sit between humanitarian short-term response to immediate needs and longer-term integrated urban planning. Interviewees also described the shelter as transitional, but more because decay was already visible. Abdulahi illustrated this with a photograph of a rusted and punctured metal roof. He also made the common complaint that the metal shelters were uncomfortable in the intense heat Bosaso is renowned for:

> 'Those metal sheet houses you see now have been there for almost seven years. Before, we used to live in makeshift houses, but we have requested the agencies to build us metal sheet houses. But those houses have many disadvantages, on hot days you cannot live in them, on cool days you cannot sleep in them.' (Bosaso, July 2018)

Abdulahi's testimony illustrates potential trade-offs that those involved in such schemes navigate. On one hand, there are benefits in lobbying for and being included in a resettlement scheme that promises (partial, albeit highly desirable) tenure security. However, this may mean enduring the transitional accommodation solution that comes with the scheme; one which is also deficient (in comparison to other makeshift options) and unsuitable for local climatic conditions. Given interviewees' general appreciation of the value of having a greater degree of security in accommodation, it was clear that most saw this as outweighing the disadvantages of the new type of housing. Nonetheless, this underscores the marginality of 'beneficiaries' of durable solution schemes, the limits of their options, and the process by which a new type of transitional settlement emerges, distinct from the wider urban morphology.

The creation of Bosaso's eastern resettlement area also had an impact on the types of gatekeeping described in Chapter 3. Chairpersons and committees have been established in the settlements, often mediating between new settlers, municipal authorities, landowners (who continued to pursue evictions in nearby or adjacent areas) and aid agencies. In contrast to humanitarian entrepreneurs in Mogadishu and Baidoa, representatives of the resettlement zones were formally acknowledged and registered by the municipality, similar to representatives of ordinary residential neighbourhoods in Bosaso. However, one representative of a new neighbourhood complained:

'The chairman of an IDP camp and the sixteen chairmen of the Bosaso neighbourhoods do not get equal rights. The neighbourhood chairman has a salary, he can participate in elections, the education fee of his family is covered by the government, he is part of the government, he has a budget, he is a known person and he is a member of the host community, so what he suggests will come into action, but my suggestion will not work. These are my specific challenges and I have the same responsibilities, or even more responsibilities than him.' (December 2017)

Ordinary gatekeeping is less evident in Bosaso's new settlements, partly due to what many people described as continuous reductions in humanitarian aid. However, according to a local NGO worker, because many displaced people continue to settle on adjacent and privately owned plots, gatekeeping does continue, as does the establishment of 'rice huts' that benefit landowners and intermediaries (NGO worker, Bosaso, January 2018).

In Bosaso, a single large resettlement area composed of multiple neighbourhoods has been created relatively close and well-connected to (but distinct from) the city 'proper'. In Hargeisa, municipal schemes have involved smaller, more dispersed resettlement villages that are generally farther away from the centre city and have varying levels of public transport connection. We discuss certain implications of these choices for settlements in the next section.

Dilemmas of distance: resettlement schemes around Hargeisa

As in Bosaso, Hargeisa's municipal authorities have collaborated with international organizations to resettle displaced people from some central settlements to new locations on the periphery. Previous chapters have detailed how returnees to Somaliland in the late 1990s established inner city settlements that evolved over time into densely populated slums. Chapter 3 illustrated how a dynamic market has developed around land and housing, and outlined practices of propertying in neighbourhoods such as Statehouse, where earlier squatters on state-owned land have been able to sell or rent plots to new arrivals. The value of land in these neighbourhoods is positively related to the option of resettlement, as those able to lay claim to it may be eligible for this or related compensation if (or when) municipal authorities follow through on stated plans to clear and redevelop neighbourhoods like Statehouse (interview with Somaliland's National Displacement and Refugee Agency, July 2019).

Such speculations have been ongoing since around 2010, when city authorities in cooperation with international organizations started to establish resettlement areas around Hargeisa, including Jimcaale to the north-east, Ayah 1, 2, 3 and 4, to the south-west, and Digaale on the south-eastern outskirts near to Hargeisa's airport. Several thousand people have been relocated from squatter settlements and rented plots in the city. As in Bosaso, land was found by municipal authorities through negotiations with owners who had an interest in formalizing their ownership and potentially adding value to adjacent plots through the related development of infrastructure. As in the other cities, land prices within Hargeisa have risen with successive reconstruction, and city authorities and businesspeople are eager to get access to the land of squatter settlements within the city. As one former city official put it, such settlements are "not in accordance with [the] town plan" and relocation has become an important state goal (former city official, 2019).

We interviewed people in Digaale, a resettlement area located around three kilometres beyond the other outskirts neighbourhoods of the city. Recipients of houses expressed different views on the resettlement scheme. Some complained about corruption in the process of moving people from the more central Mohamed Moge settlement to Digaale. Tawfiiq, previously chairman of Mohamed Moge and involved in the organization of relocation, explained:

> 'They moved 830 families and they are not actually from Mohamed Moge camp. Before they moved the people, they built metal sheet houses and instead of moving these suffering people from Mohammed Moge, they moved some people from the town because they bribed the people migrating them and only very few from Mohamed Moge were moved. […] ABC [anonymized international NGO] was moving the people and gave the contract to youths who were very corrupt and inexperienced. (Hargeisa, July 2018)

Tawfiiq observed how people from outside the designated resettlement areas managed to get access to the durable solutions scheme and obtained land and homes. We heard similar accusations from other interviewees. Tawfiiq, however, explained that he did ultimately receive the "card" that allowed him to settle in Digaale, because he was part of the Mohamed Moge committee. He also outlined that he did not give up his shelter in Mohamed Moge, as "there is someone who lives in my place [in Digaale] and I don't take any rent from him." In this way, Tawfiiq tries to maintain his social connections to and position of authority in his neighbourhood. Other interviewees used similar strategies or initially shifted to the resettlement area but subsequently moved back, thereby becoming petty landlords in the resettlement areas and renting out property to others not included in the initial scheme.

The benefits of participating in resettlement schemes were highlighted by many interviewees and related to land tenure, improved security and access to services such as basic healthcare and primary schooling. However, Digaale is located outside Hargeisa, connected only by a rough road and irregular minibuses or shared taxis. Relocating to such settlements, therefore, reduces opportunities for day labour and complicates the mobilization of social networks and resources people have built up over their years in the city. Edna, for example, lived in the Mohamed Moge neighbourhood for two years until she was resettled to Digaale in 2013. She had left Hargeisa in the 1990s because of fighting and had subsequently lived in a small village in eastern Somaliland but returned around 2011 because of drought and the loss of livestock. Edna outlined her ambivalent feelings about where the scheme had placed her:

> 'First of all, now we have an asset, a house which is ours. Before we used to pay 15,000 shillings [rent]. If we failed to pay, we were moved out immediately. But now we are free. But when it comes to the livelihoods, [Mohamed] Moge was better, we were close to our relatives and families who used to support us when we went to them. But now we are stuck, we cannot move – you can either walk to the city and suffer or stay here.' (Hargeisa, May 2019)

Edna describes the effects of spatial distance as immobilization, as being stuck, and as a disconnection. She clearly acknowledges the benefit of ownership of land and a house, but nonetheless suffers disruptions, disempowerment and loss reminiscent of the involuntary immobilization described by Lubkemann (2008). Many people weigh the benefits of tenure security against the disadvantages of distance and the potential loss of other opportunities. Despite these challenges, the Digaale neighbourhood continued to grow. According to Idil, its vice chairwoman:

> 'People are increasing, they are not decreasing. There are even some people who were about to starve in the city. They came and they live with their relatives here. Some who were unable to pay rent fees also came here and live with their relatives, others came from the rural

areas. People prefer here, because it is not a city, it is semi-rural. Now around 350 families have come here and live with their relatives. They are scattered in Digaale neighbourhood.' (Hargeisa, May 2019)

People experiencing hardship either in the rural areas or the town may be left with few other options than to move to the physically and socially detached resettlement areas. Idil's description points to the liminal character of the resettlement area, produced by both distance and flows of people out of and into Hargeisa. Digaale residents treat the settlement as both an extension of the city that can be used either in situations of need or for additional income, but also as an access point on the way into the city. In this respect, people who are driven out from the city to the peripheries often just wait for their situation to improve until they can make their way back. City newcomers, on the other side, may first decide to settle in the peri-urban Digaale maintaining both practical and affective connections with more familiar rural contexts. While Digaale residents save on rent payments, newcomers can slowly adapt to an urban lifestyle and learn to navigate the city. In both cases, however, Digaale retains its rural-urban liminality, an 'inbetweenness' that can be actively sought or simply endured. In any case, Digaale constitutes a place characterized by waiting for situations to improve, for adapting to urban livelihoods, or to diversifying options through speculation on Digaale's future integration into the wider city as rapid urban sprawl continues.

Both the Hargeisa and Bosaso examples show that resettlement schemes cannot simply be understood as practices that relocate one group of people to new, potentially better residences. Instead, these schemes are significantly influencing wider patterns of urbanization as they contribute to land and property market dynamics, shape how migration to and from the city unfolds, and thus how cities are made and expand. The next sections attend to questions of social belonging in these contexts and explore how discourses and classifications of displacement and resettlement are intertwined with locally prevalent forms of discrimination. and continue to differentiate lived experiences of citizenship in Somali cities.

Pan-Somali citizenship: layers of belonging and discrimination

In the context of violence and protracted insecurity, clan affiliation can serve as a means for social and physical protection (Mohamed, 2007). Clan membership also impacts on forms and directions of mobility, as we outlined in Chapter 2, and shapes patterns of settlement and dynamics of urbanization, as outlined in Chapter 3. Many interviewees in the three cities in Somalia (not Somaliland) identified themselves as members of the Digil and Mirifle clans (collectively known as the Rahanweyn/Reewin) and predominantly resided in rural areas of south-western regions of Somalia before they moved to the respective cities. Many other interviewees identified themselves as members of social groups and clans that are in Somalia referred to as minorities, a mixture of people considered ethnically 'non-Somali' or members of occupational castes.[3] In Mogadishu and Bosaso, places of displacement are in the public discourse associated with both minority and Digil and Mirifle clans and thus with people who are not considered indigenous to the two cities. Many Digil and Mirifle speak Maay Somali, a language that differs from Maxaa Tiri, which was in the 1970s declared the official Somali language (Eno et al, 2016). Interviewees identified these language differences as crucial for difficulties in integrating into the social fabric of Mogadishu or Bosaso, and some described how language differences led to discrimination and, especially in the 1990s, could lead to violence. Borow, who now lives in an outskirts camp in Baidoa recalled when he was first displaced from Baidoa in 1997 because of the violence of invading militias.[4] He fled to Mogadishu, where he found that

Borow: they [Hawiye/Habar Gidir militias] were there. There was a man who was my close relative who had done nothing [but] they shot him in front of me. There was no genuine reason or crime he has committed, and when we asked, they said he splashed mud on a woman. [...] He was pushing a wheelbarrow and the road was muddy, and a splash of water landed on the lady, 'Why have you made me dirty, you Ealaay man?'[5] [...] She started beating him and her brother came and without asking what was going on he started shooting and they killed him. We were told our brother was killed and came to collect the body. But they told us to leave the body or else they will kill us too. We went to a Habar Gidir man we knew, so that he would talk to them to give us the body so that we bury him. That is how we buried his body.
Interviewer: Did you meet with them to ask for blood money for the killed man [compensation]?
Borow: What will you get from a person who refused you the deceased body of your brother? Nothing, they even didn't consider that we are Somalis, that we are Muslims.
I: How did that incident make you feel?
Borow: There is proverb which says if a lion is not in his region he runs like an antelope. (Baidoa, January 2018)

Such experiences shaped the decision of many to flee to the areas where their clans held more political power (Hoehne, 2016). Beyond direct physical violence, many other practices of discrimination were experienced by interviewees. Abdille explained how he fled from his village in the Bay region when it was attacked by clan militias in the mid 1990s. He spent time in Bosaso but felt unwelcome there and decided to return after he managed to gather enough money:

'I ran from [the village] and passed through Bosaso. [...] I didn't know the [Maxaa Tiri] Somali language [...] (laughing) I never went to school to learn it. I was working in a cafeteria [in Bosaso] and I just used to give people the tea only. I did not give the customers what they requested because I did not understand the language. For 15 days, people were laughing at me (laughing). There was a man who used to encourage me not to be upset with them as I will learn the language soon. I used to know only how to cook tea and they used a name for it, that I cannot tell you (laughing). Sometimes when I brought them the wrong tea, they poured it on me because they were prideful. But after 17 days I knew everything and they allowed me to work in the place, and I worked there for about four months [...] I worked for myself in the town and then came here.' (Baidoa, January 2018)

Mohammed, who tried to make a living in Mogadishu years ago, also left the city and returned to the Bay region because he could not manage to keep a job because of language difficulties. He described his experience looking for work in Mogadishu's Bakaara market:

'[I] met a man who most probably was from northern Somalia, [...] he was working at a construction site alone. Then he called me asking me if I am looking for work. I said yes I am looking for a job. Then he instructed me to pull a rope for measuring the house he was constructing. However, language was the main challenge as I couldn't understand him. As you know, their words are difficult to understand. Then he got annoyed with me, asking me where I came from. Later, he chased me away. I became frustrated because I was looking for a job for almost three months and when I got the opportunity I couldn't manage.' (Baidoa, January 2018)

Mohammed clearly felt ashamed for his inability to learn the 'official' Maxaa Tiri Somali and repeatedly emphasized that one is better off remaining in a region where people share the same language. In Baidoa, many interviewees emphasized that ethnolinguistic differences between 'local' and 'displaced' communities were much less pronounced than in other cities, as in-migrants had travelled shorter distances and came from areas inhabited by many of the same Af Maay-speaking groups that predominate in the regional capital city. Realities of intergroup relations are, of course, more complex, and previous chapters have shown how social stratification plays out in Baidoa in material inequalities between different settlements on the margins, and in their relation to the wider city. In future, attention should be paid here to how 'transitional' resettlement areas (built since our research was conducted) contribute to these dynamics, taking account of the social make-ups of local and in-migrant populations, in comparison with Bosaso or Hargeisa.

Beyond language, distinctions between rural and urban lifestyles were used by interviewees to emphasize difference between 'original' town residents and displaced newcomers. In Baidoa, Dhaqane, the chairman of an outskirts camp, explained:

> 'Still, they [camp dwellers] do not mix completely with the town. They still look like they are in the bush. And when you ask them, "Why do you not join and settle with the [town] residents here?" they may say that they have a different culture from the town people, so they can't mix with them. These are people [...] who only know how to collect firewood from the countryside and to wash clothes. They don't know how to read and write, so they can't open their own shop. I don't know what will be in their future. But the old people are only looking for how to get on with their daily life, nothing else. They are not looking beyond this and I think they are willing to go back to their villages. Hence, they are not willing to be part of the residents here in the town. They are here temporarily for a short period of time.' (Baidoa, January 2018)

Dhaqane himself fled five years prior to the interview from the countryside to Baidoa, where he later established the camp in which he was interviewed. He nonetheless emphasized distinctions between 'indigenous' city dwellers and incoming groups, referring to differences in the appearance, education status and the related inability to find skilled jobs. Dhuhulow, an elder born and raised in Mogadishu, used rural-urban difference to express his views on how people arriving in the city adjust to urban life:

> 'People from [...] Bay and Bakool all depended on their farms. There are two rainy seasons and their income depended on the [harvest] and if they had any livestock. Here, they can find regular jobs. In the morning, they go to the market. Some families still depend on farming. Some are beggars and bring money home that way. If the husband and his wife cannot work, they become beggars. Their children, whether they had one or two, worked on the farms back home. They tell you that they never had cash in their pockets in their entire lives. The only time they had cash was after harvest or when they sold livestock. They

go to work every day [here] and earn a fair amount of money. [...] If I want to build a house that has six rooms, it will cost me around $1,500 to 2,000. I sign a contract with a man. He brings his team. They did not used to get the money they earn now. They did not have the skills they know now. They do not want to return to their hometowns. Some of them became barbers and opened barbershops [...] The youth do not want to go back to the rural areas. They've grown accustomed to the city.' (Mogadishu, January 2018)

While emphasizing advantages and opportunities rural in-migrants gain when they 'learn' to live in the city, Dhuhulow contributes to the frequent juxtaposition of town and countryside, the former described as more civilized and modern, the latter as prone to tradition, backwardness and, potentially, violence.[6] However, Dhuhulow explicitly mentions the regions of Bay and Bakool, from where many displaced people in Mogadishu fled. These two regions, and the Digil and Mirifle clans that predominantly reside there, are sometimes disparaged in public discourse as being 'backward', a narrative that Dhuhulow reproduces when he refers to the lack of monetary transactions in both regions. His reference to barbers – a stigmatized occupation – further adds to his classifications of people he sometimes referred to as "refugees", sometimes as "displaced people". Later in the interview, Dhuhulow laments the negative impact of rural-urban mobility on domestic agricultural production and claims outsiders have affected the productive capacity of 'locals' through their importation of diseases that affect poultry. These and other discourses activate and foster social boundaries and essentialize differences between social groups, here between displaced people from historically marginalized clans and 'original' residents from dominant groups in the city.

It is worth noting that many interviewees emphasized that they did not face any form of discrimination, often alluding to shared Islamic faith and a pan-Somali ethnic identity. However, several interviews gave a sense of how inequalities were felt and experienced. In Mogadishu, for example, experiences of subordination were often acute in descriptions of security and how this is embedded in clan relations. In photovoice discussions, for example, participants took pictures primarily within their own neighbourhoods, and owing to security considerations feared taking photos in the wider city. For such a reason, Fahmo explains that she was able to get someone else to take a photo (Figure 6.3) on her behalf:

Fahmo: This is a place where camels are kept and their milk is sold to the people. [...] It is located behind the highway to the town. The man who brought us milk in the morning took these pictures [...] We cannot

Figure 6.3: Photograph of camels in Mogadishu

Source: Photograph taken by Anonymous.

	take the pictures because if the men who take care of the camels see us taking pictures, they would beat us. But the person who took this photo is allowed to do so, because his people are among the men who take care of the camels. They are of the same clan [...]
Interviewer:	What would they do if you took pictures of their camels?
Fahmo:	They would beat you. Or they would ask you questions, like who sent you and why are you taking the pictures of our camels? For me they would ask that. (Fahmo, Mogadishu, July 2018)

Fahmo's explanation of how this photo was taken speaks to her fears of being identified as a suspicious outsider, questioned and potentially subjected to violence. Suspicion and tension have often characterized aspects of life in Mogadishu, where political control remains contested, and where Al Shabaab continues to exert influence. While interviewees did not speak directly about this type of violence (or Al Shabaab's shadow government), wider feelings of insecurity can be particularly acute for people from clans that are politically subordinate in the city or face more general marginalization across society.

Other interviewees belonged to groups whose ethnic identity as 'Somali' is often challenged or contested. The Somali Bantu Jareer face prejudice and hate discourse 'derived from their African origin and alleged African-like physical characteristics in comparison with the features of other Somalis' (Eno and Kusow, 2014, 91). Given historical and contemporary political marginalization, people from this (broad) group did not have an option to 'return' to an area where their social/clan groups are dominant. The term Jareer (hard hair) is used in Somalia to denote a phenotypical distinction from other Somalis. It is also often used as political self-categorization, which is why Menkhaus (2010: 323) concludes that the term, in and of itself, is not considered to be intrinsically derogatory.[7] Some people we interviewed self-identified as Jareer, others as Reer Shabelle, a group of people who predominantly live alongside the Shabelle river.[8] Being asked about discrimination, Mohammed, a self-identified Jareer elder who lived in the Hiran region (central Somalia) before he fled from famine and violence to Mogadishu, replied:

'Yes, there is discrimination. Somalis will not give up discrimination and people may think that your clan is this or that, or second class, that's common [laughs]. We face things like that. People aren't all the same, right? [...] But the inhabitants in [our] neighbourhood are welcoming. They have no problem with us living in the neighbourhood.' (Mogadishu, May 2019)

Mohammed emphasized that racism is found in wider urban society, as opposed to the neighbourhood where he lives. In Bosaso, 35-year-old Cawo, who had fled to Bosaso to escape violence in Mogadishu two decades ago, recounted:

> 'I can remember a day [in Bosaso] I was with a lady, […] we were carrying sacks in the market and people were saying "Look at that Jareer! Look at their noses!" and they threw stones at us!' (Bosaso, July 2018)

While Cawo explained that the status of Jareer in Bosaso had improved over time, she later returned to discrimination when asked about education opportunities:

> 'The discrimination used to be there, even in schools. If the student in the school is either Madhibaan or Jareer, he will never appear on the list of those who have excelled in the exams. So, the parents get disappointed and tell their children to drop out and work for them to make money. But now that habit has changed, now thank God, because people were given training and awareness raising. Last year I went with my daughter to her school to attend the closing ceremony. All the mothers and parents were there. All those who excelled were from different tribes – excelled in science and Somali and all the subjects. But I did not see any Jareer person on that podium.' (Bosaso, July 2018)

As noted by Cawo, another group that has faced marginalization and discrimination across society are people known as 'Madhibaan', one of many occupational caste groups, defined by specific origin myths and historical engagement in socially disdained handiworks such as shoemaking, metalwork, hairdressing, and circumcision (Luling, 1984; Eno and Kusow, 2014; Mire, 2017). Cawo herself reproduced the hegemonic discourse and negative stereotypes associated with occupational out-castes:

> 'They [the Madhibaan] live in a separate camp called […] The majority live there. A few live in the other camps, but the majority of them are grouped together there. No one discriminates against them now. The people are all the same who live here. But they do disturb people and cause problems. When people hear of them, they don't want them to join their camp, because they like to fight and shout with you. So those people run away from them. But other tribes are just poor and peaceful.' (Bosaso, July 2018)

Cawo's example confirms that neither forms of racism nor other 'prejudicial and discriminatory discourses and practices' are restricted to the privileged strata of the society but constitute a 'set of ideologies and practices that penetrates class and color boundaries' (Sheriff, 2001, 119). People subordinated by race- and caste-thinking are therefore not prevented from participating in the same hegemonic discourses and often employ the same concepts and categories as their oppressors (Gilroy, 2001).

Cawo and Mohamed have been confronted with discrimination throughout their lives. However, they tended either to locate discriminatory practices outside their own neighbourhoods or in the past. Here, the critique of discrimination articulated from a relatively safe place removed from the risk of contestations in the here-and-now. Both emphasize the general improvement of their situation:

> 'Now people have been educated and intermarry with each other. There has been much awareness-raising […] The religious leaders at the mosque and elders, they told them that people are equal and have the same rights, that they are Muslims and follow the Prophet and are same in front of God. Now most of the people come out from the ignorance. There are only few who haven't [Laughs]. Look, now when they are in the car, men ask us where we are going, they ask us if they will find women to marry from our camp. So, there is integration.' (Cawo, Bosaso, July 2018)

Cawo relates improvements to the length of residence of minority groups in Bosaso, as well as to (religious) education and ongoing campaigns against discrimination. Similar improvements were identified by an NGO worker in Baidoa (January 2018), albeit he linked the reduction of discrimination to the widespread experience of displacement among both majority and minority groups:

> 'No, they [displaced people] are not discriminated against. Before minority communities like Eyle [a caste group], their camps were not visited [by international organizations] and were discriminated against.[9] But now the immigrants are from the main clans and were affected by the [same] problems that the minority people found. So they become part of the community and no one is discriminating against them, the awareness of the community has changed.'

Being further probed about the Eyle and other minority groups, the NGO worker, after emphasizing that international organizations now attend to their needs too, nonetheless admits: "People still have the tradition of discriminating against them and they have problems with intermarriage, you will not marry from them, but other interactions are good right now". The recognition of discriminatory and racist practices by Mohammed, Cawo and the NGO worker is couched in a discourse of gradual social and cultural change and increased social integration of marginalized groups (Figure 6.4). The same

Figure 6.4: Photograph of painting in a community centre of a Mogadishu camp

Note: Writing reads 'awareness raising of society'.
Source: Photograph taken by Mukhtar.

interviewees, however, also show how deeply entrenched racializing and stereotyping discourses are in society, and how difference can be emphasized and fostered even in efforts to overcome them. Cawo, Mohammed and Abdille regularly laughed when describing discriminatory practices, a form of laughter that showed discomfort and, at times, even shame (of not being able to speak a language, for example) when revealing their own experiences. The stated improvements can allude to the less violent forms of discrimination to which the NGO worker points; they can also be interpreted as a sign that discriminatory discourses and practices have over the years become more subtle and covert.[10] While officially condemned, the continuation of discriminatory practices is increasingly embedded in a culture of silence and secrecy that often surround racism and tends to increase the resignation of those who are discriminated against (Sheriff, 2001, 182; Bakonyi, 2018, 265-67).

The topic of intermarriage was regularly brought up when interviewees were asked about discriminatory practices. Traditionally, marginalized groups formed endogamous units, as they were considered unmarriable by people from the dominant Somali clan groups. Many interviewees identified an increase in intermarriages as an indication or even proof of the overall decrease of discriminatory practices. See, for example, this statement from an NGO staff member in Bosaso:

'I think it is getting better. Before they [Madhibaan people] were very much discriminated against. They used to do heavy work or low jobs like repairing shoes, blacksmith, hairdressing and cutting, also digging holes. But people saw those kind of important jobs as unfit for men, so they [the Madhibaan] did them and this caused their discrimination [...] Their girls were not married by other men from different clans, they didn't send their children to school, instead they taught them manual jobs like hairdressing. But now people are getting better, they are marrying their girls. It's normal now.' (Bosaso, July 2018)

Several interviewees mentioned such marriage options. However, and often after follow-up questions, interviewees from both marginalized and more powerful social groups usually admitted that intermarriages remain more of the exception than the norm (interviews with Idil and Muuse, Bosaso, December 2017). Intermarriages are taking place, but the few known examples are also emphasized, widely shared and discussed across the city and wider society. The attention given to these marriages reveals their exceptionality. Around the time of the research, in September 2018, a Jareer man was attacked, killed and set alight by a group of people from a dominant clan group in Mogadishu because his relative planned to marry a woman related to the attackers (BBC Somali, 2018). The violence made hidden or downplayed prejudices visible and thus prompted wide discussions about persistent patterns of discrimination, including in a debate in the federal parliament.

Discourses of sameness and otherness are shaping patterns of inclusion and exclusion which, alongside gender, race, wealth and class, distribute privileges and solidify hierarchies that shape peoples' behaviours and experiences. Othering narratives and practices and the ways particular social groups and places are stigmatized emphasize the complexity of intergroup relations and point to the layers of discrimination and marginalization within and beyond the different types of settlements associated with displacement to cities. These narratives and practices contradict the long-critiqued (Ahmed, 1995) but still influential discourse of sameness of culture, religion or language in Somalia, a narrative that continues to structure debates on (pan-Somali) nationalism and citizenship. Despite the historical emphasis on nomadism as the backbone and cultural inheritance of a Somali ethnicity (Ahad, 2015), notions of belonging and citizenship do not only rely on primordial assumptions of kinship (and ideologies of blood) but additionally, and perhaps increasingly, are embedded in a sedentarist ideology of authenticity and claims of locational origins. The final sections analyse views and practices of citizenship, and the ways in which urban segregation may be enabled by resettlement schemes undertaken through the durable solution framework.

Contested citizenship: territorializing displacement and political belonging

Discourses designating and othering social groups, discriminatory practices and the distribution of stigma are often related to clan/ethnic identity.

Urbanization and urban settlement patterns, however, add another dimension to these practices and attest to the multiple ways in which status designations are territorialized (Wacquant et al, 2014). In Mogadishu and Bosaso, displacement and urban settlement are associated with clans and social groups that do not hold political power in the city. The situation in Hargeisa and Baidoa is different, where the majority of interviewees who had experienced displacement were from locally influential clans. Although this does not necessarily prevent discrimination, interviewees in these cities emphasized general feelings of belonging. Nafiso in Hargeisa immediately answered questions about discrimination by saying, "We don't have any problem with them, they are our people" (December 2017), while Salman in Baidoa simply stated that "Baidoa is our town" (January 2018). Both interviewees felt that they belonged in the city, sentiments that are related to their membership of locally important and socially accepted clan groups.

However, beyond clan affiliation, additional markers of difference were regularly highlighted to mark boundaries of belonging between those considered displaced and those considered residents of the two cities. Quresha, a post-war returnee from a refugee camp in Ethiopia who settled in Statehouse in Hargeisa, explained the spatialization of prejudice: "There is no discrimination at all. But there was a time they [city residents] sometimes used to describe us as Oromo people because the Oromos used to rent and live here" (Hargeisa, December 2017). Being designated as Oromo often carries a derogatory meaning and intention. Over the years, many people from the (non-Somali) Oromo ethnic group fled from Ethiopia to Somaliland, where they have often faced discrimination. Described as economic migrants in public discourse, Oromo have been portrayed as beggars or people who take low-status jobs.[11] The stigmatization of non-Somali ethnic groups was visible in many residential neighbourhoods in Hargeisa including the inner-city squatter settlements analysed in previous chapters. Khadra, with clear distaste in her voice, emphasized that her neighbourhood was full of people who were not Somalilanders, such as the "Oromo from Ethiopia" whom she identified as being "very many" and "very unhygienic people" (December 2017). Sarah, a resident in Statehouse explained the connection between the place of settlement and stigmatization:

Sarah:	We can interact with them [Hargeisa residents] easily, even though there is some stigma about the neighbourhood, because people outside the neighbourhood believe that this is a dirty place with refugees. That is the general assumption. But when you interact with them, they learn and realize that we are normal and good people.
Interviewer:	When you go to town do you feel any discrimination?

Sarah: No, I don't feel that. [inaudible] There is no stamp on me showing that I am from Statehouse (laughs).

Similar sentiments were emphasized in Baidoa, where most people who were living in outskirts camps came from similar clan groups as city residents. Still, as Malaakay (January 2018) outlined, the "people here, sometimes, they call you refugee, though we don't like to be called that." While refugees and internally displaced persons were rarely differentiated in popular parlance across Somalia and Somaliland, the increased attention displacement receives from policymakers and international organizations has introduced classificatory nuances. The tendency for NGOs, policy or academia to label people living in Hargeisa's inner-city squatter settlements as 'displaced', ignores the fact that many of the people we interviewed had returned, like most Hargeisa residents, from displacements during the war. The summary classification as displaced and the territorialization of stigma attached to it was particularly emphasized in the resettlement areas at the far fringes of Hargeisa. As Edna, who was part of a resettlement scheme and received a metal shack in Digaale, explained:

Edna: They [people in Hargeisa] call us the displaced people.
Interviewer: You don't like that word?
Edna: We don't like that word. When we are in the city, they say to us, these are the displaced people, this is the bus station for the displaced people. And I think this is because of the lack of roads from here to the city. If the road was built, we wouldn't be displaced people, but we would have become the corner of an expanding city. Even if you visit your relatives, children will say: 'Are you from the place of the displaced people? Are you going to that place?' These are the frequently asked questions and for me personally this is shocking, it is something bad […] Even when I go to my relatives, the children of my family say, this is [Edna], she is from the place of the displaced people. (Hargeisa, May 2019)

The territorialization of stigma is linked by Edna to the distance of Digaale from the main town, but especially to a lack of infrastructure: "Our difference is only [the] buses. For them, they use a bus to reach town, where us, we use a different car at different stations and with different names. That is why we are receiving these harassments" (Hargeisa, May 2019). Instead of connecting Digaale with the wider city, the infrastructural disconnection preconfigures it as a place different and distinct from the city proper. In this way, durable solutions initiatives that define, categorize, count, document and map displacement, as well as identify problems and plan, design and implement solutions (durable or not) are co-producing legibility and spatialization effects (Scott, 1998; Trouillot, 2001). They also introduce a vocabulary and categorization of displacement that is adapted and integrated into the moral and social order of the city. The establishment of resettlement schemes almost exclusively for people identified as displaced, such as Digaale in Hargeisa or the outskirt areas of Bosaso, contributes to the territorialization of stigma and prejudice. These can become particularly pronounced if displaced people are also associated with clans different from those of 'indigenous' city dwellers, as in Bosaso or Mogadishu. Such schemes can foster forms of 'inclusive exclusion' (Agamben, 1998, 9; Minca, 2015, 82), where specific population groups are included in urban planning initiatives, but in ways that involve socio-spatial distancing and build distinctions between insiders and outsiders.

In Bosaso, effects of the intertwinement of in-migration, clan-based distinctions and insider/outsider discourses have been exacerbated by securitization. Al Shabaab is active in many of the southern regions from where most forced migrants to Puntland originate. Although a multi-clan organization, Al Shabaab has been described to have historically recruited large numbers of Digil and Mirifle fighters into its rank and file (Ingiriis, 2020, 370). In Puntland, people affiliated with these clans have in public discourse often been considered as being potentially prone towards involvement in the group's activities. When Al Shabaab increased its attacks in the region, the Puntland government and security services built on and reinforced these narratives, subjecting in-migrants from Digil and Mirifle clan groups to intensified scrutiny. Cawo provides her view on some of these security measures, again reflecting on her own identity in relation to broader group differences among the urban in-migrants:

> 'If an explosion happens in Bosaso, that evening and then next day all the Rahanweyn [Digil and Mirifle] men in the town sitting around or in the restaurants are arrested and go through security checks. But if Jareer community [people] are arrested they will soon be freed – I am Reer Shabelle [Jareer]. But the Eelaay or those from Baidoa [Digil and Mirifle], none of them will be released until their identities are verified. [...] It is discrimination: innocent people are arrested because of what Al-Shabaab has done. It may happen that the person who does the terrorism is not from their tribe, but that day all Eelaay community are arrested. They will fill all the jails, other tribes are released but they are retained. I always see that community arrested, even the tailors, shopkeepers, also the hawkers. [...] The majority of the small business enterprise are theirs, so the suspicion is caused because they took all the business, they sell all cosmetics, clothes [...] 90 per cent of the businesses are owned by them, only 10 per cent are [owned by] the

local community, so they are suspected in regard to where they brought all this money from.' (Bosaso, July 2018)

Cawo's discussion of counterterrorist policing shows how people constituted as regional or urban outsiders can be profiled and detained in mass operations. Although Cawo counters common narratives about aid dependency, she nonetheless contributes to stereotyping Digil and Mirifle communities as important drivers of the city's economy. For Cawo, it is the apparent economic success of some in-migrants that raises suspicion of security forces and governing agents. Others rather tend to point to historical membership patterns of Al Shabaab.[12] In any case, such group designations are a precondition for clan-based police profiling and discriminatory security measures which have, at times, culminated in 'deportations', especially of young men from these clan groups to the south (Idris Haji, 2012). These deportations were only stopped after widespread criticism within Somalia and from international organizations (UNHCR, 2010).[13]

Perhaps to counter the stigma emplaced in these settlements, residents of squatter areas, camps and resettlement schemes in Hargeisa and Bosaso often emphasized social heterogeneity. In the quote that prefaces this chapter, Guuleed describes the naming and composition of his neighbourhood. He highlights a diversity of clan and ethnicity that speaks to ideas of pan-Somali solidarity and a notion of citizenship that defies contemporary clan-based political practice in which people from 'minority' groups have little power. However, it also illustrates how group identities are reproduced within settlement practices, distinguishing diverse groups of often marginalized people from the 'locals' of the wider city. Similarly, Yasmin (Bosaso, December 2017) and Waris (Hargeisa, July 2018) use the term 'federation' indicating that people from different clans are living in their neighbourhoods. However, Waris also laughingly admits that while "Daami [her neighbourhood] is a 'federation' [...] it is [name of an Isaaq subclan] who run things." In Bosaso, Guuleed spoke about how clan-based relations of power shape politics:

'Our camp is among the oldest and largest camp in this area of east Bosaso. The biggest office and the biggest mosque are located here. [...] We are working on how these poor people can get all basic needs like education, hospitals and clean water. [...] The residents of Bosaso welcomed us as brothers but there are three things that they have but we don't have as refugees. One: we are not the same in terms of employment. Always priority is given to the residents, and they get to be employed in high positions. So, for a boy [from here] who graduates secondary school, he will not be given a job, it will be given to someone local. And secondly, when the refugees are walking and meet with the soldiers, the refugees are arrested while others are being left free to move. That is discrimination. The third thing is that we do not have our own land. We are on private land and if the town reaches us then we will have only a couple of months to clear out. (Bosaso, December 2017)

In Guuleed's account, economic disadvantage, the securitization of displaced people and issues of tenure in the context of urban growth are intertwined as articulations of difference, albeit alongside the commonly expressed sentiment that in-migrants have been 'welcomed' in Bosaso. Acceptance and assistance were frequently expressed through ideas of shared Somali ethno-cultural and religious identity – *Soomaalinimo* – even if other experiences and lived realities highlighted inequalities and group differences that stratify the right to the city.

Conclusion: Making difference legible

While previous chapters have examined the different types of mobility and fixity that structure urbanization and the materiality and political economy that underpins them, this chapter has engaged with temporalities and effects of displacement conditioned by 'durable solutions' initiatives. This policy framework attempts to support long-term responses to displacement by providing spaces for resettlement and with them, if possible, tenure security to avoid further cycles of the type of evictions outlined in Chapter 3.

National and international actors are engaging here in what Foucault described as the politics of problematization, as they are generating an ensemble of discursive and material practices that identify a thing or a situation through difficulties, which are transformed into problems for which potential responses and solutions can be developed. These solutions then become part of the 'problematization as it unfolds' (Rabinow, 2009, 18, 19). In Somalia, practices of problematization have entailed the discursive identification of an ensemble of problems related to internal displacement and placed them in relation to unregulated and rapid forms of urban growth (another ensemble of problems) and the resultant demand for (urban) resources (FGS, 2021, 18). This interrelated ensemble of problems is then translated into a further set of humanitarian and development needs that also entail categorizations that define people in need. Such problematizations are, as Rabinow (2009, 19, 20) outlines, 'saturated in relations of power', as they constitute 'institutionally legitimated claims to truth'. Among these are designations of who qualifies as belonging to 'displacement affected communities', such as 'refugees, asylum seekers, refugee returnees and vulnerable host communities' (FGS, 2021, 18), and the identification of places in need of urgent and long-term intervention. We have shown how such problematizations, their discursive identification of displaced people, and proposed, planned and practiced solutions all intertwine with local social dynamics and produce legibility and spatialization effects. In Somalia, this is visible in the many attempts to translate the different categorizations of displacement and displaced people into local vocabularies. Here multiple forms of stigmatization are entangled with the delineation of displacement, which becomes particularly visible in the territorialization of stigma in distant and thus spatially segregated resettlement areas. These become, in the public imaginary, the places where 'the displaced' or 'the refugees' live.

Some of these areas evolve into liminal spaces that reflect and influence wider dynamics of mobility, urbanization and contestations of citizenship. In carceral contexts, liminality has been characterized by the blurring of boundaries (Moran, 2013) and a capacity to confine and control particular populations through site marginality and neglect (Richardson, 2017). Our approach to liminality differs slightly in emphasizing the co-production of liminal spaces by a wide range of actors who often aspire (and at times also achieve) betterment in their circumstances while nonetheless continuing to reproduce inequality and marginalization. The liminality of resettlement areas – their state of being perceived as 'betwixt and between' (Turner, 1970, 234) – can be understood in several ways. Being located on the edge of cities, resettlement areas can enable new arrivals to maintain connections that straddle urban and rural livelihoods and mobilities. From the perspective of international organizations, resettlement areas are often thought to sit between humanitarian short-term response to acute problems (including evictions) and longer-term aspirations for integrated urban planning. Their liminal character is also materially evident in the provision of what international organizations call 'transitional shelters'. The liminality of durable solutions is also clear in the experiences of populations who are defined with a range of markers as urban outsiders and are both selectively integrated into and segregated from the wider social fabric of the city.

This form of 'inclusive exclusion' (Agamben, 1998, 9) confirms Meier and Frank's (2016, 363) assertion that 'dwelling is [...] an issue of power and contestations – as it is realized in processes such as segregation, gentrification and displacement and in socio-spatial forms such as gated communities or shanty towns'. Power is here exerted in the interplay between discursive categorization and the materialization of socio-spatial forms, such as resettlement areas. Discussing refugeehood as immobilization and drawing also from Agamben's (1998) discussion of zones of indistinction, Diken (2004, 84) emphasized how refugees develop an ambiguous position and co-produce processes of ordering that places them in camps. Similar dynamics exist in resettlement areas where residents co-produce the socio-political ordering across a politically highly fragmented territory in which sovereign power is practiced by a wide array of actors ranging from municipal, regional or national authorities to an equally broad array of (international) organizations (see also Purdeková, 2017). Their co-production of the displacement discourse obfuscates socio-political contestation over the right to the city and the definition of citizenship.

We have also shown that neither camps nor resettlement spaces are static but are continuously acted upon and contested. They evolve through the agency of their residents who seek flexibility, mobility and diversification of options to improve their lives. Liminal urban spaces are conducive to this co-production. They can be transformative in enabling the coming into being of new hybrid forms through the expression of contradictory elements (see Soja, 1996; Bhabha, 2012), emergent economic activities (see Mbatha and Mchunu, 2016) and identities (Hanlon et al, 2019). Cities change, and ghettos or enclaves associated with migrant populations can eventually become central to their wider identities and economies (Hasdell, 2016, 4).

People living at the margins, tend to co-produce the displacement discourse, either to position themselves in relation to opportunities or to assert identity in relation to the wider city. This emerges in the 'federation' idea described by Yasmin and Waris, emphasizing solidarity among a diverse constituency of urban outsiders and emergent identities that emphasize the heterogeneity of marginalized groups residing within one neighbourhood, but which distinguishes the area from the wider 'local' society. Many interviewees' aspirations to become urban citizens attest to the lack of their political integration and their subordinate political position. The clan-based elements of politics in Somalia and Somaliland and undefined questions of citizenship and belonging were articulated by many, if mainly in their emphasis on the social heterogeneity of their own residential neighbourhood. If, as Simone contends, urbanization 'denotes a thickening of fields, an assemblage of increasingly heterogeneous elements into more complicated collectives' (2004, 408) then this can take place within peripheral camps and resettlement areas. These areas become reception and mooring points for in-migrants but continue to be defined vis-à-vis the wider city and placed in opposition to the 'local' and 'original'. However, the ambition of integration and citizenship also manifests in aspirational appeals to – pan-Somali connections and identities. This is evident in Guuleed's description at the very beginning of this chapter as well as in the use of the English loan word 'federation', which seems to speak to the historical notion of a pan-Somali political unity.[14] In the interviews, expressions of these ideas are often ambiguous, appearing in flux and relational to the particular aspects of inclusion or exclusion in the neighbourhood and wider city. As we have argued above, understandings of clan, ethnic or national identity are neither fixed nor simply symbolic constructions. They are constituted in multiple daily interactions and practices that also intersect with wider humanitarian and political discourses of protracted displacement.

Over the last three decades, an extensive literature has debated and deconstructed the supposed ethno-cultural homogeneity of the Somali Horn of Africa that was based on understandings of shared nomadic pastoral heritage and a single lingua franca (Ahmed, 1995; Besteman, 1996; Lewis, 1998; Besteman, 1998; Kusow, 2004; Eno et al, 2010; Kusow and Eno, 2015). Across the four cities, a large proportion of people categorized as 'internally displaced' belong to clans, ethno-linguistic and/or (out)caste groups who have been subjected to varying forms of discrimination. This chapter has shown how social diversity and differentiation interact with the flattening humanitarian-political categorizations of displacement. These forms of categorization are further reinforced by territorializations of displacement in camps and resettlement areas that spatially segregate displaced people – and thus city outsiders – vis-à-vis 'locals' or 'indigenous' inhabitants.

7

Conclusion: Living at the Precarious Edges of Planetary Urbanization

This book set out to explore the nexus of displacement and urbanization from the viewpoint of people living at the urban margins in four Somali cities. Building on narrative interviews and photovoice, and using a micro-sociological and micro-spatial lens, we explored *what people actually do* when they have been forced to flee and decide to come to and settle in a city. How do they find shelter and a place to stay? What do they (have to) do to sustain themselves and their families? What infrastructures and technologies do they use to manage their basic needs? How do they experience city life and what are their relationships with the people who are already resident in their immediate vicinity or in the wider city? Each chapter of the book has used different analytical entry points to answer these questions. It has looked at war and ecological shocks through an urban lens and explored migrants' arrival and settlement at the urban margins. Here, specific socio-spatial and socio-material constructions came into focus, along with the political and economic relations imbued in them. It then addressed material and digital infrastructures to explore the intersections of space, technology and society, both at the basic level of immediate human needs, as well as for the organization of flows and communicative networks necessary for livelihoods. Finally, it used resettlement approaches and practices to explore the spatio-social inequalities that are sustained and generated in policies that attempt to govern urbanization and city living.

Throughout the chapters, we have explored the power relations embedded in the categorizations and sorting of people by urban residents, political authorities and international organizations. While categorizing and sorting, people are policing society. Rancier (1999, 29ff.) emphasized how bodies are classified and named and thereby assigned 'to a particular place and task'. This assignment also distributes the capacity to speak, to be heard and to become visible. We have shown how the figure of the IDP is assigned to the urban margins, placed in camps or squatter settlements, problematized, subjected to interventions and experiments for solutions – whether 'durable' or not. Agamben (1998) claimed that the refugee became the counterpart of the citizen, politically included in the state-dominated international order through their encamped exclusion. Analogously, IDPs could be seen to have become the counterpart of urban denizens – included in the urban fabric through their physical separation and, in most cases, political exclusion. These conditions contribute to the constitution of life as precarious, and of people as abject, wasted, disposable (Bauman, 2004; Tyler, 2013) and 'socially dead' (Wilcox, 2019, 310–11; Mbembe, 2000, 270-271).

However, far from being the passive mass of people that policymaking and international programming often seems to assume, our focus on the ordinary lives of those categorized as internally displaced has shed some light on how people living at the margins are accommodating, appropriating or contesting these categorizations through everyday practices. Truly 'bare' life is an impossibility, and the disposed of aim to mobilize relationships and networks that improve their social standing. As we have shown in several chapters, they often do so by embedding themselves in patriarchal and clientelist structures that make their exploitation survivable; for example, through humanitarian rentierism or in precarious labour relations.

The focus on the urban margins has highlighted difference across and within the four cities. Therefore, we have told not one but multiple stories of precarious urbanism. These revealed destitution and violence, and shed light on the dramatic and often inhumane ways in which poverty and marginalization are experienced. However, in the midst of the 'injury, violence, and death' (Butler, 2009, II) that shapes precarious urbanism, we were also able to show the many ways in which people try to enhance their life chances, work towards improving their own situations, and attempt to provide better circumstances for future generations.

Each chapter has shown that it is both impossible and analytically unhelpful to develop clear categorical distinctions of displacement that differentiate, for example, conflict from poverty-driven, or economic from political displacement. In this respect we add to a wider body of literature that critically engages with the power of these forms of human sorting (Bowker and Star, 2000) and social policing (Rancier, 1999). Instead, in the Horn of Africa and elsewhere, different kinds of mobility are unfolding into and constituting processes of urbanization. By embedding micro-sociological detail in the wider historical and political context, we have also shown that the cities under focus do not constitute bounded entities but emerge as socio-spatial formations in the making. Cities are, therefore, notoriously difficult to pin down. Their continuous remaking is particularly pronounced in the context of violence-induced rapid growth. We have identified the extensive spatial expansion and densification of cities through physical and social practices of urban in-migrants. We have also shown how these practices are blurring distinctions between the rural and urban, human-made and natural, technological and social, material and immaterial, as well as associated morphologies and modes of living. The focus on settlements associated with displacement and on the everyday lives of their inhabitants has demonstrated how people at the margins are actively contributing to this city-making. City-newcomers are assembling relations, artefacts and materials, interweave ideas and aspirations, and with their bodies and labour power they are literally building and expanding the city. Some of the installations people establish are makeshift, cobbled together from leftover materials, rubble and debris and made in the expectation of needing to move again. Others are more durable and expected to last, if only as a 'transitional' measure for a few years. But all of these activities and assemblages are part of the 'relentless "churning"' on all spatial scales that characterizes cities (Brenner and Schmid, 2015, 165).

Building on the displacement experiences of interviewees, Chapter 2 explored the histories of violent conflicts and displacement in Somalia/Somaliland through the experiences of the four cities. The different trajectories of these urban centres were largely shaped by the dynamics of the civil war that started at the end of the 1980s and unleashed waves of displacement, both inwards and outwards to and from the cities. This attests to the need to move from the state-centred perspective on (civil) wars to the exploration of micro- and site-specific processes of violence (see Kalyvas, 2003; Bakonyi and Bliesemann de Guevara, 2009) that contribute to different trajectories of urbanization, and shape spatially and socially distinct forms of urbanism. In more recent studies the term 'conflict urbanism' (Saldarriaga et al, 2017; Danielak, 2020) has been coined to emphasize the place-specific effects and dynamics of violence and to assess the intertwinement of violence and city-making. Although multiple forms of violence feature prominently in the experiences of people in all four cities, we have not dedicated a specific chapter of the book to this topic. This is partly due to the emphasis that interviewees put on improvements to their physical security. Although such testimonies should be evaluated relative to experiences in wider society of mass violence and large-scale destruction, the decision not to use violence as separate analytical device also reflects our concern about placing ourselves on either side of an ongoing narrative contest around urban destruction and reconstruction in Somalia. The global gaze is often only drawn to Somalia at moments of crisis, whether around the urban mass influx of impoverished in-migrants or instances of spectacular violence, such as terrorist attacks. More recently, however, this narrative is challenged in reports of international organizations, which now tend to emphasize political, economic and social improvements. While such emphasis may be used by these organizations to justify their own presence and activities, the narrative of progress is even more prevalent in the social media discourse of Somali journalists, activists, entrepreneurs, civil servants and popular culture 'influencers', many of whom are young and transnationally connected. Much of the content created here foregrounds a 'Somalia rising' narrative with imagery of beaches, new hotels and vibrant city life all indicating improvements in urban security and pointing to the cities' economic dynamism. These narratives are themselves part of the urban reconstruction process as they encourage diaspora return and investment. There are inevitable tensions in navigating between different framings and imaginaries of Somali urbanism. As we have tried to show, the very issue of displacement connects these contrasting narratives around both the violence and economic growth that underpins contemporary forms of camp urbanization in Somalia and Somaliland. By presenting and analysing the experiences of people who live at the margins of these rising cities, we aim to critically engage with reductive and sensationalist perspectives of political instability and humanitarian crisis, but also the jubilant perspective of a (re)emerging middle and upper class (and their international networks) that tends to overlook some of the costs of capitalist urban development that is still paid primarily by the cities' most impoverished inhabitants.

The Somalia and Africa 'rising' narratives can be interpreted as part of the wider capitalist projection of a frictionless world of economic growth and consumption (Appel, 2012). They also attest to our emphasis that Somali cities, while located at the global peripheries of capital, are nonetheless integrated in international circuits of profit and power. They are global cities, being nodes that enable flows of people, commodities, money, aid and information. We have examined these internationalized urban nodes from the perspectives of their margins and with a focus on the ordinary, emphasizing, for example, the connections between urban land, the global aid regime, infrastructural development, mobile connectivity and the emergence of various forms of rentierism and (labour) exploitation across the cities.

Our decision to use the concept of 'camp urbanization' highlights mobility as driver of urbanization and expression of urbanism. This includes the experiences and choices in-migrants make when they journey to cities, and their mobilization of material and social relations in attempts to find secure places where they can erect shelter, settle and rebuild their lives. These efforts have resulted in the emergence of three socially and spatially distinct types of settlements which we have identified across the cities as: inner-city (squatter) settlements, camps at the edges of cities, and planned resettlement areas – the latter often spatially segregated from the main city. Residents in each type of settlement are building up social relations and material structures which integrate these places into the wider urban fabric. Although the different forms of integration have their own consequences for inhabitants, various practices are contributing to the expansion, densification and (often) gentrification of cities, a process we aim at capturing with the notion of camp urbanization.

We recognize that every place-specific focus runs the risk of inadvertently producing a 'localized otherness' (Sheppard et al, 2013, 897). In thick ethnographic studies, this may involve the creation of a variety of local-parochial Others seemingly unconnected to the wider world. Although we tried to engage with the four cities without a priori assumptions and from a non-essentializing perspective, we have also been wary of the creeping in of a 'new particularism' (Brenner et al, 2010, 206; Scott and Storper, 2015) that limits the purchase of broader theorization of the urban. The comparative gesture we adopt throughout the book – and the common patterns of camp urbanization and experiences of urbanism we identified and contrasted with findings from other studies from multiple world regions – aimed at guarding against this tendency. Above all, we have tried to be attentive to the ways that interview testimonies and photos present the multiscalar relations in which people's activities and experiences were embedded. Oscilating between the particular urban settings and the wider relations in which these environments are entangled contributes to what others have described as the 'worlding' of cities (Simone, 2001, 2004; Mbembe and Nuttall, 2004; Ong, 2011; McCann et al, 2013). The specific worldings of the urban margins emphasizes activities and performativity but simultaneously takes into account the multilevelled engagements and encounters of both actors and institutions, not all of them necessarily located in the city, and many of them drawn together only temporarily to fix problems that they or others have previously identified (see also Ong, 2011, 3, 11).

The multiscalar links and activities were particularly evident in Chapter 3's analysis of the politcial economy of the four cities. Here, we identified the emergence of a (mostly small-scale) humanitarian rentierism and demonstrated how humanitarian entrepreneurs – aka camp managers, leaders or gatekeepers – acquire power through their facilitation of relations between three actor groups: destitute arrivals to the city, landowners, and actors working in the aid industry. The interplay of these actor groups, along with their lopsided power relations, shapes the forms, morphologies and social dynamics of camp urbanization. The emergence of intermediaries between local and international actors is, of course, nothing new in Somalia. Often building on Bayart's (2000) influential exploration of extraversion, intermediaries and the wider socio-political relations in which they are embedded have been studied in many different contexts, including the Horn of Africa (Bierschenk et al, 2002; Engle Merry, 2006; Bakonyi, 2011; Hagmann, 2016; Münch and Veit, 2018). To this literature we have added empirical cases that identify how power and intermediation are multilayered and cut across too-static conceptions of the local and international. As such, we are less focused on the relations between international aid agencies and their local staff or partners who operate between these institutions and the recipients of their engagement. Instead, we highlight the interplay of different actors in a wider network of interests, where the identities of aid recipients, intermediaries and distributors may be blurred. This is particularly evident in micro-level camp leadership and this form of small-scale humanitarian entrepreneurship is embedded in complex relations of power that we disaggregate in Chapter 3. Above all, although decision-making power is clearly unevenly distributed, we emphasize the emotive and affective aspects of patron–client relations that exist between camp leaders and city newcomers. The former not only welcome people in dire need but also often provide initial support that is experienced as relief by those who would otherwise be stranded in an unfamiliar urban environment. The affective ties and mutual obligations that underscore these and other types of moral economies also render socio-economic differentiation and forms of exploitation acceptable to people (Narotzky and Besnier, 2014, S7). Comparisons between the cities and the experiences of settlement allowed us to flesh out similarities and differences in the flow of power. For example, we examined relations between city newcomers and long-time settlers, some of whom may become gatekeepers themselves. Their activities and encounters successively interweave the settlements into the wider social and material composition of the city. Again, while the dynamics we describe are specific to the four cities in Somalia and Somaliland, the process of camp urbanization, and thus the moulding of settlements associated with displacement into the city, is not. Comparative examples from the literature on both conflict and humanitarian urbanism in other contexts such as Kabul, Goma, Gulu and Beirut, have displayed similar patterns of displacement-linked urban transformations.

We have further shown how in-migrants to Somali cities might initially be protected through the patron–client relations they enter into with camp leaders and also, indirectly, with landowners. However, the more the settlements are embedded in the urban environment and the more infrastructural developments, urban reconstruction and urban sprawl accelerates, the more likely land speculation becomes. These processes have shed light on the unequal relations that constitute property and the violence imbricated in property relations. Once land and housing speculations reach the urban margins, evictions become likely, displacing people once more to ever more peripheral settlements and camps at the city outskirts. Although visible in cities across the globe, gentrification takes on different forms depending on local policies, economic structures and class relations (Atkinson and Bridge, 2005, 17). In Somalia and Somaliland, the contribution of in-migrants to the making of cities often, ironically, also contributes to their further marginalization. Here, the establishment of settlements, including land clearances and the assembling of social and physical infrastructures, is frequently followed by evictions and thus contributes to continued cycles of displacement that are forcing people at the margins to be forever on the move. The destruction of the built environment of camp-like settlements is followed by concerted efforts to rebuild the city on a (more) permanent basis. As these new installations are replacing the makeshift and transitional structures characteristic of displacement-affected populations, they are also replacing the socio-economic networks people have established to manage their survival. In this way, violence continues to inscribe itself in urban spaces, shaping the layered urban landscapes of built forms that are assembled and superimposed upon each other over time while distributing and stratifying the life chances of its residents.

Initial settlement practices and petty humanitarian entrepreneurship contribute to this dynamic of evictions and gentrification. Humanitarian engagement is but one driver of these processes. The forms of humanitarian rentierism analysed in the book are evolving within a longer history of extraversion in Somalia. This has involved the mobilization of social relations and divisions during postcolonial state formation, their transformation during the civil war and later periods of violence, and the related rise of political and economic elites, many of whom are currently engaged in building a new state. Among the latter are also many people from the global Somali diaspora, who knowingly or inadvertently contribute to gentrification as they invest in real estate and buy properties in the cities. Disputes over land ownership have increased in Mogadishu since 2012. This is related to security improvements and the (not necessarily permanent) return of people from the diaspora, including previously exiled landowners. This contributes further to the commodification of land and services, alongside the powerful banking and communication companies and many other commercial actors involved in the internationally supported development of infrastructure, and the institutional and physical reconstruction of the cities. International humanitarian regimes and both diasporic and other capital investments make the reconstruction of these cities and the commodification and regulation of property relations an inherently transnational process. However, in the course of urban reconstruction and institutional development, people living at the margins are pushed further and further outside the city proper and into peripheral camps.

Chapter 4 sustained the focus on the built environment through its discussion of infrastructural improvisations. Looking at and comparing the building, management and use of infrastructure in the different settlements, the chapter shows how sanitation, water and healthcare facilities mediate and stratify bodily experiences in and of the city. This chapter contributes to the rapidly growing literature on infrastructures and logistics as it draws attention to the multiple ways technology intersects with space and society. The sites of our research, however, are located in a region that is not often explored in science and technology studies' accounts of quotidian infrastructural life. We have outlined how people at the urban margins have continuously adapted layered ensembles of infrastructural connections reacting to redundancies or risks, and in ways that are fostering precarious lives. All examples showed that infrastructure both produces and is produced by processes of social differentiation. The lack and malfunctioning of infrastructures generates uncertainty and puts people under tremendous stress, as they use their bodies and labour power to bridge gaps, replace missing pieces or search for other solutions. These improvisations also rely on creative collaborations and (often parochial) social solidarities. Although mutual care can help to compensate for some gaps, infrastructural improvisations are also promoting new forms of petty commodification of services, goods and labour. Above all, improvisation is time consuming, and the daily effort and time people need to access basic services and fulfil elementary needs, such as having access to a toilet or being able to fetch water, significantly contributes to their precarity and marginalization. In addition, the chapter introduced schooling as an infrastructure that holds the promise to break the cycle of precarity. This may only be possible for the next generation, and we also highlighted the significant challenges associated with accessing this highly commodified infrastructure.

The chapter also outlined how infrastructures are part of ongoing struggles over land and are direct expressions of relations of property and contestations of belonging and citizenship. Barry (2020) refers to this as infrastructure's material politics. We point to the mundane yet life-sustaining aspects of material politics. Infrastructures are not just technologies or things external to and used by humans but are deeply interwoven into their own biophysical existence. They shape life itself when mediating bodily functions and insert the human metabolism into the metabolism of the city. The corporeal experiences of eating, drinking, excreting, suffering and dying demonstrate this and show how infrastructures are constituting subjects, relating them to each other and in space, and shaping the daily rhythms and emotive experiences of precarious lives at the edges of Somali cities.

In this way the chapter contributes to recent academic attention to infrastructures and logistics (Cowen 2014, Chua et al, 2018; Enns and Bersaglio, 2020) but moves beyond megaprojects that immediately signal their international or global character, such as the Chinese Belt and Road Initiative, or the Ethiopian Grand Renaissance Dam (Blanchard and Flint, 2017; Nordin and Weissmann, 2018; Ho, 2020; Gebresenbet and Wondemagegnehu, 2021). The study of mundane and localized infrastructural practices to some extent counters the wider literatures' focus on global mobilities, flows, interconnections and hubs as it foregrounds heterogeneity and fragmentation along with corrosions, break-downs and disruptions (see Graham, 2010; McFarlane, 2018; Barry, 2020). However, the chapter also demonstrates how intimate and situated bodily practices remain in many respects interwoven with transnational and global networks that unevenly stretch out across the cities and beyond. Prominent again is aid infrastructure, but also roads, business ventures or financial services, all of which link localized infrastructural practices to multiple and often less heterogeneous networks that allow for a smoother flow of communication, ideas, skills, financial investments and money.

Money is further examined in Chapter 5. Here we shifted our focus from localized, fragmented materialities to the ways in which urban margins are linked to the more tightly meshed global and virtual worlds that ICTs enable. Moving beyond the spaces of the camp, people actively make connections with the wider city, often in order to make money. The focus on labour relations and their links to ICTs emphasized radically different types of connectivity and mobility and in doing so, the chapter further zoomed into precarious lifeworlds. The analytical value of too broad a notion of precarity – as the generalized insecurity and uncertainty that we introduced initially from the work of Butler (2006) and Ettlinger (2007) – can here be questioned. Some authors have called for a re-rooting of precarity studies in an 'analysis of specific labour conditions' (Millar, 2017, 1, 4–5). Sympathetic to this critique, Chapter 5 foregrounded descriptions and visualizations of the lived experiences of working people at the urban margins.

These marginalized urban settlements constitute large reservoirs of manual labour. Camp urbanization fosters social stratification. This in turn increases demand from people from wealthier classes for, for example, women to support them in their reproductive and caring duties; for men to work in the booming construction industry; and for both men and women to support the production and circulation of goods and materials as petty entrepreneurs, porters and traders in local markets, or through door-to-door hawking. After outlining the type and organization of livelihoods strategies people at the urban margins develop, we drew attention to the importance of digital connectivity for the organization of labour and other social relations that underpin these means of (precarious) survival. The locally focused approach enabled an exploration of how marginalized urban populations engage with and understand ICTs without, however, detaching these local, specific uses of technology from the wider flows that enable and shape them. As elsewhere in the book, we identified entanglements of both locally particular and globally mobile practices that govern displaced populations, and we discussed people's agency to comply or resist these forms of government. ICT infrastructures play a distinctive role in enabling connections that are vital for people to access and circulate resources - among people at the urban margins, with employers, international telecommunications companies, humanitarian agencies and, indirectly, with national and international policymakers. We used mobile telephony – both the devices and their related data infrastructure – as a lens through which to explore the local dimension of (virtual) global connectivity. We concur with Brinkman et al (2017) that this approach can be more illuminating of urban (displacement-linked) precarity than policy or research focus on the impacts of these technologies on particular population groups.

The links between precarity and ICT-enabled connectivity provide some understanding of how people at the urban margins relate to urban reconstruction and economic growth, the roles they play in the urban economy, and the effects that this labour has on them. At the same time, ICTs themselves have acquired a particularly prominent position within debates about vulnerable, mobile populations. Expanding and developing access to ICTs for such marginalized groups is a frequently articulated objective of international development actors, and is often linked with various forms of empowerment (World Bank, 2016; Hatayama, 2018). Following the refugee (reception) crisis in Europe 2015–16, the trope of the 'connected migrant' (Diminescu, 2008) has risen in prominence in scholarly and policy debates. This has led to discussions about digitally mediated migration and an emphasis on the practical value of different functions of mobile phones for mobile populations (UNHCR, 2016), especially those who are making dangerous journeys into 'fortress Europe'. A growing academic literature explores how connectivity helps migrants access practical journey-relevant information, navigate border regimes, access or avoid human-trafficking/smuggling networks, connect with humanitarians and obtain resources on arrival that may foster social integration (Dekker and Engbersen, 2014; Frouws et al, 2016; Gillespie et al, 2016; Borkert et al, 2018). Earlier research on 'digital diasporas' (Brinkerhoff, 2009) describes how the internet has contributed to the deepening and broadening of transnational social networks and influenced further migration (Hiller and Franz, 2004; Vertovec, 2004; Komito, 2011; Madianou and Miller, 2012; Oiarzabal and Reips, 2012; Schaub, 2012) including in relation to globally dispersed Somali communities (Horst, 2007; Lindley, 2009; Charmarkeh, 2013).

Much of this literature focuses on migrants en route to the global North, whereas there are fewer studies on people moving within countries in the global South, for instance in terms of rural-urban migration (Cartier et al, 2005; Muto, 2012; Onitsuka and Hidayat, 2019). In Somalia and Somaliland, the mobile phone has undoubtedly helped people to navigate the uncertainties of enforced mobility and urban settlement. Ethnographic studies of the use of mobile phones and their role in mobility within the global South have also highlighted the impact of ICTs on social networks and how they further entangle rural and urban economies and livelihood-related movements (Steel et al, 2017). The interviewees in cities in Somalia and Somaliland confirm, in this respect, the findings of such research on ICTs in Cameroon, Rwanda or Sudan, as they enable regular communication between the city and countryside, but also within the city.

They can decrease the perceived distance between people and can help sustain social and at times even economic capital. They contribute to the remote organization of livelihood-related mobilities, not only in relation to (more studied) pastoral nomadism (De Bruijn et al, 2010; Tofik, 2014; Butt, 2015; Ngowi et al, 2015; Debsu et al, 2016; Asaka and Smucker, 2016; Baird and Hartter, 2017; Djohy et al, 2017) but, as we emphasize, also within urban centres. With respect to the latter, we have specifically contributed to the small number of studies that have examined the use of ICTs by displaced people who are attempting to make a living in precarious urban conditions, such as Boas's (2020) account of the online social networking of people displaced by climate change-linked ecological events in Bangladesh. Like Boas, we have pointed to the complexity of internal population movement, along with the role of mobile phones to allow migrants to maintain long-distance and dispersed social ties that could be used when necessary and the attempt to use mobile phones to reduce risks of migration. The links people establish through virtual communication are important, although they are also often disrupted by a lack of rural network coverage, factors relating to the ongoing armed conflict or limited access to electricity or functioning mobile phones.

Ultimately, the chapter cautions against overly simplistic or 'tech-solutionist' approaches to policymaking. Research in the 'ICT for development' (ICT4D) field often stresses the empowering potential of connectivity, highlighting how devices may provide access to market-relevant information or increase entrepreneurial capacity (Komunte, 2015; Kusimba et al, 2015; Suri and Jack, 2016). In this respect, we follow a more critical trend that questions the egalitarian and emancipatory promises of technology for marginalized groups. While mobile telephony eases many of the connectivity issues that people used to compensate for with physical movement, it can also reinforce spatialized inequalities in the city and foster power imbalances between mobile work forces and their employers. Mobile connectivity does not by itself transform or transcend existing social structures. Instead, multiple studies from various African and Asian contexts have shown that the way in which ICTs are often used can reinforce gendered inequalities (Hahn and Kibora, 2008; Wallis, 2013; Wyche and Olson, 2018; Porter et al, 2020; Natile, 2020; Summers et al, 2020). The Somali city examples confirm some of these findings. Women are more likely than men to be illiterate and therefore had greater difficulties in navigating text-based messaging and mobile money systems. This can open up new avenues for exploitation and for some people – the elderly, some women – mobile use can reinforce dependence on others with the skills to use the new affordances of the technology. Nonetheless, both men and women emphasized how the mobile phone – and particularly mobile money – supports their organization of everyday duties, facilitates work relations, allows for interpersonal access to financial assistance, and saves people time. However, the ubiquity of mobile money and their compulsion to use these systems due to a lack of physical cash seemed to increase the risk of delayed or denied (remote) payments by employers.

The sixth and final chapter of the book examined the longer-term position of in-migrant populations in the four cities in Somalia and Somaliland. The attention that large-scale displacement and rapid urbanization have received in aid circles was conceptualized here as an example of the practices of problematization that Foucault outlined as being central to biopolitics. Before (liberal) government can operate, problems need to be identified and problem spaces need to be carved out (Joyce, 2003, 20). These problematizations transform a set of issues into an 'ensemble of problems' while suggesting, or at least promising to develop, solutions that may help to transform the identified phenomenon (Rabinow, 2009, 18–20; Ong, 2011, 3–4). This then enables a shift from analysis to intervention. In Somalia, problematization is predominantly practiced by international organizations, who currently provide the bulk of quantitative and qualitative information on the (government) problems in the country and its cities. A whole array of reports and webpages are currently operated with the aim of identifying, counting and (dynamically) mapping humanitarian problems. These carved out problem spaces are then supposed to be acted upon by the government (in the making). Displacement and urbanization are prominent among the phenomena that over recent decades have been formulated in this way – a type of problematization that we recognize our own contribution to with the framing of this book.

We have only briefly, but within several chapters, touched upon the way knowledge and power are interwoven in both the identification of problems and the interventions designed to address them. The example of 'durable solutions' initiatives provided an example, and the resettlement schemes they have led to were analysed through the views of their beneficiaries. Partly designed to address the continuing problem of evictions and cycles of displacement, such interventions were indeed providing people with various tangible opportunities. They increased tenure security, relieved people from the uncertainty of displacement, provided the potential to diversify livelihoods through subletting, enabled people to invite relatives to settle nearby, and provided generally better options for sanitation and water. Most of the schemes included infrastructure and services that were experienced as improvements compared to those found in inner-city squatter settlements and or peripheral camps. It was notable here how the resettlement schemes were brought to life through new material assemblages that cut across the carefully designed and disciplined spaces laid out by the international organizations and municipal authorities that planned them. However, because these settlements are usually established at the far outskirts of cities, they can also increase social and material disconnection, disrupt established networks and work relations, and contribute to further precarity.

The chapter also showed how people's sense of belonging is intrinsically tied to their experiences and strategies of mobility. Brun's (2016) analysis of internally displaced people in Georgia, who move between temporary rented accommodation, shows how the deterritorialization caused by displacement is not followed by a reterritorialization of identity and status. In the Somali case studies, the resettlement area is designed to reduce the constant mobility and provide people with routes to land and tenure security, which is often associated with possibilities for belonging. However, increased tenure security does not preclude other types of mobility important for securing livelihoods, as people look to maximize or expand available options to get by. Brun notes that 'the IDP category changes content during protracted situations of displacement, as it shifts from a humanitarian category to a social category' (2016, 429; 2010). This is confirmed in our analysis of multiple forms of categorization that accompany resettlement and intertwine with the categorization as displaced.

Overall, however, resettlement schemes have contributed to and further shaped patterns of (camp) urbanization as they have led to the establishment of new residential areas. These reconfigure land and property relations, generate new centres of gravity for continuing in-migration, redefine mechanisms of in- and exclusion, and contribute to the renegotiation of citizenship. In this respect, durable solutions programming runs the risk of alignment with locally prevailing prejudices and practices of discrimination as they carve out specific settlements for the most vulnerable – now identified as displaced populations and categorized as such in a state-centric fashion. These practices tend to reinforce binary distinctions between urban locals and rural in-migrants, between autochthonous city dwellers and outsiders, and thus of people assigned with a genuine right to the city and people who are merely endured by rightful citizens. While these discourses are co-produced by a broad number of actors, including the people who are themselves living at these margins (see also Ettlinger and Bose, 2020), they are also reflected and can be reinforced in resettlement schemes, which distinguish spaces for 'the displaced' and mark out urban segregation. This also speaks to how categorizations introduced through policy discourse – here the figure of the IDP relevant across the cities in ordinary daily practices – continue to contribute to exclusion and reproduce urban inequalities.

Similar patterns of inclusion and exclusion were identified by Purdeková (2017), who analysed peace-building through the planning of ethnically integrated villages in post-war Burundi. Drawing from the perspectives of people who have been resettled or affected by resettlement schemes, Purdeková examines how these initiatives represent 'struggles over the power to posit order, name its constituent parts, their nature and relations' (2017, 542). Her analysis highlights the 'public production of space and its involvement in the (re)construction or remodelling of collective identities'

(2017, 541). Likewise, we show how people appropriate meta-discourses such as 'displacement' and 'integration' to make claims to urban space, but conversely how spatial arrangements play a significant role in predefining and constituting social groups as insiders or outsiders, with differing capacities to advance their interests in – and belonging to – the city. In many of the outer resettlement areas, social distinctions of displacement take an immediately visible spatial form, attesting to both 'territorial stigmatization in action' (Wacquant et al, 2014), and ongoing contestations and struggles for citizenship and thus modalities of inclusion (Holston and Appadurai, 1996). While we have emphasized the liminality of these resettlement areas, they nonetheless point to the further 'explosion of urban spaces' Lefebvre once identified, and a tendency towards the planetary generalization of a form of urbanism (Brenner and Schmid, 2012; Brenner, 2014) characterized by the sprawl of urban agglomerations and the expansion and simultaneous transformation of urban morphologies. Throughout the book we have discussed this type of urbanism with respect to the transformation of refugee camps in cities, camp urbanization more generally and the related contribution of resettlement schemes.

Building an analysis of migration-linked urbanization through comparison of the experiences of in-migrant populations across four cities has brought with it several challenges. Some details pertaining to the social and political make-up of the cities and emphasizing difference have inevitably been glossed over – particularly those that relate to the modalities and capacities of municipal and regional administrations that hold authority in the cities. The role of the state(s) in these contexts of camp urbanization is undoubtedly an area that requires further research. This is particularly evident in the context of the ongoing (if uncertain) federalization project in Somalia, where the status and representation of displaced populations will be an important indicator of the extent to which federal member states can develop more inclusive political identities.

Although we interviewed government officials and (where possible) corroborated claims made about policy or programming, our analysis has primarily relied on the experiences, perspectives and subjectivities of inhabitants of neighbourhoods associated with displaced populations. This was a conscious decision that was framed in relation to an overall methodology that emphasized maximizing the expression of marginalized research participants, at least in comparison to the modes of knowledge production that are more commonly pursued in a frequently, and at times, acutely restrictive research environment. In doing so, we have attempted to foreground as many perspectives as possible from people who live at the marginalized and precarious edges of an urbanizing society. In the process, we have learned a great deal from these individuals and can only hope that our synthesis and comparative analysis does justice to their insights.

APPENDIX

Table A.1: Subclan self-identifications by interviewees (where given) in first round of narrative interviews

City	Clan family (where given)	Subclan (where given)
Mogadishu	Digil and Mirifle	Boqol Hore
		Eelay
		Hadamo
		Heletha
		Hubeyr
		Leysaan
		Shanta Caleemood
		Wanjeel
	Dir	Biimaal
	Bantu Jareer	Reer Shabelle
		Shiidla
	Hawiye	Duduble
		(*Unspecified*)
		(*Unspecified*)
Baidoa	Digil and Mirifle	Boqol Hore
		Garwale
		Gelidle
		Haraw
		Harin
		Jiron
		Leysaan
		Luwaay
		Qomaal
		Wanjeel

(continued)

Table A1: Subclan self-identifications by interviewees (where given) in first round of narrative interviews (continued)

City	Clan family (where given)	Subclan (where given)
Bosaso	Digil and Mirifle	(*Multiple, unspecified*)
	Bantu Jareer	Reer Shabelle
	Madhibaan	(*Unspecified*)
	Darood	Marehan
	Hawiye	Gaaljecel
	Dir	(*Unspecified*)
	Dir / Isaaq	(*Unspecified*)
Hargeisa	Dir / Isaaq	Arab
		Habir Yoonis
		Habar Awal / Sacad Muuse
		Arab
	Dir	Gadabuursi
	Gabooye	(*Unspecified*)

Notes

Chapter 1

1. In general, place names in the book are written according to their conventional (or most commonly used) English spellings.
2. The term 'displacement-affected communities' is increasingly used to acknowledge that displacement does not only impact on the people forced to move but also the societies and places where those people seek refuge. However, we refrain from using this notion of community, as this implies social ties that may not exist and risks obscuring processes of stratification that we explore throughout the book.
3. The debate as to how far refugee camps have developed an urban form is ongoing (Montclos and Kagwanja, 2000; Agier, 2002a, 2002b; Malkki, 2002; Bauman, 2002; Agier et al, 2002; Turner, 2005; Crisp, 2015; Jansen, 2016; Jansen, 2018).
4. Along with one other person who assisted but who wished to remain anonymous.
5. A discussion of such negotiations and how they shape the 'politics of narrative' is found in Lesutis (2018).
6. An example can be provided by the reports produced through the IOM displacement tracker matrix: https://dtm.iom.int/somalia [last accessed 26 August 2021].
7. For an attempt to initiate a more open discussion among researchers about these practices, see Mwambari and Owor (2019).
8. With respect to the exhibitions in the research cities, Jutta Bakonyi and Abdirahman Edle were present during all exhibitions, while Peter Chonka and Kirsti Stuvoy participated in Bosaso and Hargeisa respectively.
9. See securityonthemove.co.uk/events/ for details of dissemination activities undertaken before the publication of this book, and future updates of this ongoing process.

Chapter 2

1. *Hanti-Wadaag* means 'Shared Property' is a legacy of naming during the socialist (*Hantiwadaagnimo*) phase of the military regime under General Siyaad Barre who ruled the country between 1969 and 1991.
2. Some sources summarize the Digil and Mirifle as Rahanweyne/Reewin, others keep them separate as two clan families. Others differentiate the Isaaq as a separate clan family from the Dir. Clans develop, some groups separate, others merge, while others are erased. For this reason, we have decided not to visualize kin relations in a 'clan tree' in this book, as such visualizations tend to freeze a given moment in time and, thus, to obfuscate social dynamics that characterize segmentary lineage and other kinship-based relations. Such representations are reminiscent of colonial-era classificatory systems intended to bring order to messy social realities. However, beyond our narrative accounts in this and subsequent chapters the Appendix includes a table summarizing the clan and subclan names that were mentioned as self-identifications by some interviewees.

3   The boundary between businesspeople and warlords remained fluid. Successful business owners often started to recruit their own militias and may then compete with their former political allies. Vice versa, warlords could shift their interest towards business ventures.
4   See Table 1 in the Appendix.
5   The RRA was the only clan militia that openly displayed its clan base (Rahanweyn) in its name, probably because it considered itself to be a self-defence unit resisting 'foreign' occupation from clan militias external to the region.

Chapter 3
1   Again, it is important to note that return is often cyclical, and many people from the wider diaspora are often moving between Somalia and other countries of settlement in the East Africa region and beyond.

Chapter 4
1   Ezeh et al (2017) argue that the scientific literature on 'slum health' is underdeveloped in comparison to more general studies of urban health, and links between poverty and health. Specific focus on slum health thus considers the connections between health and urban space.
2   Although improving, Somalia faces the world's highest rates of child mortality and maternal deaths, with one in twelve women dying from causes related to pregnancy and childbirth, see https://www.unicef.org/somalia/health; https://childmortality.org/ [accessed 1 April 2021].

Chapter 5
1   This chapter builds on, brings together and expands the arguments we have made in two previous articles: Bakonyi, J. and Chonka, P. (2019) 'Precarious labour – Precarious lives: Photographic glimpses from displaced people in Somali cities', *Afrique contemporaine* 1–2: 205-224; and Chonka, P. and Bakonyi, J. (2021) 'Precarious technoscapes: Forced mobility and mobile connections at the urban margins' *Journal of the British Academy*, 9 (S11): 67–91.
2   Khat is imported from Ethiopia or Kenya, constitutes a major import good, and is important for taxation (customs) and state income in both Somalia and Somaliland (Bakonyi 2011, chapter 7.2). Women play various roles in the trade (Koshin, 2022), although none of our interviewees relied on this for income.
3   *Ayuuto* is derived from the Italian *aiuto* (meaning 'help'). *Hagbad* is another Somali word for the same type of group saving scheme.
4   Somaliland has its own currency, the Somaliland shilling, and mobile money services there operate in both this local currency and US dollars.
5   'Worldwide mobile data pricing 2021: The cost of 1GB of mobile data in 230 countries', Cable.co.uk, Available from: https://www.cable.co.uk/mobiles/worldwide-data-pricing/#resources
6   These enterprises were established around 2002 and emerged from earlier infrastructure created by the Al Barakaat communication and remittance company (Marchal, 2002; Lochery, 2015; Hagmann and Stepputat, 2016, 10).
7   Some studies have posited that saving to fund the migration of a family member is itself a livelihood strategy, given the expectation that subsequent remittances will help sustain a household back home (De Haas, 2007). However, research in Somali contexts suggests that the economic profile of migrants sending back remittances tends to be more affluent and

NOTES

that the poorest groups do not have the resources to send family members (Ali and Rift Valley Institute, 2016). Similar research also questions whether many families do actively encourage young people to migrate, given the prevalence of initiatives and activities in Somaliland to prevent these outflows (Ali, 2016).

Chapter 6

1. For the political context and dynamics of violence in that period see Bakonyi, 2013.
2. Casanelli (2015) and Hoehne (2016) have explored the political dynamics linked to historical (and conflict-related) internal migration patterns, rather than the micro-level livelihood considerations of marginalized people, such as those featured in this book.
3. We do not have the clan affiliation of every interviewee. People from minority groups are often aligned to a majority clan and may provide this affiliation if asked.
4. The history of violence in the Bay and Bakool regions is analysed in Bakonyi (2013).
5. Eelaay are from the Mirifle lineage and are known to predominantly live in the Burhakaba district of Bay region. However, the term is in Mogadishu often used with derogatory intention for all people speaking Af Maay.
6. In the early 1990s, and particularly in the context of the battle for Mogadishu, rural-urban distinctions were mobilized to distinguish 'authochtonous' and allegedly more 'civilized' urban clans, from the pastoralist clans that 'invaded' the city in the fight against Siyaad Barre (see Bakonyi 2011, 165–167).
7. Eno and Kusow (2014) detail numerous racist and derogatory terms used against what they call the 'Somali Bantu Jareer' peoples, but do not describe 'Jareer' itself in the same way, presumably because of its use for self-identification. Nonetheless, the classification of people as Jareer uses physical markers to demarcate group boundaries and phenotypically encodes forms of belonging and identities that could be described as racist.
8. Among the many attempts at group classification is the subdivision of the main Jareer groups into Gosha, Shabelle, Shidle and Boni (SIDRA 2019).
9. Minority groups often seem to lack access to humanitarian and development aid, either because they do not have middlemen in Nairobi from where many international programmes in Somalia are coordinated, or in federal and regional governmental structures.
10. See for example van Dijk's (1993) discussion of elite disourse and racism in Europe.
11. The Somaliland government has organized periodic mass round-ups and deportations of Oromo since the 2000s (Lindley, 2009a). The position of the sizeable group of Oromo and other in-migrants from Ethiopia and other countries in Somaliland and Somalia has received scant research attention.
12. Al Shabaab is also renowned for its targeted recruitment from Somali Bantu Jareer communities in southern regions (Ingiriis, 2020). This can involve specific outreach or the forced recruitment of children/young people.
13. More recently, Somaliland authorities have also expelled hundreds of long-established Digil and Mirifle migrants from eastern parts of *its* territory, a move condemned by Puntland officials who received these people before many moved onwards 'back' to what is now the Southwest State (Hiiraan, 2021).
14. This unity was epitomized in the merger of the former British and Italian colonies into an independent state in 1960 and symbolized in the five points of the Somali flag. This spoke to the political goal of unification of all regions in the Horn that are predominantly inhabited by ethnic Somalis, including parts of Djibouti, Ethiopia and Kenya.

References

Abdi, A.A. (1998) 'Education in Somalia: History, destruction, and calls for reconstruction', *Comparative Education*, 34(3): 327–340.

Abourahme, N. (2015) 'Assembling and spilling-over: Towards an "ethnography of cement" in a Palestinian refugee camp', *International Journal of Urban and Regional Research*, 39(2): 200–217.

Aceska, A., Heer, B. and Kaiser-Grolimund, A. (2019) 'Doing the city from the margins: Critical perspectives on urban marginality', *Anthropological Forum*, 29(1): 1–11.

Adam, H.M. (1995) 'Somalia: A Terrible Beauty Being Born?' in W. Zartman (ed) *Collapsed States: The Disintegration and Restoration of Legitimate Authority*, Boulder and London: Lynne Rienner, pp 69–90.

Ademolu, E. and Warrington, S. (2019) 'Who gets to talk about NGO images of global poverty?', *Photography and Culture*, 12(3): 365–376.

AFP (2016) 'Somalia housing boom as Mogadishu emerges from ashes of war', 3 January, Available from: https://english.alarabiya.net/features/2016/01/03/Somalia-housing-boom-as-Mogadishu-emerges-from-ashes-of-war [Accessed 14 April 2022].

Africa Watch (1990) 'Somalia: A government at war with its own people' January, Available from: https://www.hrw.org/sites/default/files/repomaliamalia_1990.pdf [Accessed 1 September 2021].

Agamben, G. (1998) *Homo Sacer: Sovereign Power and Bare Life*. Stanford: Stanford University Press.

Agier, M. (2002a) 'Between war and city: Towards an urban anthropology of refugee camps', translated by R. Nice and L. Wacquant, *Ethnography*, 3(3): 317–341.

Agier, M. (2002b) 'Still stuck between war and city: A response to Bauman and Malkki', translated by R. Nice and L. Wacquant, *Ethnography*, 3(3): 361–366.

Agier, M., and Lecadet, C. (2014) *Un monde de camps*. Paris: La Découverte.

Ahad, A.M. (2015) *Somali Oral Poetry and the Failed She-Camel Nation State: A Critical Discourse Analysis of the Deelley Poetry Debate (1979–1980)*. New York: Peter Lang.

REFERENCES

Ahmad, A. (2015) 'The security bazaar: business interests and Islamist power in civil war Somalia', *International Security*, 39(3): 89–117.

Ahmed, A.J. (ed) (1995) *The Invention of Somalia*. Trenton: The Red Sea Press.

Ahmed, I.I. (2000) 'Remittances and their economic impact in post-war Somaliland', *Disasters*, 24(4): 380–389.

Aidid, S. (2015) 'Can the Somali speak?', Africa Is a Country, 30 March, Available from: https://africasacountry.com/2015/03/can-the-somali-speak-cadaanstudies [Accessed 20 May 2020].

Al-Bulushi, S. (2014) '"Peacekeeping" as occupation: Managing the market for violent labor in Somalia', *Transforming Anthropology*, 22(1): 31–37.

Ali, N. (2016) 'Parents in Somaliland are going to great lengths to stop their children from migrating to Europe', Africa at LSE, 8 June, Available from: https://blogs.lse.ac.uk/africaatlse/2016/06/08/parents-in-somalil and-are-going-to-great-lengths-to-stop-their-children-from-migrating-to-europe/ [Accessed 1 June 2021].

Ali, N. and Rift Valley Institute (2016) 'Going on Tahriib: The Causes and Consequences of Somali Youth Migration to Europe', Nairobi: Rift Valley Institute.

Amis, P. (1984) 'Squatters or tenants: The commercialization of unauthorized housing in Nairobi', *World Development,* 12(1): 87–96.

Amnesty International (2017) 'Not time to go home: unsustainable returns of refugees to Somalia', 21 December, Available from: https://www.amne sty.org/en/documents/afr52/7609/2017/en/ [Accessed 4 August 2021].

Andreucci, D., García-Lamarca, M., Wedekind, J. and Swyngedouw, E. (2017) '"Value grabbing": A political ecology of rent', *Capitalism Nature Socialism,* 28(3): 28–47. https://doi.org/10.1080/10455752.2016.1278027.

Appadurai, A. (1996) *Modernity at Large: Cultural Dimensions of Globalization*, Minneapolis: University of Minnesota Press.

Appel H (2012) Offshore work: Oil, modularity, and the how of capitalism in Equatorial Guinea. *American Ethnologist* 39(4): 692–709.

Apthorpe, R. (2005) 'Postcards from Aidland, Or: Love from Bubbleland', Graduate seminar paper, IDS, University of Sussex (10) 2005.

Asaka, J.O. and Smucker, T.A. (2016) 'Assessing the role of mobile phone communication in drought-related mobility patterns of Samburu pastoralists', *Journal of Arid Environments*, 128: 12–16.

Atkinson, R. and Bridge, G. (eds) (2005) *Gentrification in a Global Context*, London: Routledge.

Awotwi, J., Ojo, A. and Janowski, T. (2011) 'Mobile governance for development: Strategies for migrant head porters in Ghana'. 5th International Conference on Theory and Practice of Electronic Governance (ICEGOV2011), Tallinn, ACM International Conference Proceeding Series: 175–184.

Baird, T.D. and Hartter, J. (2017) 'Livelihood diversification, mobile phones and information diversity in Northern Tanzania', *Land Use Policy*, 67: 460–471.

Bakewell, O. (2008a) 'Research beyond the categories: The importance of policy irrelevant research into forced migration', *Journal of Refugee Studies*, 21(4): 432–453.

Bakewell, O. (2008b) '"Keeping them in their place": The ambivalent relationship between development and migration in Africa', *Third World Quarterly*, 29(7): 1341–1358.

Bakewell, O. and Jónsson, G. (2011) 'Migration, mobility and the African city'. Oxford: International Migration Institute.

Bakonyi, J. (2009) 'Moral economies of mass violence: Somalia 1988–1991', *Civil Wars*, 11(4): 434–454.

Bakonyi, J. (2011) *Land ohne Staat. Wirtschaft und Gesellschaft im Krieg am Beispiel Somalias*. Frankfurt am Main: Campus.

Bakonyi, J. (2013) 'Authority and administration beyond the state: Local governance in southern Somalia, 1995–2006', *Journal of Eastern African Studies*, 7(2): 272–290.

Bakonyi, J. (2018) 'Seeing like bureaucracies: rearranging knowledge and ignorance in Somalia', *International Political Sociology*, 12(3): 256–273.

Bakonyi, J. (2021) 'The political economy of displacement: Rent seeking, dispossession and precarious mobility in Somali cities', *Global Policy*, 12(S2): 10–22.

Bakonyi, J. (2022a) 'Modular sovereignty and infrastructural Power: The elusive materiality of international statebuilding', *Security Dialogue*, 53(3): 256–278.

Bakonyi, J. (2022b) 'War's Everyday: Normalizing Violence and Legitimizing Power', *Partecipazione & Conflitto*, 15(1): 121–138.

Bakonyi, J. and Bliesemann de Guevara, B. (2009) 'The mosaic of violence – An introduction', *Civil Wars*, 11(4): 397–413.

Bakonyi, J. and Chonka, P. (2019) 'Precarious labour – precarious lives: Photographic glimpses from displaced people in Somali cities', *Afrique contemporaine*, 2019/1(269–270): 205–224.

Bakonyi, J., Chonka, P. and Stuvøy, K. (2019) 'War and city-making in Somalia: Property, power and disposable lives', *Political Geography*, 73: 82–91.

Bakonyi, J., Kappler, S, Nag E-M. and Opfermann, L. (2021) 'Precarity, mobility and the City: Introduction to the Special Issue', *Global Policy*, 12(S2): 5–9.

Balthasar, D. (2013) 'Somaliland's best kept secret: Shrewd politics and war projects as means of state-making', *Journal of Eastern African Studies*, 7(2): 218–238.

Barnes, C. (2006) 'U dhashay—Ku dhashay: Genealogical and territorial discourse in Somali history', *Social Identities*, 12: 487–498.

Barnes, C. and Hassan, H. (2007) 'The rise and fall of Mogadishu's Islamic courts', *Journal of Eastern African Studies,* 1(2): 151–160.

Barnes, J. and Alatout, S. (2012) 'Water worlds: Introduction to the special issue of *Social Studies of Science*', *Social Studies of Science,* 42(4): 483–488.

Barry, A. (2020) 'The Material Politics of Infrastructure' in S. Maasen, S. Dickel and C. Schneider (eds) *TechnoScienceSociety: Technological Reconfigurations of Science and Society*, Heidelberg: Springer, pp 91–109.

Bartlett, A., Alix-Garcia, J. and Saah, D. S. (2012) 'City growth under conflict conditions: The view from Nyala, Darfur', *City and Community,* 11(2): 151–170.

Bauman, Z. (2002) 'In the lowly nowherevilles of liquid modernity: Comments on and around Agier', *Ethnography,* 3(3): 343–349.

Bauman, Z. (2004) *Wasted Lives: Modernity and its Outcasts*. Cambridge: Polity.

Bayat, A. (2000) 'From "dangerous classes" to "quiet rebels": Politics of the urban subaltern in the global South', *International Sociology,* 15(3): 533–557.

Bayat, A. (2010) *Life as Politics: How Ordinary People Change the Middle East*. Amsterdam: Amsterdam University Press.

Bayart, J.F. (2000) 'Africa in the world: a history of extraversion', *African Affairs,* 99(395): 217–267.

Baxter, J., Gibson, D. and Lynch-Blosse, M. (1990) *Double Take: The Links Between Paid and Unpaid Work*. Canberra: Australian Government Publishing Service.

BBC Somali (2018) 'Nin loo gubay beeshiisa oo gabar ka guursatay beel ka mid ah kuwa ku xooggan Muqdisho' [Man burned because girl from his clan married into one of the dominant clans in Mogadishu], 21 September, Available from: https://www.bbc.com/somali/war-45602063 [Accessed 25 August 2021].

Beall, J., Goodfellow, T. and Rodgers, D. (2011) 'Cities, conflict and state fragility', working paper 85, London: Crisis States Research Centre.

Berns-McGown, R. (2016) 'Towards an academic praxis of integrity', *Journal of Somali Studies,* 3(1): 85–106.

Besteman, C. (1996) 'Representing violence and" othering" Somalia', *Cultural Anthropology,* 11(1): 120–133.

Besteman, C. (1998) 'Primordialist blinders: A reply to I.M. Lewis', *Cultural Anthropology,* 13(1): 109–120.

Besteman, C. (2017) 'Experimenting in Somalia: The new security empire', *Anthropological Theory,* 17(3): 404–420.

Besteman, C. and Cassanelli, L. (eds) (1996) *The Struggle for Land in Southern Somalia: The War Behind the War*. Boulder, CO: Westview Press.

Betts A., Bloom, L. and Weaver, N. (2015) *Refugee innovation: Humanitarian innovation that starts with communities*. Oxford: University of Oxford, Refugee Studies Centre.

Beveridge, R. and Koch, P. (2018) 'Urban everyday politics: Politicising practices and the transformation of the here and now', *Environment and Planning D: Society and Space,* 37(1): 142–157.

Bhabha, H.K. (2012) *The Location of Culture,* London: Routledge.

Bierschenk, T, Chauveau, J. P. and de Sardan, O. (2002) 'Local Development Brokers in Africa: The rise of a new category', Institut fuer Ethnology and Africa Studies, Working Papers 13.

Bjarnesen, J. and Turner, S. (eds) (2020) *Invisibility in African Displacements: From Structural Marginalization to Strategies of Avoidance.* London: Zed Books.

Blanchard, J-M.F. and Flint, C. (2017) 'The geopolitics of China's Maritime Silk Road initiative', *Geopolitics,* 22(2): 223–245.

Bliesemann de Guevara, B. and Bøås, M. (eds) (2020) *Doing Fieldwork in Areas of International Intervention: A Guide to Research in Violent and Closed Contexts.* Bristol: Bristol University Press.

Blomley, N. (2003) 'Law, property, and the geography of violence: The frontier, the survey, and the grid', *Annals of the Association of American Geographers,* 93(1): 121–141.

Blundo, G. and Le Meur, P-Y. (2008) 'Introduction: An Anthropology of Everyday Governance: Collective Service Delivery and Subject-Making' in G. Blundo and P-Y. Le Meur (eds) *The Governance of Daily Life in Africa: Ethnographic Explorations of Public and Collective Services,* Leiden: Brill, pp 1–37.

Boas, I. (2020) 'Social networking in a digital and mobile world: The case of environmentally-related migration in Bangladesh', *Journal of Ethnic and Migration Studies,* 46(7): 1330–1347.

Boltanski, L. (1999) *Distant Suffering: Morality, Media and Politics.* Cambridge: Cambridge University Press.

Borkert, M., Fisher, K.E. and Yafi, E. (2018) 'The best, the worst, and the hardest to find: How people, mobiles, and social media connect migrants in(to) Europe', *Social Media + Society,* 4(1): 1–11.

Bourdieu, P. (2001) *Meditationen. Zur Kritik der scholastischen Vernunft,* Frankfurt: Suhrkamp.

Bowker, G.C. and Star, S.L. (2000) *Sorting Things Out: Classification and Its Consequences.* Cambridge, MA: MIT Press.

Bradbury, M. (2008) *Becoming Somaliland.* London: James Currey.

Brankamp, H. (2020) 'Refugees in uniform: Community policing as a technology of government in Kakuma refugee camp, Kenya', *Journal of Eastern African Studies,* 14(2): 270–290.

Brenner, N. (ed) (2014) *Implosions/Explosions: Towards a Study of Planetary Urbanization.* Berlin: Jovis.

Brenner, N. and Schmid, C. (2012) 'Planetary Urbanization' in M. Gandy (ed) *Urban Constellations.* Berlin: Jovis, pp 10–13.

Brenner, N. and Schmid, C. (2015) 'Towards a new epistemology of the urban?', *City,* 19(2–3): 151–182.

Brenner, N., Peck, J. and Theodore, N. (2010) 'Variegated neoliberalization: Geographies, modalities, pathways', *Global Networks,* 10(2): 182–222.

Brinkerhoff, J.M. (2009) *Digital Diasporas: Identity and Transnational Engagement.* Cambridge: Cambridge University Press.

Brinkman, I., Both, J. and De Bruijn, M. (2017) 'The mobile phone and society in South Sudan: A critical historical-anthropological approach', *Journal of African Media Studies,* 9(2): 323–337.

Brun, C. (2010) 'Hospitality: Becoming 'IDPs' and 'Hosts' in Protracted Displacement', *Journal of Refugees Studies,* 23(3): 337–355.

Brun, C. (2016) 'Dwelling in the Temporary: The involuntary mobility of displaced Georgians in rented accommodation', *Cultural Studies,* 30(3): 421–440.

Burton, J. (2020) '"Doing no harm" in the digital age: What the digitalization of cash means for humanitarian action', *International Review of the Red Cross,* 102(913): 43–73.

Büscher, K. (2018) 'African cities and violent conflict: The urban dimension of conflict and post conflict dynamics in Central and Eastern Africa', *Journal of Eastern African Studies,* 12(2): 193–210.

Büscher, K., and Vlassenroot, K. (2010) 'Humanitarian presence and urban development: New opportunities and contrasts in Goma, DRC', *Disasters,* 34(2): 256–273.

Büscher, K., Komujuni, S. and Ashaba, I. (2018) 'Humanitarian urbanism in a post-conflict aid town: Aid agencies and urbanization in Gulu, Northern Uganda', *Journal of Eastern African Studies*: 12(2): 348–366.

Butler, J. (1990) *Gender Trouble: Feminism and the Subversion of Identity.* New York: Routledge.

Butler, J. (2006) *Precarious Life: The Powers of Mourning and Violence.* New York: Verso.

Butler, J. (2009) 'Performativity, precarity and sexual politics', *AIBR, Revista de Antropología Iberoamericana,* 4(3): i–xiii.

Butt, B. (2015) 'Herding by mobile phone: Technology, social networks and the "transformation" of pastoral herding in East Africa', *Human Ecology,* 43(1): 1–14.

Butz, D. and Cook, N. (2017) 'The epistemological and ethical value of autophotography for mobilities research in transcultural contexts', *Studies in Social Justice,* 11(2): 238–274.

Cadman, L. (2009) 'Nonrepresentational theory/Nonrepresentational geographies' in R. Kitchin and N. Thrift (eds) *International Encyclopedia of Human Geography* (1st ed), Oxford: Elsevier, pp 456–463.

Carrier, N. (2016) *Little Mogadishu: Eastleigh, Nairobi's Global Somali Hub*. London: Hurst.

Carrier, N., and Scharrer, T. (eds) (2019) *Mobile Urbanity: Somali Presence in Urban East Africa*. Oxford: Berghahn Books.

Cassanelli, L. (2015) *Hosts and guests: A historical interpretation of land conflicts in southern and central Somalia*. Nairobi: Rift Valley Institute.

Cassanelli, L., and Abdikadir, F.S. (2008) 'Somalia: Education in transition', *Bildhaan: An International Journal of Somali Studies*, 7(1): 91–125.

Castleden, H., and Garvin, T. (2008) 'Modifying photovoice for community-based participatory Indigenous research', *Social Science & Medicine*, 66(6): 1393–1405.

Cartier, C., Castells, M. and Qiu, J.L. (2005) 'The information have-less: Inequality, mobility, and translocal networks in Chinese cities', *Studies in Comparative International Development*, 40: 9–34.

Chandler, D. and Reid, J. (2016) *The Neoliberal Subject: Resilience, Adaptation and Vulnerability*. Lanham: Rowman and Littlefield.

Chant, S. and McIlwaine, C. (2016) *Cities, Slums and Gender in the Global South: Towards a Feminised Urban Future*, London and New York: Routledge.

Charmarkeh, H. (2013) 'Social media usage, tahriib (migration), and settlement among Somali refugees in France', *Refuge: Canada's Journal on Refugees*, 29(1): 43–52.

Chonka, P. (2018) 'New media, performative violence, and state reconstruction in Mogadishu', *African Affairs*, 117(468): 392–414.

Chonka, P. (2019a) '#Bookfairs: New 'old' media and the digital politics of Somali literary promotion', *New Media and Society*, 21(11–12): 2628–2647.

Chonka, P. (2019b) 'The Empire tweets back? #HumanitarianStarWars and memetic self-critique in the aid industry', *Social Media + Society*, 5(4): 1–13.

Chonka, P. (2019c) 'News media and political contestation in the Somali territories: defining the parameters of a transnational digital public', *Journal of Eastern African Studies*, 13(1): 140–157.

Chonka, P. and Bakonyi, J. (2021) 'Precarious technoscapes: forced mobility and mobile connections at the urban margins', *Journal of the British Academy* 9 (S11): 67–91.

Chonka, P., Edle, A. and Stuvøy, K. (2022) 'Eyes on the ground and eyes in the sky: Security narratives, participatory visual methods, and knowledge production in "danger zones', *Security Dialogue:* 1–22.

Chouliaraki, L. (2010) 'Post-humanitarianism: Humanitarian communication beyond a politics of pity', *International Journal of Cultural Studies*, 13(2): 107–126.

Chua, C., Danyluk, M., Cowen, D. and Khalili, L. (2018) 'Introduction: Turbulent circulation: Building a critical engagement with logistics', *Environment and Planning D: Society and Space*, 36(4): 617–629.

Coetzee, C. (2019) 'Ethical?! Collaboration?! Keywords for our contradictory times', *Journal of African Cultural Studies*, 31(3): 257–264.

Collier, S. and Lakoff, A. (2005) 'On Regimes of Living' in A. Ong and S. Collier (eds), *Global Assemblages: Technology, Politics, and Ethics in Anthropological Problems*, Malden: Blackwell, pp 22–39.

Collins, G. (2009). 'Connected: Exploring the extraordinary demand for telecoms services in post-collapse Somalia', *Mobilities*, 4(2): 203–223.

Compagnon, D. (1998) 'Somali armed units: The interplay of political entrepreneurship and clan-based factions' in C. Clapham (ed) *African Guerrillas*, London: James Currey, pp 73–90.

Cowen, D. (2014) *The Deadly Life of Logistics: Mapping Violence in Global Trade*, Minneapolis: University of Minnesota Press.

Crawley, H. and Skleparis, D. (2018) 'Refugees, migrants, neither, both: Categorical fetishism and the politics of bounding in Europe's "migration crisis"', *Journal of Ethnic and Migration Studies*, 44(1): 48–64.

Crisp, J. (2015) 'Zaatari: A camp and not a city', Urban Refugees, 13 October, Available from: http://www.urban-refugees.org/debate/zaatari-camp-city/ [Accessed 25 March 2019].

Cronin-Furman K. and Lake M. (2018) 'Ethics abroad: Fieldwork in fragile and violent contexts', *PS: Political Science and Politics*, 51(3): 607–614.

Dahir, A.L. and Kazeem, Y. (2017) 'Homegrown technology is being used to help millions at risk from a devastating famine in Africa', Quartz Africa, 23 March, Available from: https://qz.com/938093/homegrown-technology-is-being-used-to-help-millions-at-risk-from-a-devastating-famine-in-africa/ [Accessed 25 March 2019].

Dahya, N. and Dryden-Peterson, S. (2017) 'Tracing pathways to higher education for refugees: The role of virtual support networks and mobile phones for women in refugee camps', *Comparative Education*, 53(2): 284–301.

Dalal, A. (2015) 'A socio-economic perspective on the urbanization of Zaatari Camp in Jordan', *Migration Letters*, 12(3): 263–278.

Danielak, S. (2020) 'Conflict urbanism: Reflections on the role of conflict and peacebuilding in post-apartheid Johannesburg', *Peacebuilding*, 8(4): 447–459.

Danyluk, M. (2017) 'Capital's logistical fix: Accumulation, globalization, and the survival of capitalism', *Environment and Planning D: Society and Space*, 36(4): 630–647.

Darling, J. (2017) 'Forced migration and the city: Irregularity, informality, and the politics of presence', *Progress in Human Geography*, 41(2): 178–198.

de Bruijn, M., Nyamnjoh, F. and Angwafo, T. (2010) 'Mobile interconnections: Reinterpreting distance, relating and difference in the Cameroonian Grassfields', *Journal of African Media Studies*, 2(3): 267–285.

de Certeau, M. (1984) *The Practice of Everyday Life*. Berkeley, Los Angeles: University of California Press.

de Haas, H. (2007) 'Remittances, migration and social development', *Social Policy and Development Programme Paper Number 34*, United Nations Research Institute for Social Development.

de Waal, A. (1997) *Famine Crimes: Politics and the Disaster Relief Industry in Africa*. Bloomington: Indiana University Press.

Debsu, D.N., Little, P.D., Tiki, W., Guagliardo, S.A.J. and Kitron, U. (2016) 'Mobile phones for mobile people: The role of information and communication technology (ICT) among livestock traders and Borana pastoralists of Southern Ethiopia', *Nomadic Peoples*, 20(1): 35–61.

Declich, F. (1995) 'Identity, dance and Islam among people with Bantu origins in riverine areas of Somalia', in A.J. Ahmed (ed) *The Invention of Somalia*. Trenton: The Red Sea Press.

Dekker, R. and Engbersen, G. (2014) 'How social media transform migrant networks and facilitate migration', *Global Networks*, 14(4): 401–418.

Del Ministro, T. (2021) 'Unraveling spaces of exceptions through durable solutions', *Global Policy*, 12(2): 23–27.

Denov, M., Doucet, D. and Kamara, A. (2012) 'Engaging war affected youth through photography: Photovoice with former child soldiers in Sierra Leone', *Intervention: International Journal of Mental Health, Psychosocial Work and Counselling in Areas of Armed Conflict*, 10(2): 117–133.

Desai, R., McFarlane, C. and Graham, S. (2015) 'The politics of open defecation: Informality, body, and infrastructure in Mumbai', *Antipode*, 47(1): 98–120.

Diken, B. (2004) 'From refugee camps to gated communities: Biopolitics and the end of the city', *Citizenship Studies*, 8(1): 83–106.

Dillon, M. (2004) 'The security of governance' in W. Larner and W. Walters (eds) *Global Governmentality: Governing International Spaces*, London: Routledge, pp 76–94.

Diminescu, D. (2008) 'The connected migrant: An epistemological manifesto', *Social Science Information*, 47(4): 565–579.

Djohy, G., Edja, H. and Schareika, N. (2017) 'Mobile phones and socioeconomic transformation among Fulani pastoralists in Northern Benin', *Nomadic Peoples*, 21(1): 111–135.

Dodsworth, S. and Cheeseman N. (2018) 'The potential and pitfalls of collaborating with development organizations and policy makers in Africa', *African Affairs*, 117(466): 130–145.

Douglas, M. (1970) *Purity and Danger: An Analysis of Concepts of Pollution and Taboo*, London: Penguin.

Duale, A. (2011) 'How displaced communities use technology to access financial services', *Forced Migration Review*, 38: 28–29.

Duffield M. (2013) 'Disaster-resilience in the network age: Access-denial and the rise of cyber-humanitarianism', *DIIS Working Paper 2013/23*, Copenhagen: Danish Institute for International Studies.

Duffield, M. (2018) *Post-Humanitarianism: Governing Precarity in the Digital World*. Cambridge: Polity Press.

El-Bushra, J. and Gardner, J. (2016) 'The impact of war on Somali men: Feminist analysis of masculinities and gender relations in a fragile context', *Gender and Development*, 24(3): 443–458.).

Engle Merry, S. (2006) 'Transnational human rights and local activism: Mapping the middle', *American Anthropologist*, 108(1): 38–51.

Eno, M.A., and Kusow, A.M. (2014) 'Racial and caste prejudice in Somalia', *Journal of Somali Studies* 1(2): 91–118.

Eno, M.A., Dammak, A. and Eno, O.A. (2016) 'From linguistic imperialism to language domination: "Linguicism" and ethno-linguistic politics in Somalia', *Journal of Somali Studies*, 3(1): 9–52.

Eno, O.A., Eno, M.A. and Van Lehman, D.J. (2010) 'Defining the problem in Somalia: Perspectives from the southern minorities', *Journal of the Anglo-Somali Society*, 47: 19–30.

Enns, C., and Bersaglio, B. (2020) 'On the coloniality of "new" mega-infrastructure projects in East Africa', *Antipode*, 52(1): 101-123.

Eriksson Baaz, M., and Verweijen, J. (2018) 'Confronting the colonial: The (re)production of "African" exceptionalism in critical security and military studies', *Security Dialogue*, 49(1–2): 57–69.

Ettlinger, N. (2007) 'Precarity unbound', *Alternatives*, 32(3): 319–340.

Ettlinger, N. and Bose, D. (2020) 'The ordinariness of struggle and exclusion: A view from across the north–south urban "divide"', *Cambridge Journal of Regions, Economy and Society*, 13(3): 509–526.

Evans-Agnew, R.A. and Rosemberg, M-A.S. (2016) 'Questioning photovoice research: Whose voice?', *Qualitative Health Research*, 26(8): 1019–1030.

Ezeh, A., Oyebode, O., Satterthwaite, D., Chen, Y-F., Ndugwa, R., Sartori, J., Mberu, B., Melendez-Torres, G.J., Haregu, T., Watson, S.I., Caiaffa, W., Capon, A. and Lilford, R. (2017) 'The history, geography, and sociology of slums and the health problems of people who live in slums', *The Lancet*, 389(10068): 547–558.

Fahim, K. (2021) 'In Syria's war without end, refugee tent camps harden into concrete cities', Washington Post [online], 19 July, Available from: https://www.washingtonpost.com/world/middle_east/idlib-syria-war-refugees/2021/07/19/db8d514e-e0e2-11eb-a27f-8b294930e95b_story.html [Accessed 26 July 2021].

Federal Government of Somalia (FGS), (2021) 'Somalia: The National Durable Solutions Strategy 2020–2024', Available from: https://data.unhcr.org/en/documents/details/85880 [Accessed 13 August 2021].

Feldman, B. (2007) 'Somalia: Amidst the rubble, a vibrant telecommunications infrastructure', *Review of African Political Economy*, 34(113): 565–572.

Foucault, M. (1998) 'Polemics, politics and problematizations: An interview by Paul Rabinow, May 1984', in *Ethics: Subjectivity and Truth, (Essential Works of Michel Foucault, 1954–1984, Vol. 1)*. New York: The New Press, pp 381–390.

Frouws, B., Phillips, M., Hassan, A. and Twigt, M. (2016) 'Getting to Europe the "WhatsApp" way: The use of ICT in contemporary mixed migration flows to Europe', Briefing Paper 2, Regional Mixed Migration Secretariat.

Fukui, R. and Arderne, C.J. (2018) 'Mogadishu's first tech hub', World Bank Blogs, 25 June, Available from: https://blogs.worldbank.org/digital-development/mogadishu-s-first-tech-hub [Accessed 24 August 2021].

Furlong, K. (2014) 'STS beyond the "modern infrastructure ideal": Extending theory by engaging with infrastructure challenges in the South', *Technology in Society*, 38: 139–147.

Gandy, M. (2004) 'Rethinking urban metabolism: Water, space and the modern city', *City*, 8(3): 363–379.

Gebresenbet, F. and Wondemagegnehu, D.Y. (2021) 'New dimensions in the Grand Ethiopian Renaissance Dam negotiations: Ontological security in Egypt and Ethiopia', *African Security* 14(1): 80–106.

Gillespie, M., Ampofo, L., Cheesman, M., Faith, B., Iliadou, E., Issa, A., Osseiran, S. and Skleparis, D. (2016) 'Mapping Refugee Media Journeys: Smartphones and Social Media Networks', Milton Keynes: Open University/France Médias Monde.

Gilroy, P. (2001) *Against Race: Imagining Political Culture beyond the Color Line*. Cambridge, MA: Harvard University Press.

Goodfellow, T. (2020) 'Finance, infrastructure and urban capital: The political economy of African "gap-filling"', *Review of African Political Economy*, 47(164): 256–274.

Graham, S. (ed) (2010) *Disrupted Cities: When Infrastructure Fails*. London: Routledge.

Green, E. and Kloos, B. (2009) 'Facilitating youth participation in a context of forced migration: A photovoice project in northern Uganda', *Journal of Refugee Studies*, 22(4): 460–482.

Gregory, D. (2011) 'From a view to a kill: Drones and late modern war', *Theory, Culture & Society*, 28(7–8): 188–215.

Gupta, A. and Ferguson, J. (1997) 'Discipline and Practice: "The Field" as Site, Method, and Location in Anthropology' in A. Gupta and J. Ferguson (eds) *Anthropological Locations: Boundaries and Grounds of a Field Science*. Berkeley: University of California Press, pp 1–46.

Hagmann, T. (2016) *Stabilization, extraversion and political settlements in Somalia*. Nairobi: Rift Valley Institute.

Hagmann, T. and Stepputat, F. (2016) 'Corridors of trade and power: Economy and state formation in Somali East Africa', *DIIS-GOVSEA Working Paper 2016/8*, Copenhagen: Danish Institute for International Studies.

REFERENCES

Hagmann, T., et al. (2022) *Commodified Cities – Urbanization and public goods in Somalia*. Nairobi: Rift Valley Institute.

Hahn, H.P. (2010) 'Urban life-worlds in motion: In Africa and beyond', *Africa Spectrum*, 45(3): 115–129.

Hahn, H.P. and Kibora, L. (2008) 'The domestication of the mobile phone: Oral society and new ICT in Burkina Faso', *The Journal of Modern African Studies*, 46(1): 87–109.

Haji, A. (2019) 'Somalia—Data Protection Overview', Data Guidance, 24 August 2020, Available from: https://www.dataguidance.com/notes/somalia-data-protection-overview [Accessed 24 August 2021].

Hammar, A. (2014) 'Displacement economies: paradoxes of crisis and creativity in Africa', in A. Hammar (ed) *Displacement Economies in Africa: Paradoxes of Crisis and Creativity*. London and New York: Zed Books, pp 3–32.

Hammond, L. (2013) 'Somalia rising: things are starting to change for the world's longest failed state', *Journal of Eastern African Studies*, 7(1): 183-193.

Hanlon, T.M., Richmond, A.K., Shelzi, J. and Myers, G. (2019) 'Cultural identity in the peri-urban African landscape: A case study from Pikine, Senegal', *African Geographical Review*, 38(2): 157–171.

Hansen, P. (2007) 'Revolving returnees: Meanings and practices of transnational return among Somalilanders', PhD thesis, Department of Anthropology, University of Copenhagen.

Hansen, S.J. (2013) *Al-Shabaab in Somalia: The History and Ideology of a Militant Islamist Group*. Oxford: Oxford University Press.

Harley A. (2012) 'Picturing reality: Power, ethics, and politics in using photovoice', *International Journal of Qualitative Methods*, 11(4): 320–339.

Harvey, D. (1982) *The Limits to Capital*. Oxford: Basil Blackwell.

Hasdell, P. (2016) 'Liminal urbanism: The emergence of new urban "states"', Contested Cities Working Paper Series, IV-1A(1-0003): 1–12.

Hatayama, M. (2018) 'ICTs and livelihood supports of refugees and IDPs'. K4D helpdesk report, Department for International Development, Available from: https://assets.publishing.service.gov.uk/media/5c6c01dd40f0b61a20f90f3f/504_ICTs_and_Livehoods_of_Refugees_and_IDPs.pdf [Accessed 28 September 2020].

Helander, B. (1997) 'Clanship, Kinship and Community Among the Rahanweyn: A Model for Other Somalis' in H.M. Adam and R. Ford (eds) *Mending Rips in the Sky: Options for Somali Communities in the 21st Century*. Trenton: Red Sea Press.

Hendriks, S. (2019) 'The role of financial inclusion in driving women's economic empowerment', *Development in Practice*, 29(8): 1029–1038.

Herz, M. (ed) (2012) *From Camp to City: Refugee Camps of the Western Sahara*. Zurich: Lars Müller.

Hiiraan (2021) 'Mudug governor condemns Somaliland's deportation of people from southwestern Somalia', Hiiraan Online, 3 October, Available from: https://www.hiiraan.com/news4/2021/Oct/184121/mudug_governor_condemns_somaliland_s_deportation_of_people_from_southwestern_somalia.aspx [Accessed 25 April 2022].

Hill, M. (2010) 'No redress: Somalia's forgotten minorities', Minority Rights Group International report, London: Minority Rights Group International.

Hiller, H.H. and Franz, T.M. (2004) 'New ties, old ties and lost ties: The use of the internet in diaspora', *New Media and Society*, 6(6): 731–752.

Ho, S. (2020) 'Infrastructure and Chinese power', *International Affairs*, 96(6): 1461–1485.

Hoehne, M. V. (2013) 'Limits of hybrid political orders: The case of Somaliland', *Journal of Eastern African Studies*, 7(2): 199–217.

Hoehne, M.V. (2016) 'The rupture of territoriality and the diminishing relevance of cross-cutting ties in Somalia after 1990', *Development and Change*, 47(6): 1379–1411.

Holston, J. and Appadurai, A. (1996) 'Cities and citizenship', *Public Culture*, 8: 187–204.

Horst, C. (2007) *Transnational Nomads: How Somalis Cope with Refugee Life in the Dadaab Camps of Kenya*. New York: Berghahn Books.

Horst, C. and Nur, A.I. (2016) 'Governing mobility through humanitarianism in Somalia: Compromising protection for the sake of return', *Development and Change*, 47(3): 542–562.

Horst, H.A. (2006) 'The blessings and burdens of communication: Cell phones in Jamaican transnational social fields', *Global Networks*, 6(2): 143–159.

Hounsell, B. and Owuor, J. (2018) 'Innovating mobile solutions for refugees in East Africa', Available from https://www.samuelhall.org/s/Innovating_mobile_soultions_report_2018.pdf [Accessed 16 July 2020].

Howe, P. (2019) 'The triple nexus: A potential approach to supporting the achievement of the Sustainable Development Goals?', *World Development*, 124 (article 104629).

Hughes, N. and Lonie, S. (2007) 'M-PESA: Mobile money for the "unbanked": Turning cellphones into 24-hour tellers in Kenya', *Innovations: Technology, Governance, Globalization*, 2(1–2): 63–81.

Hujale, M. (2021) 'Displaced Somalis and refugees struggle to recover as climate change brings new threats', 17 August, Available from: https://www.unhcr.org/news/stories/2021/8/611a2bca4/displaced-somalis-refugees-struggle-recover-climate-change-brings-new-threats.html [Accessed 22 April 2022].

Human Rights Watch (HRW) (2020) 'Letter to Somalia Authorities on Gololey Investigations', 5 October, Available from: https://www.hrw.org/news/2020/11/20/letter-somalia-authorities-gololey-investigations [Accessed 31 July 2021].

Huq, E. and Miraftab, F. (2020) ' "We are all refugees": Camps and informal settlements as converging spaces of global displacements', *Planning Theory & Practice,* 21(3): 351–370.

Hutcheon, L. (1993) 'Beginning to theorize postmodernism', in J.P. Natoli and L. Hutcheon (eds) *A Postmodern Reader.* Albany: SUNY Press, pp 243–272.

Iazzolino, G. (2015) *Following Mobile Money in Somaliland.* Nairobi: Rift Valley Institute.

Idris Haji, H. (2012) 'Economic Migrants or Internal Displaced Persons? An Empirical Analysis of Urban IDPs in Bosaso City', MA thesis, Aarlborg University, Denmark.

Ikanda, F.N. (2019) 'Forging associations across multiple spaces: How Somali kinship practices sustain the existence of the Dadaab Camps in Kenya' in J.D. Schmidt, L. Kimathi and M.O. Owiso (eds) *Refugees and Forced Migration in the Horn and Eastern Africa: Trends, Challenges and Opportunities.* Springer International Publishing, pp 287–304.

Ingiriis, M.H. (2020) 'The anthropology of Al-Shabaab: The salient factors for the insurgency movement's recruitment project', *Small Wars & Insurgencies,* 31(2): 359–380.

Inter-Agency Standing Committee (IASC) (2010) 'IASC Framework on Durable Solutions for Internally Displaced Persons', Available from: https://www.unhcr.org/50f94cd49.pdf [Accessed 26 August 2021].

Internal Displacement Monitoring Centre (2018) 'City of Flight: New and secondary displacements in Mogadishu, Somalia', Available from https://www.internal-displacement.org/sites/default/files/inline-files/201811-urban-displacement-mogadishu.pdf [Accessed 31 July 2021].

International Committee of the Red Cross (ICRC) (2018) 'ICRC staff member abducted in Somalia', 2 May, Available from: https://www.icrc.org/en/document/icrc-staff-member-abducted-somalia [Accessed 31 July 2021].

International Committee of the Red Cross (ICRC) and Privacy International (2018) 'The Humanitarian Metadata Problem – Doing No Harm in the Digital Era', 11 December, Available from: http://privacyinternational.org/report/2509/humanitarian-metadata-problem-doing-no-harm-digital-era [Accessed: 16 July 2020].

International Organization for Migration (IOM) (2021) 'IOM Somalia Relocates Nearly 7,000 Internally Displaced Families Facing Eviction', 9 March, Available from: https://reliefweb.int/report/somalia/iom-somalia-relocates-nearly-7000-internally-displaced-families-facing-eviction [Accessed 4 August 2021].

Jacobs, J.M. (1996) *Edge of Empire: Postcolonialism and the City.* London: Routledge.

Jaji, R. (2012) 'Social technology and refugee encampment in Kenya', *Journal of Refugee Studies*, 25(2): 221–238.

Jansen, B.J. (2016) 'The protracted refugee camp and the consolidation of a "humanitarian urbanism"', *International Journal of Urban and Regional Research*, Available from: https://www.ijurr.org/spotlight-on/the-urban-refugee-crisis-reflections-on-cities-citizenship-and-the-displaced/the-protracted-refugee-camp-and-the-consolidation-of-a-humanitarian-urbanism/.

Jansen, B.J. (2018) *Kakuma Refugee Camp: Humanitarian Urbanism in Kenya's Accidental City*. London: Zed Books.

Jaspars, S., Adan, G.M. and Majid, N. (2019) 'Food and power in Somalia: Business as usual? A scoping study on the political economy of food following shifts in food assistance and in governance', *Conflict Research Programme*, London: London School of Economics.

Jewitt, S. (2011) 'Geographies of shit: Spatial and temporal variations in attitudes towards human waste', *Progress in Human Geography*, 35(5): 608–626.

Johnsen S., May J. and Cloke P. (2008) 'Imag(in)ing "homeless places": Using auto-photography to (re)examine the geographies of homelessness', *Area*, 40(2): 194–207.

Joyce, P. (2003) *The Rule of Freedom: Liberalism and the Modern City*. London: Verso.

Kahiye, M. (2015) 'Mogadishu International Book Fair deemed a huge success', 31 August, Available from: http://www.warscapes.com/blog/mogadishu-international-book-fair-deemed-huge-success [Accessed 31 July 2021].

Kälin, W. (2019) 'Somalia: Displaced populations and urban poor no longer left behind', Available from: https://unsom.unmissions.org/sites/default/files/un_somalia_dsi_dis_pop.pdf [Accessed 8 August 2021].

Kalyvas, S.N. (2003) 'The ontology of "political violence": Action and identity in civil wars', *Perspectives on Politics,* 1(3): 475–494.

Kapteijns, L. (2012) *Clan Cleansing in Somalia: The Ruinous Legacy of 1991*. Philadelphia: University of Pennsylvania Press.

Kessi, S., Marks, Z. and Ramugondo, E. (2020) 'Decolonizing African Studies', *Critical African Studies,* 12(3): 271–282.

Komito, L. (2011) 'Social media and migration: Virtual community 2.0.', *Journal of the American Society for Information Science and Technology*, 62(6): 1075–1086.

Komunte, M. (2015) 'Usage of mobile technology in women entrepreneurs: A case study of Uganda', *The African Journal of Information Systems*, 7(3): 52–74.

Koshin, S.A. (2022) *Galkayo's khat economy: The role of women traders in Puntland, Somalia*. Nairobi: Rift Valley Institute.

Kundu, R. and Chatterjee, S. (2020) 'Pipe dreams? Practices of everyday governance of heterogeneous configurations of water supply in Baruipur, a small town in India', *Environment and Planning C: Politics and Space,* 39(2): 318–335.

Kusimba, S., Yang, Y. and Chawla, N. (2015) 'Family Networks of Mobile Money in Kenya', *Information Technologies and International Development,* 11(3): 1–21.

Kusow, A.M. (ed) (2004) *Putting the Cart before the Horse: Contested Nationalism and the Crisis of the Nation-state in Somalia.* Trenton: Red Sea Press.

Kusow, A.M., Eno, M.A. (2015) 'Formula narratives and the making of social stratification and inequality', *Sociology of Race and Ethnicity,* 1(3): 409–423.

Lawhon, M., Ernstson, H. and Silver, J. (2014) 'Provincializing urban political ecology: Towards a situated UPE through African urbanism', *Antipode,* 46(2): 497–516.

Lawhon, M., Nilsson, D., Silver, J., Ernstson, H. and Lwasa, S. (2017) 'Thinking through heterogeneous infrastructure configurations', *Urban Studies,* 55(4): 720–732.

Lefebvre, H. (1996) *Writings on Cities.* Oxford: Blackwell.

Lehman, D.V. and Eno, O. (2003) 'The Somali Bantu: Their History and Culture', Washington, DC: Center for Applied Linguistics, Cultural Orientation Resource Center, Available from: https://files.eric.ed.gov/fulltext/ED482784.pdf [Accessed 4 August 2021].

Lemke, T. (2005) 'A zone of indistinction: A critique of Giorgio Agamben's concept of biopolitics' *Outlines. Critical Practice Studies,* 7(1): 3-13.

Lennon, K. (2019) 'Feminist perspectives on the body ' in E.N. Zalta (ed) *The Stanford Encyclopedia of Philosophy* (Fall 2019 edn), Available from: https://plato.stanford.edu/archives/fall2019/entries/feminist-body/ [Accessed 28 March 2021].

Lesutis, G. (2018) 'The politics of narrative: Methodological reflections on analysing voices of the marginalized in Africa', *African Affairs,* 117(468): 509–521.

Lewis, I.M. (1994) *Blood and Bone: The Call of Kinship in Somali Society.* Trenton: The Red Sea Press.

Lewis, I.M. (1998) 'Doing violence to ethnography: A response to Catherine Besteman's "Representing violence and 'othering' Somalia"', *Cultural Anthropology,* 13(1): 100–108.

Lindley, A. (2009a) 'The early-morning phonecall: Remittances from a refugee diaspora perspective', *Journal of Ethnic and Migration Studies,* 35(8): 1315–1334.

Lindley, A. (2009b) 'Seeking refuge in an unrecognized state: Oromos in Somaliland', *Refuge: Canada's Journal on Refugees,* 26(1): 187–189.

Little, P.D. (2021) 'Trusting in Somalia's stateless money: The persistence of the Somali shilling', *African Affairs,* 120(478): 103–122.

Lochery, E. (2015) 'Generating power: Electricity provision and state formation in Somaliland', PhD thesis, Oxford University.

Long, K. (2012) 'Rethinking durable solutions for refugees' in G.K. Brown and A. Langer (eds) *Elgar Handbook of Civil War and Fragile States*, Cheltenham: Edward Elgar Publishing, pp 153–175.

Lubkemann, S.C. (2008) 'Involuntary immobility: On a theoretical invisibility in forced migration studies', *Journal of Refugee Studies,* 21(4): 454–475.

Luling, V. (1984) 'The other Somali: Minority groups in traditional Somali society', in *Proceedings of the Second International Congress of Somali Studies*, Hamburg: Helmut Buske Verlag, pp 39–55.

Luther, W.J. (2012) 'The monetary mechanism of stateless Somalia', SSRN Scholarly Paper ID 2047494. Social Science Research Network.

MacGinty, R., Brett, R. and Vogel, B. (eds) (2020) *The Companion to Peace and Conflict Fieldwork*. London: Palgrave Macmillan.

Maclean, K., and Woodward, E. (2013) 'Photovoice evaluated: An appropriate visual methodology for Aboriginal water resource research', *Geographical Research*, 51(1): 94–105.

Madianou, M. (2019) 'Technocolonialism: Digital innovation and data practices in the humanitarian response to refugee crises', *Social Media + Society*, 5(3): 1–13.

Madianou, M. and Miller, D. (2012) *Migration and New Media: Transnational Families and Polymedia*. London: Routledge.

Majid, N., Abdirahman, K. and Hassan S. (2018) 'Remittances and vulnerability in Somalia', Nairobi: Rift Valley Institute, Available from: https://riftvalley.net/publication/remittances-and-vulnerability-somalia [Accessed 14 May 2020].

Malkki, L. (2002) 'News from nowhere: Mass displacement and globalized "problems of organization"', *Ethnography,* 3(3): 351–360.

Manzo, K. (2008) 'Imaging humanitarianism: NGO identity and the iconography of childhood', *Antipode*, 40(4): 632–657.

Marchais, G. (2020) 'Contemporary research must stop relying on racial inequalities', *Africa at LSE*, 30 January, Available from https://blogs.lse.ac.uk/africaatlse/2020/01/30/research-must-stop-racial-inequalities-colonialism/ [Accessed 25 April 2020].

Marchal, R. (2002) *A Survey of Mogadishu's Economy*. Nairobi: European Commission/Somali Unit.

Marchal, R. (2010) 'The Puntland state of Somalia. A tentative social analysis', Paris: HaL Sciences Po, CERI: Centre d'études et de recherches internationales.

Martin, D (2015) 'From spaces of exception to "campscapes": Palestinian refugee camps and informal settlements in Beirut', *Political Geography*, 44: 9–18.

Massey, D. (1983) 'Industrial restructuring as class restructuring: Production decentralization and local uniqueness', *Regional Studies*, 17(2): 73–89.

Massey, D. (1991) 'A global sense of place', *Marxism Today*, June: 24–29.

Massey, D. (1996) 'Space/power, identity/difference: Tensions in the city' in A. Merrifield, and E. Swyngedouw (eds) *The Urbanization of Injustice*. London: Lawrence & Wishart, pp 100–117.

Massey, D. (2005) *For Space*. London: Sage.

Massy-Beresford, H. (2015) 'Where is the fastest growing city in the world?', *The Guardian* [online], 18 November, Available from: https://www.theguardian.com/cities/2015/nov/18/where-is-the-worlds-fastest-growing-city-batam-niamey-xiamen [Accessed 31 July 2021].

Mateja, P. and Strazzari, F. (2017) 'Securitization of research: Fieldwork under new restrictions in Darfur and Mali', *Third World Quarterly*, 38(7): 1531–1550.

Mayer-Schönberger, V. and Cukier, K. (2013) *Big Data: A Revolution That Will Transform How We Live, Work, and Think*, London: John Murray.

Mbatha, S. and Mchunu, K. (2016) 'Tracking peri-urban changes in eThekwini Municipality – beyond the "poor–rich" dichotomy', *Urban Research & Practice*, 9(3): 275–289.

Mbembe, A. (2000) 'At the edge of the world: Boundaries, territoriality, and sovereignty in Africa', *Public Culture*, 12(1): 259–284.

Mbembe, A. and Nuttall, S. (2004) 'Writing the world from an African metropolis', *Public Culture* 16(23): 347–372.

McCann, E., Roy, A. and Ward, K. (2013) 'Assembling/worlding cities', *Urban Geography*, 34(5): 581–589.

McFarlane, C. (2011) *Learning the City: Knowledge and Translocal Assemblage*. Chichester: Wiley-Blackwell.

McFarlane, C. (2018) 'Fragment urbanism: Politics at the margins of the city', *Environment and Planning D: Society and Space*, 36(6): 1007–1025.

McFarlane, C. (2019) 'The urbanization of the sanitation crisis: Placing waste in the city', *Development and Change*, 50(5): 1239–1262.

Meier, L. and Frank, S. (2016) 'Dwelling in mobile times: Places, practices and contestations', *Cultural Studies*, 30(3): 362–375.

Menkhaus, K. (2010) 'The question of ethnicity in Somali studies: The case of Somali Bantu identity', in M.V. Hoehne and V. Luling (eds) *Milk and Peace, Drought and War: Somali Culture, Society and Politics*. London: Hurst and Co, pp 87–104.

Mignolo, W.D. and Walsh, C.E. (2018) *On Decoloniality: Concepts, Analytics, Praxis*. Durham: Duke University Press.

Milko, V. and Hammond, C. (2019) 'The World's Largest Refugee Camp Is Becoming a Real City', Bloomberg UK, 27 September, Available from: https://www.bloomberg.com/news/articles/2019-09-27/how-the-rohingya-refugee-camp-turned-into-a-city [Accessed 27 August 2021].

Millar, K.M. (2017) 'Toward a critical politics of precarity', *Sociology Compass* 11(6), e12483.

Minca, C. (2015) 'Geographies of the camp', *Political Geography*, 49: 74–83.

Mire, H.Y. (2017) 'Qof Ma Dhiban: Somali Orality and the Delineation Of Power', Major Research Paper, York University, Toronto, Available from: https://yorkspace.library.yorku.ca/xmlui/handle/10315/34823 [Accessed 1 August 2021].

Mohamed, J. (2007) 'Kinship and contract in Somali politics', *Africa*, 77(2): 226–249.

Momodu, S. (2016) 'Somalia rising from the ashes', *Africa Renewal*, 30(1): 36–40.

Moran, D. (2013) 'Between outside and inside? Prison visiting rooms as liminal carceral spaces', *GeoJournal*, 78(2): 339–351.

Mosse, D. (ed) (2011) *Adventures in Aidland. The Anthropology of Professionals in International Development*, New York: Berghahn Books.

Muggah, R. and Abdenur, A.E. (2018) 'Refugees and the city: The twenty-first-century front line', World Refugee Council Research Paper No. 2, July, Available from: https://www.cigionline.org/publications/refugees-and-city-twenty-first-century-front-line/ [Accessed: 27 March 2019].

Müller, T.R. (2013) 'The long shadow of Band Aid humanitarianism: Revisiting the dynamics between famine and celebrity', *Third World Quarterly*, 34(3): 470–484.

Münch, P. and Veit, A. (2018) 'Intermediaries of intervention: How local power brokers shape external peace- and state-building in Afghanistan and Congo', *International Peacekeeping*, 25(2): 266–292.

Murphy, J. and McDowell, S. (2018) 'Transitional optics: Exploring liminal spaces after conflict', Urban Studies, 56(12): 2499–514.

Muto, M. (2012) 'The impacts of mobile phones and personal networks on rural-to-urban migration: Evidence from Uganda', *Journal of African Economies*, 21(5): 787–807.

Mwambari, D. and Owor, A. (2019) 'The black market of knowledge production', Governance in Conflict Network, 20 March, Available from: https://www.gicnetwork.be/the-black-market-of-knowledge-production/ [Accessed 25 April 2020].

Mwangi, O.G. (2010) 'The Union of Islamic Courts and security governance in Somalia', *African Security Review*, 19(1): 88–94.

Myers, G. (2011) *African Cities: Alternative Visions of Urban Theory and Practice*, London, New York: Zed Books.

Narotzky, S. and Besnier, N. (2014) 'Crisis, value, and hope: Rethinking the economy', *Current Anthropology* 55(S9): S4–S16.

Natile, S. (2020) *The Exclusionary Politics of Digital Financial Inclusion: Mobile Money, Gendered Walls*. London: Routledge.

Neves Alves, S. (2019) 'Everyday states and water infrastructure: Insights from a small secondary city in Africa, Bafatá in Guinea-Bissau', *Environment and Planning C: Politics and Space,* 39(2): 247–264.

Ngowi, E., Mwakalobo, A. and Mwamfupe, D. (2015) 'Making ICTs work for agro-pastoral livelihood: Using the telecentre as learning tool for agro-pastoralists communities in Tanzania', *Journal of Sustainable Development* 8(2): 89–98.

Nguya, G., and Siddiqui, N. (2020) 'Triple nexus implementation and implications for durable solutions for internal displacement: On paper and in practice', *Refugee Survey Quarterly,* 39(4): 466–480.

Nikielska-Sekula, K. (2021) '"Have you just taken a picture of me?": Theoretical and ethical implications of the use of researcher-produced photography in studying migrant minorities' in K. Nikielska-Sekula and A. Desille (eds) *Visual Methodology in Migration Studies: New Possibilities, Theoretical Implications, and Ethical Questions.* Cham: Springer International Publishing, pp 31–49.

Nordin, A.H.M. and Weissmann, M. (2018) 'Will Trump make China great again? The belt and road initiative and international order', *International Affairs,* 94(2): 231–249.

Norwegian Refugee Council (NRC) (2018) 'Back to square one: Post-eviction assessment in Somalia', Report, 25 January, Available from: https://www.nrc.no/resources/reports/back-to-square-one/ [Accessed 23 April 2019].

Nurhussein, S. (2008) 'Global networks, fragmentation, and the rise of telecommunications in stateless Somalia', MA thesis, University of Oregon.

Nyberg Sørensen, N. (2004) 'Opportunities and pitfalls in the migration-development nexus: Somaliland and beyond', *DIIS Working Paper 2004/21,* Copenhagen: Danish Institute for International Studies.

O'Reilly, K. (2010) 'Combining sanitation and women's participation in water supply: An example from Rajasthan', *Development in Practice,* 20(1): 45–56.

Oesch, L. (2017) 'The refugee camp as a space of multiple ambiguities and subjectivities', *Political Geography,* 60: 110–120.

Ogallo, L.A., Omondi, P., Ouma, G. and Wayumba, G. (2018) 'Climate change projections and the associated potential impacts for Somalia', *American Journal of Climate Change,* 7(2): 153–170.

Oiarzabal, P.J. and Reips, U.D. (2012) 'Migration and diaspora in the age of information and communication technologies', *Journal of Ethnic and Migration Studies,* 38(9): 1333–1338.

Oka, R. (2011) 'Unlikely cities in the desert: The informal economy as causal agent for permanent "urban" sustainability in Kakuma refugee camp, Kenya', *Urban Anthropology and Studies of Cultural Systems and World Economic Development,* 40(3–4): 223–262.

Ong, A. (2011) 'Introduction. Worlding cities, or the art of being global', in A. Roy and A. Ong (eds) *Worlding Cities: Asian Experiments and the Art of Being Global*. Oxford: Malden, Blackwell, pp 1–28.

Onitsuka, K. and Hidayat, A.R.R.T. (2019) 'Does ICT facilitate or impede rural youth migration in Indonesia?', Proceedings of the 9th International Conference Rural Research and Planning Group, Universitas Mahasaraswati Denpasar, Bali, 34–43.

Owino, B. (2020) 'Harmonising data systems for cash transfer programming in emergencies in Somalia', *Journal of International Humanitarian Action*, 5(1): 1-16.

Paris, R. (2001) 'Warten auf Amtsfluren', *Kölner Zeitschrift für Soziologie und Sozialpsychologie*, 53(4): 705–733.

Pech, L., Büscher, K. and Lakes, T. (2018) 'Intraurban development in a city under protracted armed conflict: Patterns and actors in Goma, DR Congo', *Political Geography*, 66: 98–112.

Pénicaud, C. and McGrath, F. (2013) 'Innovative inclusion: How Telesom ZAAD brought mobile money to Somaliland', GSMA Mobile for Development, Available from: https://www.gsma.com/mobilefordevelopment/wp-content/uploads/2013/07/Telesom-Somaliland.pdf [Accessed 24 August 2021].

Pérouse de Montclos, M-A. and Kagwanja, P.M. (2000) 'Refugee camps or cities? The socio-economic dynamics of the Dadaab and Kakuma camps in northern Kenya', *Journal of Refugee Studies*, 13(2): 205–222.

Picker, G., and Pasquetti, S. (2015) 'Durable camps: The state, the urban, the everyday', *City*, 19(5): 681–688.

Porter, G., Hampshire, K., Abane, A., Munthali, A., Robson, E., De Lannoy, A., Tanle, A. and Owusu, S. (2020) 'Mobile phones, gender, and female empowerment in sub-Saharan Africa: Studies with African youth', *Information Technology for Development*, 26(1): 180–193.

Potvin, M. (2013) 'Humanitarian urbanism under a neoliberal regime: Lessons from Kabul (2001–2011)', Paper presented at the International Resourceful Cities 21 Conference, Berlin, 29–31 August.

Pratt, A. (2019) 'Formality as exception', *Urban Studies*, 56(3): 612–615.

Purdeková, A. (2017) 'Respacing for peace? Resistance to integration and the ontopolitics of rural planning in post-war Burundi', *Development and Change*, 48(3): 534–566.

Rabinow, P. (1995) *French Modern: Norms and Forms of the Social Environment*. Chicago and London: The University of Chicago Press.

Rabinow, P. (2009) *Anthropos Today: Reflections on Modern Equipment*. Princeton: Princeton University Press.

Radjou, N. and Prabhu, J. (2015) *Frugal Innovation: How to Do Better with Less*. London: Profile Books.

Renders, M. (2012) *Consider Somaliland: State-Building with Traditional Leaders and Institutions* Leiden: Brill.

Richards, P. (ed) (2005) *No Peace, No War: The Anthropology of Contemporary Armed Conflicts*. London, James Currey.

Richardson, J. (2017) 'Precarious living in liminal spaces: Neglect of the Gypsy–Traveller site', *Global Discourse*, 7(4): 496–515.

Ritchie, H.A. (2022) 'An institutional perspective to bridging the divide: The case of Somali women refugees fostering digital inclusion in the volatile context of urban Kenya', *New Media & Society*, 24(2): 345–364.

Robinson, J. (2006) *Ordinary Cities: Between Modernism and Development*. London and New York: Routledge.

Robinson, J. (2011) 'Cities in a world of cities: The comparative gesture', *International Journal of Urban and Regional Research*, 35(1): 1–23.

Robinson, J. (2016) 'Thinking cities through elsewhere: Comparative tactics for a more global urban studies', *Progress in Human Geography*, 40(1): 3–29.

Rodgers, D. and O'Neill, B. (2012) 'Infrastructural violence: Introduction to the special issue', *Ethnography*, 13(4): 401–412.

Rose, G. (2016) *Visual Methodologies: An Introduction to Researching with Visual Materials* (4th edn). Los Angeles: Sage.

Rothe, D. (2017) 'Seeing like a satellite: Remote sensing and the ontological politics of environmental security', *Security Dialogue*, 48(4): 334–353.

Roy, A. (2010) *Poverty Capital: Microfinance and the Making of Development*. New York: Routledge.

Roy, A. (2011) 'Slumdog cities: Rethinking subaltern urbanism', *International Journal of Urban and Regional Research*, 35(2): 223–238.

Roy, A. (2016) 'Who's afraid of postcolonial theory?', *International Journal of Urban and Regional Research*, 40(1): 200–209.

Rift Valley Institute/Heritage Institute for Policy Studies (RVI/HIPS) (2017) 'Land matters in Mogadishu: Settlement, ownership and displacement in a contested city', Joint report, Nairobi: Rift Valley Institute.

RSF, Reporters Without Borders (2014), 'Al-Shabaab bans Internet in areas it controls', Available from: https://rsf.org/en/news/al-shabaab-bans-internet-areas-it-controls [Accessed 24 August 2021].

Saldarriaga, J. F., Kurgan, L. and Brawley, D. (2017) 'Visualizing conflict: Possibilities for urban research', *Urban Planning*, 2(1): 100–107.

Samara, T.R., He, S. and Chen, G. (eds) (2013) *Locating Right to the City in the Global South*, London: Routledge.

Samatar, A.I. (1989) *The State and Rural Transformation in Northern Somalia, 1884–1986*. Madison: University of Wisconsin Press.

Sanyal, R. (2016) 'From camps to urban refugees: Reflections on research agendas', *International Journal of Urban and Regional Research* [online], Available from: https://www.ijurr.org/spotlight-on/the-urban-refugee-crisis-reflections-on-cities-citizenship-and-the-displaced/from-camps-to-urban-refugees-reflections-on-research-agendas/ [Accessed 27 August 2021].

Schaub, M.L. (2012) 'Lines across the desert: Mobile phone use and mobility in the context of trans-Saharan migration', *Information Technology for Development*, 18(2): 126–144.

Schwarz, K.C. and Richey, L.A. (2019) 'Humanitarian humor, digilantism, and the dilemmas of representing volunteer tourism on social media', *New Media & Society*, 21(9): 1928–1946.

Scott, A. and Storper, M. (2015) 'The nature of cities: The scope and limits of urban theory', *International Journal of Urban and Regional Research*, 39(1): 1–15.

Scott, J.C. (1998) *Seeing Like a State: How Certain Schemes to Improve the Human Condition Have Failed.* New Haven: Yale University Press.

Scott, M. (2014) *Media and Development.* London: Zed Books.

Sheppard, E., Leitner, H. and Maringanti, A. (2013) 'Provincializing global urbanism: A manifesto', *Urban Geography,* 34(7): 893–900.

Sheriff, R.E. (2001) *Dreaming Equality: Color, Race, and Racism in Urban Brazil.* New Brunswick: Rutgers University Press.

SIDRA, Somali Institute for Development Research and Analysis (2019) 'Towards an improved understanding of vulnerability and resilience in Somalia' Report, June 2019, Available from: https://sidrainstitute.org/wp-content/uploads/2019/07/Report_Towards-an-improved-understanding-of-vulnerability-and-resilience-in-Somalia.pdf [Accessed 15 July 2022].

Simone, A. (2001) 'On the worlding of African cities', *African Studies Review,* 44(2): 15–41.

Simone, A. (2004) *For the City Yet to Come: Changing African Life in Four Cities.* Durham, NC: Duke University Press.

Simone, A. (2004) 'People as infrastructure: Intersecting fragments in Johannesburg', *Public Culture,* 16(3): 407–429.

Simone, A. (2018) *Improvised Lives: Rhythms of Endurance in an Urban South.* Cambridge: Polity Press.

Şimşek-Çağlar, A. and Glick Schiller, N. (2018) *Migrants and City-Making: Dispossession, Displacement, and Urban Regeneration.* Durham, NC: Duke University Press.

Skjelderup, M., Ainashe, M. and Abdulle "Qare" A.M. (2020) 'Militant Islamism and local clan dynamics in Somalia: The expansion of the Islamic Courts Union in Lower Jubba province', *Journal of Eastern African Studies*, 14(3): 553–571.

Skran, C. and Easton-Calabria, E. (2020) 'Old concepts making new history: Refugee self-reliance, livelihoods and the "refugee entrepreneur", *Journal of Refugee Studies,* 33(1): 1–21.

Slovic, P., Västfjäll, D., Erlandsson, A. and Gregory, R. (2017) 'Iconic photographs and the ebb and flow of empathic response to humanitarian disasters', *Proceedings of the National Academy of Sciences,* 114(4): 640–644.

Smirl, L. (2015) *Spaces of Aid: How Cars, Compounds, and Hotels Shape Humanitarianism.* London: Zed Books.

Smith, M., and Yanacopulos, H. (2004) 'The public faces of development: An introduction', *Journal of International Development,* 16(5): 657–664.

Smith, N. (1996) *The New Urban Frontier: Gentrification and the Revanchist City.* London and New York: Routledge.

Smith, N. (2002) 'New globalism, new urbanism: Gentrification as global urban strategy', *Antipode,* 34(3): 427–450.

Soja, E.W. (1996) *Thirdspace: Journeys to Los Angeles and Other Real-and-Imagined Places.* Hoboken: Wiley-Blackwell.

Somali Public Agenda (SPA) (2019) 'Land prices in Mogadishu and its impact on the urban poor and IDPs', SPA Governance Brief 06, Available from: http://somalipublicagenda.org/wp-content/uploads/2019/11/SPA_Governance_Briefs_06_2019_ENGLISH.pdf [Accessed 14 April 2022].

Somali Public Agenda (SPA) (2022) 'Turkey's role in public service and infrastructural development in Mogadishu', SPA report, Available online at: https://somalipublicagenda.org/turkeys-role-in-public-service-and-infrastructural-development-in-mogadishu/ [Accessed 14 April 2022].

Sossouvi, K. (2013) 'E-transfers in emergencies: Implementation support guidelines', Cash Learning Partnership Network, Available from: https://www.calpnetwork.org/publication/e-transfers-in-emergencies-implementation-support-guidelines/ [Accessed 20 August 2020].

Spencer, K.L., Mrig, E.H., and Bouchard, E.G. (2021) 'Unpacking gatekeeping in medical institutions: A case study of access to end-of-life patients', *Qualitative Research,* 1-15.

Spivak, G.C. (1994) 'Can the subaltern speak?', in P. Williams and L. Chrisman (eds) *Colonial Discourse and Postcolonial Theory: A Reader.* New York: Columbia University Press, pp 66–111.

Steel, G., Cottyn, I. and van Lindert, P. (2017) 'New connections – new dependencies: Spatial and digital flows in sub-Saharan African livelihoods', in L. de Haan (ed), *Livelihoods and Development.* Leiden: Brill, pp 148–167.

Stepputat, F. (2004) 'Dynamics of return and sustainable reintegration in a "mobile livelihoods"-perspective', *DIIS Working Paper 2004/10.*

Stepputat, F. (2012) 'Knowledge production in the security–development nexus: An ethnographic reflection', *Security Dialogue,* 43(5): 439–455.

Sturridge, C., Bakewell, O. and Hammond, L. (2018) 'Return and (re)integration after displacement: Belonging, labelling and livelihoods in three Somali cities', London and Nairobi: EU Trust Fund for Africa (Horn of Africa Window) Research and Evidence Facility, Available from: https://blogs.soas.ac.uk/ref-hornresearch/files/2020/02/Return-and-ReIntegration.pdf [Accessed 4 August 2021].

Stuvøy, K., Bakonyi, J. and Chonka, P. (2021) 'Precarious spaces and violent site effects: Experiences from Hargeisa's urban margins', *Conflict, Security & Development*, 21(2): 153–176.

Sultana, F. (2009) 'Fluid lives: Subjectivities, gender and water in rural Bangladesh', *Gender, Place and Culture*, 16(4): 427–444.

Summers, K.H., Baird, T.D., Woodhouse, E., Christie, M.E., McCabe, J.T., Terta, F. and Peter, N. (2020) 'Mobile phones and women's empowerment in Maasai communities: How men shape women's social relations and access to phones', *Journal of Rural Studies*, 77: 126–137.

Suri, T. and Jack, W. (2016) 'The long-run poverty and gender impacts of mobile money', *Science*, 354(6317): 1288–1292.

Sutton-Brown, C.A. (2014) 'Photovoice: A methodological guide', *Photography and Culture*, 7(2): 169–185.

Swyngedouw, E. (1996) 'The city as a hybrid: On nature, society and cyborg urbanization', *Capitalism Nature Socialism* 7(2): 65–80.

Swyngedouw, E. (2006) 'Circulations and metabolisms: (Hybrid) natures and (cyborg) cities', *Science as Culture*, 15(2): 105–121.

Thieme, T., Lancione, M. and Rosa, E. (2017) 'The city and its margins', *City*, 21(2): 127–134.

Thrift, N. (2006) 'Space', *Theory, Culture & Society*, 23(2–3): 139–146.

Tofik, I. (2014) 'The use of mobile phone in camel marketing: The case of Babille district of Fafan zone, Somali region, Ethiopia', *RUFORUM Working Document Series*, 14(3): 247–251.

Totah, F. (2020) 'Palestinian refugees between the city and the camp', *International Journal of Middle East Studies*, 52(4): 607–621.

Trouillot, M-R. (2001) 'The anthropology of the state in the age of globalization: Close encounters of the deceptive kind', *Current Anthropology*, 42(1): 125–138.

Truelove, Y. (2011) '(Re-)Conceptualizing water inequality in Delhi, India through a feminist political ecology framework', *Geoforum*, 42(2): 143–152.

Truelove, Y. and Cornea, N. (2020) 'Rethinking urban environmental and infrastructural governance in the everyday: Perspectives from and of the global South', *Environment and Planning C: Politics and Space*, 39(2): 231–246.

Tsing, A.L. (2005) *Friction: An Ethnography of Global Connection*. Princeton: Princeton University Press.

Turner, S. (2005) 'Suspended spaces: Contesting sovereignties in a refugee camp', in T.B. Hansen and F. Stepputat (eds) *Sovereign Bodies: Citizens, Migrants, and States in the Postcolonial World*. Princeton: Princeton University Press, pp 312–332.

Turner, S. (2012) *Politics of Innocence: Hutu Identity, Conflict and Camp Life*. New York and Oxford: Berghahn Books.

Turner, V. (1970) *The Forest of Symbols: Aspects of Ndembu Ritual*. Ithaca: Cornell University Press.

Tyler, I. (2013) *Revolting Subjects: Social Abjection and Resistance in Neoliberal Britain*. London: Zed Books.

UN Habitat (2020) 'Somalia Programme Country Briefing Note 2020', May, Available from: https://unhabitat.org/sites/default/files/2020/05/somalia_programme_country_briefing_note_2020.pdf [Accessed 31 July 2021].

UNHCR, United Nations High Commissioner for Refugees (2010) 'Somalia: UNHCR works to reverse deportations from Puntland', Press release, 28 July, Available from: https://reliefweb.int/report/ethiopia/somalia-unhcr-works-reverse-deportations-puntland [Accessed 30 August 2021].

UNHCR, United Nations High Commissioner for Refugees (2016) 'Connecting refugees, how Internet and Mobile Connectivity can Improve Refugee Well-Being and Transform Humanitarian Action', Available from: https://reliefweb.int/report/world/connecting-refugees-how-internet-and-mobile-connectivity-can-improve-refugee-well-being [Accessed 20 August 2020].

UNOCHA, United Nations Office for the Coordination of Humanitarian Affairs (2001, 2nd edn) 'Guiding Principles on Internal Displacement', Available from: https://www.unhcr.org/uk/protection/idps/43ce1cff2/guiding-principles-internal-displacement.html [Accessed 10 July 2022].

Urry, J. (2007) *Mobilities*. Cambridge: Polity.

van Dijk, T.A. (1993) *Elite Discourse and Racism*. London: Sage.

van Noorloos, F., and Kloosterboer, M. (2018) 'Africa's new cities: The contested future of urbanization', *Urban Studies*, 55(6): 1223–1241.

Vasudevan, A. (2014) 'The makeshift city: Towards a global geography of squatting', *Progress in Human Geography*, 39(3): 338–359.

Vertovec, S. (2004) 'Cheap calls: The social glue of migrant transnationalism', *Global Networks*, 4(2): 219–224.

Wacquant, L. (2008) *Urban Outcasts. A Comparative Sociology of Advanced Marginality*. Cambridge: Polity Press.

Wacquant, L., Slater, T. and Borges Pereira, V. (2014) 'Territorial stigmatization in action', *Environment and Planning A: Economy and Space*, 46(6): 1270–1280.

Wallis, C. (2011) 'Mobile phones without guarantees: The promises of technology and the contingencies of culture', *New Media and Society*, 13(3): 471–485.

Wallis, C. (2013) *Technomobility in China: Young Migrant Women and Mobile Phones*. New York: NYU Press.

Walls, M. (2014) *A Somali Nation-State: History, Culture and Somaliland's Political Transition*. Pisa: Ponte Invisible.

Wang, C. and Burris, M.A. (1997) 'Photovoice: Concept, methodology, and use for participatory needs assessment', *Health Education & Behavior*, 24(3): 369–387.

Warsame, A.A. Sheik-Ali, I.A., Ali, A.O. and Sarkodie, S.A. (2021) 'Climate change and crop production nexus in Somalia: An empirical evidence from ARDL technique', *Environmental Science and Pollution Research*, 28(16): 19838–19850.

Wasuge, M. (2019) 'Re-introducing the Somali Shilling in Beledweyne', Somali Public Agenda, 14 January, Available from: https://somalipublicagenda.org/re-introducing-the-somali-shilling-in-beledweyne/ [Accessed 20 August 2021].

Wernick, A. (2019) 'In Uganda, a refugee camp becomes a city', *The World*, 9 May, Available from: https://www.pri.org/stories/2019-05-09/uganda-refugee-camp-becomes-city [Accessed 26 July 2021].

Wilcox, L. (2019) 'Bodies and embodiment in IR', in J. Edkins (ed) *Routledge Handbook of Critical International Relations*. New York: Routledge, pp 305–318.

Wimmer, A., and Schiller, N.G. (2002) 'Methodological nationalism and the study of migration', *European Journal of Sociology*, 43(2): 217–240.

World Bank (2010) 'Africa's infrastructure: a time for transformation', Washington DC: World Bank Group Open Knowledge Repository, Available from: https://openknowledge.worldbank.org/handle/10986/2692 [Accessed 15 April 2022].

World Bank (2016) 'World Development Report 2016: Digital Dividends', World Bank, Available from https://www.worldbank.org/en/publication/wdr2016 [Accessed 24 August 2021].

World Bank (2019) 'Somali Poverty and Vulnerability Assessment: Findings from Wave 2 of the Somali High Frequency Survey', World Bank Group Open Knowledge Repository, Available from: https://openknowledge.worldbank.org/handle/10986/32323 [Accessed: 27 July 2021].

World Bank (2021) 'Somalia Urbanization Review: Fostering cities as anchors of development', World Bank Group Open Knowledge Repository, Available from: https://openknowledge.worldbank.org/handle/10986/35059 [Accessed 31 July 2021].

Wyche, S. and Olson, J. (2018) 'Kenyan women's rural realities, mobile Internet access, and "Africa Rising"', *Information Technologies and International Development*, 14: 33–47.

REFERENCES

Wyche, S. and Steinfield, C. (2016) 'Why don't farmers use cell phones to access market prices? Technology affordances and barriers to market information services adoption in rural Kenya', *Information Technology for Development*, 22(2): 320–333.

Young, I.M. (1980) 'Throwing like a girl: A phenomenology of feminine body comportment, motility and spatiality', *Human Studies*, 3(2): 137–156.

Zetter, R. (1991) 'Labelling refugees: Forming and transforming a bureaucratic identity', *Journal of Refugee Studies*, 4(1): 39–62.

Index

A
addiction 111
Afghanistan 75, 210
Agamben, G. 13, 54, 75, 104, 167, 170, 174, 192, 207
agency 15, 19, 53–55, 71, 135, 171, 181
Agier, M. 5, 72, 73, 189, 192, 195
agriculture 32, 34, 37, 55, 124, 158
aid 10, 13, 15, 20, 23, 33, 34, 41, 53, 58–65, 67, 74–6, 98, 108, 124, 130, 136–8, 146, 168, 178, 191
airport 40, 65, 75, 78, 152
Al Shabaab 9, 13, 21, 22, 28–9, 32–5, 38–41, 55, 64, 66, 68, 124–5, 137, 160, 167–8
AMISOM 13, 32–35, 38–40, 55
assemblage 4, 7, 76, 87–9, 94, 99, 103–5, 171, 175, 184
Ayuuto (also *hagbad*) 118, 190

B
Bakaara 156
Bakool 30, 34, 38, 39, 43, 115, 157, 158, 191
bank 122
banking 65, 75, 108, 124, 129, 179
Bardera 112, 144
Barre, Siad 31, 37, 42–3
begging 35, 119, 122, 157, 165
Beledweyne 43
Berbera 42
biometrics 124, 130, 136
biopolitics 54, 136, 184
blacksmith 163
border 2, 13, 51, 147
borehole 63
boundaries 7, 38, 48, 58, 73
Bourdieu, P. 49
Burao 46
Burhakaba 191
burial 36, 43, 45, 87, 155
bus 41, 48, 166
business 33, 38, 42, 65–6, 75, 80, 118–9, 122, 124, 128, 145, 149, 167, 181
businesspeople 33, 38, 42, 64, 79, 90, 144, 152, 190

Butler, J. 8, 76, 174, 181
Buuhoodle 143

C
Cakaara 46, 90
camel 29, 115, 158–60
campscape 73, 76
capitalism 4, 53–4, 65, 78, 104, 118, 121, 176, 179
care 100, 111, 181, 121
cart 40, 89, 118
cash 18, 58, 60, 67, 109, 122, 124, 129–32, 134, 135, 157, 184
caste 2, 14, 30, 43, 49, 50, 140, 161, 162, 172
chairman 90, 96, 100, 101, 138, 144, 151, 152, 157
chairwoman 153
charcoal 38, 39, 121
cholera 92
citizenship 7, 12–3, 29, 42, 67, 74–5, 79, 138, 141, 154, 164, 168, 170–1, 180, 185–6
circulation 7, 78, 88, 181
classification 7, 12, 13, 46, 140, 154, 166, 173, 188
climate 13, 33–4, 183
clothes 18, 26, 45, 58, 110–1, 115–6, 118, 132, 143, 157, 167
colonialism 8, 20, 29, 30, 31, 46
committee 60–1, 67, 89, 90, 125, 141, 151, 153
company 40, 65, 90, 109, 121–2, 124, 129, 132, 136, 179, 181
compensation 30, 72, 74, 152, 155
Congo 62
construction 27, 41–2, 61–5, 67, 71, 79, 100, 111–2, 114, 116, 133, 156, 181, 185
contamination 90, 92
corruption 152
countryside 114, 125, 127–9, 143, 145, 157–8, 183
cow 114–5
crime 129, 155
crops 34, 40, 124, 146

INDEX

D
Daami 49, 98, 168
Dadaab 41, 72
data 122, 136–7, 182
Daynile 37, 65
debt 119, 127, 133
Degehabur 45
deportation 50, 168
diarrhoea 45, 82, 92, 98
diaspora 3–4, 16, 33, 42, 46, 54, 64–5, 75, 121, 127–8, 134, 176, 179, 182
Digaale 47, 152–4, 166–7
disabilities 18, 119
discrimination 21, 24, 30, 34, 50, 94, 140–1, 147, 154–6, 158, 160–5, 167–9, 172, 185
disease 99, 158
divorce 120, 146, 149
doctor 45, 99
documentation 72, 149
drought 13, 26, 31, 33–5, 37–8, 40–1, 44, 47, 49, 143–6, 153
drugs 26, 45, 79, 98
dugsi 64, 101–2, 146
Dulcad 48
durable solutions 7, 41, 78–9, 138, 140–2, 148, 150, 152, 164, 166–7, 169, 170, 174, 184–5

E
Eastleigh 2
education 16, 37, 40–1, 61, 63, 65, 79–84, 100–3, 106, 121, 136, 143–6, 151, 153, 156, 157, 161–2, 168, 180
elder 11, 30–1, 38, 52, 94, 157, 160, 162
elderly 15, 92, 100, 119, 123, 132, 135, 145, 183
electricity 63, 79–80, 84, 109, 133, 183
employer 23, 109, 115–6, 130–6, 181, 183–4
Ethiopia 28, 31–3, 38, 43–8, 50, 68, 70–1, 79, 138, 143, 165, 180
eviction 5, 13, 23–4, 34, 37, 45, 50, 54–55, 59, 63–8, 72–5, 81, 142, 151, 169–70, 178–9, 184
exhibition 16, 19, 21, 19–22

F
famine 13, 27, 33–4, 37–8, 56, 134, 143, 160
farming 21, 30, 34–5, 37–40, 58, 114, 124–5, 144–6, 157
fees 39, 41, 67, 71, 100–3, 122, 124, 153
fencing 60, 70, 74, 93, 95, 112
fighting 35, 39, 44, 55, 79, 153
firewood 39, 116, 118, 121, 157
flooding 33, 146
food 13, 18, 26, 31–7, 41, 45, 49, 58–61, 80, 99, 100–3, 110–1, 114–5, 121, 124, 130, 143–6

Foucault, M. 14, 138, 169, 184
fragmentation 8, 12, 16, 27, 29, 31–3, 42, 78, 88, 122, 170, 180, 181
fundraising 15–6
future 49, 60, 71, 95, 100, 138–54, 174

G
Gaalkacyo 42–3
Galgaduud 43
Galmudug 43
Garowe 45
gatekeeping 3, 10–1, 41–3, 53–4, 58–62, 67, 69, 76, 81, 83, 89, 130, 151, 177, 178
Gedo 30, 112, 144
gentrification 23, 37, 54, 55, 66, 69, 73, 75–6, 81, 170, 177–9
Golis 124
Goma 62, 178
goof 58–60, 63
governance 6, 30–1, 54, 66, 74–5
grave 36, 43
gravel 116–7, 133

H
hairdressing 158, 161, 163, 164
health 61–5, 79, 81, 83, 90, 92, 96–100, 104–6, 121, 143, 145, 149
healthcare 80, 96–100, 143, 153, 179
Hiran 160, 191
Hormuud 124
hospital 36, 79, 96, 98–100, 104, 168
human-trafficking 182

I
IASC 141–2
ICTs 24, 107–9, 122–5, 133–5, 181–3
illiteracy 132, 183
import 124
improvisation 4, 23, 73, 77, 80–4, 94, 98–9, 104–5, 121, 138, 179–80
injury 18, 22, 98, 110–1, 149, 174
investor 33, 54, 63, 65
Islam 29, 101

J
jaahilnimo 84
jerrycan 82, 89, 93, 95
Jordan 74, 199
Jowhar 35, 146
Jubaland 142
Jubba 30, 37, 215

K
Kabul 178
Kahda 37, 65
Kakuma 74
Kenya 2, 9, 28, 39, 41, 66, 72–4, 122, 191
khat 111
kiosk 63, 89, 133
Kismayo 38

L

labour 3, 9, 19, 23–4, 42, 45, 50, 63–4, 89, 93–4, 101, 104–12, 115–21, 125, 128, 131–6, 143–6, 153, 156–7, 163–5, 168, 174–6, 180–2
labourer 39, 42, 112, 132–5, 146
landowner 10, 23, 45, 53–4, 57–8, 60–3, 67–8, 76, 80–1, 83, 88–90, 100, 105, 125, 130, 148–51, 177–9
Lebanon 74
literacy 16, 24, 110, 132, 135
livestock 30, 34, 40, 42, 44, 49, 114, 119, 129, 143, 145–6, 153, 157
logistics 78, 179–80
looting 31, 37
lottery 148–50

M

Maay 30, 39, 155–6
malaria 98
marriage 94–5, 162, 164
Maxaa Tiri 30, 155–6
mayor 21–2
Mbembe, A. 3, 8, 174, 177
MCH 63, 79, 96–8
measles 98
media 1, 16, 50, 176
military 20, 29, 31, 37–9, 42–3, 46, 75
militia 31–4, 37, 39, 144, 155–6
morphology 68, 69, 76, 150
mosque 3, 35, 64, 149, 162, 168
Muslim 29, 40, 155, 162

N

Nairobi 2
nationalism 12, 96, 164

O

Ogaden 31
Oromo 44, 49–50, 70, 138, 165

P

Palestine 73–74
pastoralism 29–30, 38–9, 191, 172, 183
patriarchy 108–9, 116, 135, 174
phone (also mobile) 3–4, 19, 23, 67, 89, 107–9, 110, 115, 121–36, 182–3, 193
pipe 89, 94
police, policing 149, 168, 173–4
poultry 158
poverty capital 53
pregnancy 35, 45, 79, 190
privacy 81, 84, 86
progress (narrative of) 78, 80, 84, 135, 175

Q

Qalaafe 44
Qansaxdheere 39–40
Qoryoley 26, 27
queuing 93, 104

R

racism 34, 161–3
rain 34–5, 114, 116, 125, 157
religion 80, 101–2, 122, 162, 164, 169
remittance 3, 33, 65, 124, 127–8, 147
rent 26, 41, 47–9, 53, 58–61, 70–2, 76, 81–2, 89, 98, 119, 129–30, 148–9, 152–4, 165
rentierism 53, 81, 125, 174–9
repatriation 41, 47–8, 147
rice 61–2, 67, 82, 110, 144, 151
river 34, 35, 37, 43, 55, 160
RRA 38
rubbish 84, 87, 112, 118

S

Sahara 127
savings 24, 118, 122, 128–9, 135
seaport 65, 78, 112
sesame 34
sexual violence 44, 116
Shabelle 27, 30, 34, 35, 37, 38, 43
shame 84, 88, 163
Shilling 18, 118–9, 122, 132, 153, 218
shoes 101, 120, 161, 163
shoeshiner 26, 120
shop 18, 63, 111, 119, 121, 132–3, 144, 149, 157
shopkeeper 132, 167
shopping 116, 122, 131
sickness 8, 35, 36, 90, 98–100, 110–1, 119, 130
Simone, A. 3–4, 7–8, 89, 92, 95, 100, 103–4, 171, 177
SNM 31, 46
solidarity 45, 99, 140, 168, 171
sovereignty 13, 54, 141, 170
SSDF 31, 42
Statehouse 6, 46–9, 69–72, 74, 84, 87, 94, 152, 165, 166
Sudan 72, 124, 127, 182
sugar 57, 144

T

tahriib 13
tank 79, 82, 88–90, 94
tanker 90, 92
tax 34, 38–40, 48
techno–colonialism 136
tech–solutionism 24, 183
Telesom 122, 124
temporary 6, 9, 54, 68, 71–3, 76, 105, 147, 185
tenure 24, 45, 70, 140, 149–50, 153, 169, 184–5
territory 12, 16, 31, 74, 170, 191
terrorism 16, 167, 175
thief 129, 149
toilet 61, 63, 65, 80–88, 112, 149, 180
Turkey 65

INDEX

U
UN Habitat 1, 19
UNHCR 41, 74, 168, 182
UNICEF 79
United Nations 1, 32, 41, 78, 138, 141
USC 26, 31–2, 37

V
vaccination 98
vegetables 111, 116

W
waiting 33, 59, 86, 88, 93–4, 98, 104, 112–3, 145–6, 149, 154
walking 35–6, 40, 115, 129, 153, 168
washing 84, 110–1, 115–6, 132, 143, 157
wells 89–90, 92
WhatsApp 127
worlding 7, 177
writing 16, 52, 101, 125, 157

Y
Yarisow, Abdirahman Omar Osman 22
Yemen 28, 43, 127

Z
Zaad 122
zakat 39

www.ingramcontent.com/pod-product-compliance
Lightning Source LLC
Chambersburg PA
CBHW071157070526
44584CB00019B/2825